FAST, FRESH AND DELICIOUS

150 Quick & Healthy Everyday Meals

TIME-LIFE BOOKS, ALEXANDRIA, VIRGINIA

TIME-LIFE BOOKS IS A DIVISION OF TIME LIFE INC.

FAST, FRESH AND DELICIOUS
Project Manager Sally Collins
Vice President of Sales and Marketing Neil Levin
Director of Special Sales Liz Ziehl
Production Manager Carolyn Mills Bounds
Quality Assurance Manager Miriam P. Newton

PRODUCED BY REBUS, INC.
NEW YORK, NEW YORK

Photographers: Christopher Lawrence, Steven Mays, Steven Mark Needham,
Alan Richardson, Ellen Silverman, John Uher

FAST, FRESH AND DELICIOUS is an adaptation of CREATIVE EVERYDAY COOKING.

Second printing
Printed in U.S.A.

TIME-LIFE is a trademark of Time Warner Inc. U.S.A.

Library of Congress Cataloging–in–Publication Data

Fast, fresh and delicious : 150 quick & healthy everyday meals.
      p.   cm.
   Includes index.
   ISBN 0-7835-5285-8
   1. Quick and easy cookery.   I. Time-Life Books.
TX833.5.F37   1996
641.5'55–dc20   96-24415
                                                             CIP

Books produced by Time-Life Custom Publishing are available at special bulk discount for
promotional and premium use. Custom adaptations can also be created to meet your specific
marketing goals. Call 1-800-323-5255.

CONTENTS

Curry-Broiled Chicken with Raisin Chutney (page 41)

CHAPTER 1
POULTRY

Fajitas with Stir-Fried Chicken

▼

Fajitas make a wonderfully unfussy do-it-yourself meal. All of the components—chicken, lettuce, spicy sauce and sour cream—are put on the table and each diner rolls his own fajitas. The chicken for this version of fajitas is quickly stir-fried, although traditionally meat for this dish would be grilled. To cut calories and cholesterol, use plain yogurt in place of the sour cream.

Working time: 25 minutes
Total time: 25 minutes

Fajitas with Stir-Fried Chicken

4 Servings

1 pound skinless, boneless chicken breast	**1 teaspoon salt**
½ cup lemon juice	**½ teaspoon pepper**
6 tablespoons chopped cilantro or parsley (optional)	**8 flour tortillas**
	1 cup mild red or green salsa
4 teaspoons cumin	**8 large Romaine lettuce leaves**
2 teaspoons cornstarch	**2 tablespoons vegetable oil**
	½ cup sour cream

1 Preheat the oven to 200°.

2 Cut the chicken breast crosswise into ¼-inch-thick strips. Place the chicken in a small bowl.

Step 2

3 Add 6 tablespoons of the lemon juice, 2 tablespoons of the cilantro (if using), the cumin, cornstarch, salt and pepper and mix gently until the chicken is well coated; set aside.

4 Stack the tortillas and wrap them in foil. Place them in the oven to warm for 5 to 10 minutes.

5 Meanwhile, make the sauce: In a small bowl, stir together the salsa and the remaining 2 tablespoons lemon juice and 4 tablespoons cilantro (if using).

6 Shred the lettuce.

Step 3

7 In a medium skillet, warm the oil over medium-high heat. Add the chicken and sauté until white and firm, about 5 minutes.

8 Place the tortillas, the chicken, shredded lettuce, sauce and sour cream in serving dishes. The diners can then assemble their own fajitas by topping a tortilla with some of each of the ingredients, ending with a dollop of sour cream, and then rolling it up.

TIME-SAVERS

■ *Microwave tip: Just before serving, stack the tortillas and wrap them in a damp paper towel. Cook at 100% for 1 minute.*

■ *Do-ahead: Since the fajitas are fine served at room temperature, much of the preparation can be done ahead of time. The sauce (Step 5) can be made and the chicken marinated in advance. Just be sure to cook the chicken and warm the tortillas as close to serving time as possible.*

Values are approximate per serving: Calories: 515 Protein: 35 gm Fat: 15 gm
Carbohydrates: 58 gm Cholesterol: 78 mg Sodium: 1429 mg

Step 7

Chicken Breasts with Red Pepper Purée

▼

Slices of thyme-scented broiled chicken are especially appealing when presented in a pool of red bell pepper sauce. To make a somewhat richer and mellower sauce, stir in 2 tablespoons of sour cream just before serving. For a variation on this dish, try tarragon, basil or oregano in place of the thyme, both on the chicken and in the sauce.

Working time: 20 minutes
Total time: 35 minutes

Chicken Breasts
with Red Pepper Purée

4 Servings

2 tablespoons lemon juice
1 tablespoon olive or other
   vegetable oil
1 teaspoon thyme
¼ teaspoon black pepper
4 skinless, boneless chicken breast
   halves (about 1¼ pounds total)
1 large red bell pepper

1 medium onion
2 tablespoons butter
2 cloves garlic, minced or crushed
   through a press
2 teaspoons tomato paste
1½ teaspoons grated lemon zest
   (optional)
¼ teaspoon salt

1 Preheat the broiler. Line a broiler pan with foil.

2 In a medium bowl, combine 1 tablespoon of the lemon juice, the oil, ½ teaspoon of the thyme and the black pepper. Add the chicken breasts and turn to coat thoroughly.

Step 2

3 Cut the bell pepper into bite-size pieces. Coarsely chop the onion.

4 In a small saucepan, warm the butter over medium-high heat until it is melted. Add the onion and garlic and cook until the onion is translucent, 2 to 3 minutes. Add the bell pepper, the remaining 1 tablespoon lemon juice, the tomato paste, lemon zest (if using), the remaining ½ teaspoon thyme and the salt. Reduce the heat to low, cover and cook until the peppers are softened, about 12 minutes.

5 Meanwhile, place the chicken on the broiler pan and broil 4 inches from the heat for 7 minutes. Turn the chicken over and broil for 7 minutes, or until golden brown.

Step 4

6 Transfer the contents of the saucepan to a food processor or blender and purée. Dividing evenly, spoon some sauce onto a dinner plate and place the chicken breast on top. If desired, slice the chicken breast before serving.

TIME-SAVERS

■ *Microwave tip: To make the sauce (Step 4), in a medium microwave-safe bowl, combine the butter, onion, garlic, bell pepper, lemon juice, tomato paste, lemon zest (if using), ½ teaspoon thyme and salt. Cover and cook at 100% until the peppers are softened, about 6 minutes, stirring once. Finish the sauce as directed in Step 6 above.*

■ *Do-ahead: The chicken can be marinated (Step 2) ahead; or broiled ahead and served at room temperature. The red pepper sauce can be made ahead and served gently reheated or at room temperature.*

Values are approximate per serving: Calories: 257 Protein: 34 gm Fat: 11 gm
Carbohydrates: 5 gm Cholesterol: 98 mg Sodium: 311 mg

Step 6

Chicken Stroganoff

▼

*In this variation on the classic beef Stroganoff, chicken and mushrooms in a
sour cream sauce are served over egg noodles. Like the original dish, it's fast-cooking.
Instead of strips of beef, bite-size chicken pieces are quickly sautéed, combined
with mushrooms and enriched with sour cream and yogurt. Don't let the sauce
boil once you've added the dairy products, or it may curdle.*

Working time: 25 minutes
Total time: 30 minutes

Chicken Stroganoff

4 Servings

1 medium onion	½ pound egg noodles
½ pound small mushrooms	1 tablespoon Dijon mustard
4 skinless, boneless chicken breast halves (about 1¼ pounds total)	1 tablespoon paprika
⅓ cup flour	½ cup chicken broth
½ teaspoon salt	¼ cup sour cream, at room temperature
¼ teaspoon pepper	¼ cup plain yogurt, at room temperature
4 tablespoons butter	
2 tablespoons vegetable oil	

Step 2

1 Bring a large pot of water to a boil. Meanwhile, cut the onion into wedges. Halve the mushrooms. Cut the chicken into bite-size pieces.

2 In a plastic or paper bag, combine the flour, salt and pepper and shake to mix. Add the chicken and shake to coat lightly. Remove the chicken and reserve the excess seasoned flour.

3 In a large skillet, preferably nonstick, warm 1 tablespoon of the butter in 1 tablespoon of the oil over medium heat until the butter is melted. Add the onion and mushrooms and sauté until the onion is translucent, about 4 minutes. Remove the onion and mushrooms to a plate and set aside.

4 Add the remaining 1 tablespoon oil to the skillet and increase the heat to medium-high. Add the chicken and stir-fry until light golden but not completely cooked through, about 3 minutes. Transfer the chicken to a plate and cover loosely to keep warm.

5 Add the noodles to the boiling water and cook until al dente, 10 to 12 minutes, or according to package directions.

Step 7

6 Meanwhile, add the remaining 3 tablespoons butter to the skillet and stir in the reserved seasoned flour. Cook, stirring, until the butter and flour are blended, about 1 minute.

7 Stir the mustard and paprika into the skillet. Stir in the chicken broth. Bring the mixture to a boil over medium heat. Return the chicken, onion and mushrooms to the skillet. Reduce the heat to medium-low, cover and simmer for 5 minutes.

8 Stir in the sour cream and yogurt and continue cooking until the mixture is heated through, about 2 minutes.

9 Drain the noodles and serve topped with the Stroganoff.

Values are approximate per serving: Calories: 645 Protein: 45 gm Fat: 27 gm
Carbohydrates: 56 gm Cholesterol: 174 mg Sodium: 751 mg

Step 8

Oven-Baked Chicken Nuggets

▼

These delicious and moist oven-baked chicken nuggets will draw raves not only from children but from grownups as well. If your kids are not garlic lovers, you may want to leave this ingredient out. After you've made this recipe once, you can experiment with adding other spices and herbs to the breading mixture to vary its flavor. For example, try some chili powder or ground cumin for a Southwestern accent.

Working time: 20 minutes
Total time: 35 minutes

4 Servings

2 garlic cloves (optional)
¼ cup parsley sprigs (optional)
4 slices whole wheat or white
    bread, preferably stale
½ teaspoon salt
½ teaspoon pepper

¼ cup grated Parmesan cheese
    (about 1 ounce)
2 tablespoons chilled butter
1 pound skinless, boneless chicken
    breasts
2 tablespoons milk

Step 4

1 Preheat the oven to 425°. Line a baking sheet with foil and grease it lightly.

2 Make the breading: Peel the garlic cloves (if using) and place them in a food processor or blender. Process until finely chopped. Add the parsley (if using) and process until finely chopped.

3 Tear the bread into small pieces and add it to the processor, then add the salt, pepper and Parmesan, and process, pulsing the machine on and off, until the bread is coarsely crumbed.

4 Cut the butter into small pieces and add it to the processor. Process until the butter is completely incorporated. Transfer the breading to a paper or plastic bag.

5 Cut the chicken into 1-inch cubes. Place the milk in a small bowl. Add the chicken and stir to moisten well.

Step 5

6 Drain the chicken cubes in a colander, then place them in the bag of breading and shake until well coated.

7 Place the chicken nuggets on the prepared baking sheet, leaving space between them, and bake them for 12 to 15 minutes, or until crisp. Turning them halfway through the cooking time will improve the allover crispness.

TIME-SAVERS

■ *Do-ahead: The breading mixture can be made ahead; just be sure to refrigerate it because of its butter content. The chicken nuggets can also be breaded well ahead and frozen. Make a double or triple batch, freeze them and then bake them or microwave them (although this will not produce crisp nuggets) at a moment's notice.*

Values are approximate per serving: Calories: 269 Protein: 32 gm Fat: 10 gm
Carbohydrates: 12 gm Cholesterol: 89 mg Sodium: 663 mg

Step 6

Chinese Chicken Salad with Sesame-Ginger Dressing

▼

This flexible recipe is open to all sorts of variations and inspirations. The constant is a light but flavorful dressing, made with just a tablespoon of oil (chicken broth is the secret). Cooked asparagus, broccoli florets, snow peas or green beans could be added to or substituted for the bell pepper and carrots. And although the chicken cooks in minutes, leftover cooked chicken or turkey could be used, if you prefer.

Working time: 20 minutes
Total time: 25 minutes

Chinese Chicken Salad with Sesame-Ginger Dressing

4 Servings

¾ pound skinless, boneless chicken breast
8 leaves of red leaf or Romaine lettuce
1 large red bell pepper
2 medium carrots
3 scallions
2 quarter-size slices (¼ inch thick) fresh ginger, unpeeled
1 tablespoon Oriental sesame oil

⅓ cup rice wine vinegar or other mild vinegar
¼ cup chicken broth
1 teaspoon reduced-sodium or regular soy sauce
1 tablespoon Dijon mustard
2 cloves garlic, minced or crushed through a press
1 can (8 ounces) sliced bamboo shoots, drained

Step 4

1 Place the chicken in a steamer, cover and bring the water to a boil. Reduce the heat to medium-low and cook 5 minutes longer, until the chicken is just done. Remove the chicken, cover loosely and set aside.

2 Meanwhile, tear the lettuce and cut the bell pepper into bite-size pieces. Cut the carrots into ¼-inch-thick slices. Coarsely chop the scallions. Mince the ginger.

3 In a small bowl, make the dressing: Combine the sesame oil, vinegar, chicken broth, soy sauce, mustard, garlic and ginger. Add any juices that have accumulated under the chicken and stir to combine.

4 Cut the chicken across the grain into ¼-inch-thick slices.

5 Pour half the dressing into a skillet and warm it over medium heat. Add the scallions and cook until they start to wilt, about 1 minute.

Step 5

6 Add the bell pepper, carrots, bamboo shoots and chicken, and cook, stirring, until just heated through, about 3 minutes.

7 In a serving bowl, toss the chicken and vegetables with the lettuce and the remaining dressing.

TIME-SAVERS

■ *Microwave tip: To cook the chicken, place it in a shallow microwave-safe baking dish. Loosely cover with waxed paper and cook at 100% for 7 minutes, rotating the dish once.*

■ *Do-ahead: The chicken can be steamed and the bell pepper, carrots and scallions cut up ahead. The dressing (Step 3) can be made ahead; add the chicken juices to the dressing whenever you cook the chicken.*

Values are approximate per serving: Calories: 170 Protein: 22 gm Fat: 5 gm
Carbohydrates: 9 gm Cholesterol: 49 mg Sodium: 301 mg

Step 6

Chicken Breasts in Caper Sauce

▼

Capers are the buds of a Mediterranean shrub, pickled in vinegar and salt. Small, tender French capers—look for a jar labeled "nonpareil" (French for "unequalled") —are superior to the larger Spanish ones. If you don't have capers on hand (or don't care for them), use finely chopped pickles. The chicken breasts are pounded lightly to make cooking faster and more even, but you can skip this step to save time.

Working time: 20 minutes
Total time: 30 minutes

4 Servings

4 skinless, boneless chicken breast
  halves (about 1¼ pounds total)
1 medium onion
2 tablespoons capers, drained
1 tablespoon olive or other
  vegetable oil
2 tablespoons butter

2 tablespoons flour
1 cup chicken broth
1 tablespoon lemon juice
2 teaspoons grated lemon zest
  (optional)
¼ teaspoon pepper

1 Place the chicken breasts between two sheets of plastic wrap and pound lightly with a meat pounder or rolling pin to an even thickness of about ½ inch.

2 Coarsely chop the onion. Coarsely chop the capers.

Step 1

3 In a large skillet, warm the oil over medium-high heat until hot but not smoking. Add the chicken and brown all over, about 5 minutes per side. Remove the chicken to a plate and cover loosely to keep warm.

4 Add the butter to the skillet and heat until melted. Add the onion and cook until it begins to brown, about 3 minutes.

5 Stir in the flour and cook, stirring, until the flour is no longer visible, about 30 seconds. Stir in the chicken broth, lemon juice, lemon zest (if using), capers and pepper, and bring to a boil over medium-high heat. Return the chicken (and any juices that have accumulated on the plate) to the skillet. Reduce the heat to low, cover and simmer until the chicken is cooked through, about 3 minutes.

Step 2

Values are approximate per serving: Calories: 266 Protein: 34 gm Fat: 11 gm
Carbohydrates: 5 gm Cholesterol: 98 mg Sodium: 509 mg

Step 3

Pineapple-Grilled Chicken Breasts with Salsa

▼

A tart sauce made with yogurt, pineapple juice and lemon juice ensures that the grilled chicken in this dish will be golden brown and moist. Look forward to leftovers—the chicken is also tasty at room temperature or cold. The salsa is made from crushed pineapple, honey, lemon zest, shallots and ginger. Keep an eye on the chicken as it grills, as fruit-based barbecue sauces can scorch easily.

Working time: 20 minutes
Total time: 35 minutes

4 Servings

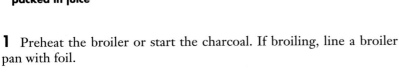

8 medium shallots or 2 small onions	**⅓ cup plain yogurt**
4 quarter-size slices (¼ inch thick) fresh ginger, unpeeled	**3 tablespoons lemon juice**
2 cloves garlic	**¾ teaspoon salt**
1 small fresh or pickled jalapeño pepper, seeded	**¾ teaspoon black pepper**
⅓ cup (packed) cilantro sprigs (optional)	**4 skinless, boneless chicken breast halves (about 1¼ pounds total)**
1 can (8 ounces) crushed pineapple, packed in juice	**2 teaspoons honey**
	2 teaspoons grated lemon zest (optional)

1 Preheat the broiler or start the charcoal. If broiling, line a broiler pan with foil.

2 In a food processor, finely chop the shallots (or onion), ginger, garlic, jalapeño and cilantro (if using).

3 Drain the pineapple, reserving the juice.

4 In a large bowl, combine ¼ cup of the pineapple juice, half of the shallot-ginger mixture, the yogurt, 2 tablespoons of the lemon juice and ½ teaspoon each of the salt and pepper. Add the chicken and toss to coat thoroughly.

5 If broiling, place the chicken on the prepared broiler pan. Grill or broil the chicken 4 inches from the heat for 10 minutes. Turn the chicken over and grill or broil until golden brown and cooked through, about 10 minutes.

6 Meanwhile, in a medium bowl, combine the remaining pineapple juice, 1 tablespoon lemon juice, the honey, lemon zest (if using), the remaining ¼ teaspoon each salt and pepper, the remaining shallot-ginger mixture and the drained pineapple.

7 Serve the chicken with the pineapple salsa on the side.

TIME-SAVERS

■ *Do-ahead: The marinade (Steps 2 through 4) and the pineapple salsa (Steps 2, 3 and 6) can both be made ahead. The chicken can be marinated ahead, or even grilled ahead and served at room temperature.*

Values are approximate per serving: Calories: 234   Protein: 35 gm   Fat: 2 gm
Carbohydrates: 18 gm   Cholesterol: 83 mg   Sodium: 523 mg

Step 3

Step 4

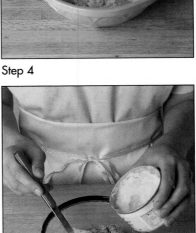

Step 6

Chicken Parmesan Sandwich

▼

To add extra flavor to this Italian-style sandwich, the rolls are cut apart and the cut sides coated with the olive oil used to sauté the chicken. If you are fond of the very olive-y flavor of extra-virgin olive oil, this would be a good place to use it. On the other hand, if you are watching calories, you might want to skip this step and simply serve the chicken on plain toasted rolls.

Working time: 20 minutes
Total time: 20 minutes

Chicken Parmesan Sandwich

4 Servings

2 medium plum tomatoes
4 kaiser or other hard rolls
¼ cup fine unseasoned
 breadcrumbs
¼ cup plus 4 teaspoons grated
 Parmesan cheese (about 1 ounce)
¾ teaspoon oregano

¼ teaspoon pepper
4 chicken cutlets (about 1¼
 pounds total)
¼ cup olive or other vegetable oil
¼ cup mayonnaise (optional)
4 leaves lettuce

Step 4

1 Slice the tomatoes. Cut the rolls in half horizontally.

2 In a plastic or small paper bag, combine the breadcrumbs, ¼ cup of the Parmesan, the oregano and pepper.

3 Add the chicken cutlets and toss to coat them lightly.

4 In a large skillet, warm 3 tablespoons of the oil over medium-high heat until hot but not smoking. Add the chicken and sauté until browned and cooked through, 2 to 3 minutes per side, adding the remaining 1 tablespoon oil if necessary to prevent sticking. Remove the chicken to a plate and cover loosely.

5 While the skillet is still hot, place one half of each of the rolls in the skillet to absorb some of the flavored oil.

Step 5

6 Spread the other half of each roll with mayonnaise (if using). Top with the lettuce, chicken cutlets, tomato slices and a dusting (about 1 teaspoon) of additional Parmesan.

TIME-SAVERS

■ *Do-ahead: The sandwiches can be made ahead and served at room temperature, although they should not sit very long with the lettuce and tomato in them or the rolls will get soggy.*

Step 6

Values are approximate per serving: Calories: 495 Protein: 42 gm Fat: 19 gm
Carbohydrates: 36 gm Cholesterol: 90 mg Sodium: 585 mg

Cider-Sautéed Chicken Breasts

▼

This simple sauté is a lightened version of a French dish in which chicken breasts are cooked with heavy cream and apple brandy. Here, fresh apple cider and a small amount of light cream are used instead. Tart cider is best, but a squeeze of lemon juice will sharpen the flavor of a sweet cider. For an extra finishing touch, garnish the chicken with toasted sliced almonds.

Working time: 20 minutes
Total time: 30 minutes

Cider-Sautéed Chicken Breasts

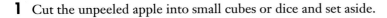

4 Servings

1 small tart green apple, such as Granny Smith	**1 tablespoon butter**
3 tablespoons flour	**2 tablespoons olive or other vegetable oil**
½ teaspoon salt	**About 1¼ cups apple cider or apple juice**
¼ teaspoon pepper	**½ cup golden raisins**
¼ teaspoon cinnamon	**2 tablespoons half-and-half or light cream**
4 skinless, boneless chicken breast halves (about 1¼ pounds total)	

Step 4

1 Cut the unpeeled apple into small cubes or dice and set aside.

2 In a shallow bowl, combine the flour, salt, pepper and cinnamon. Dredge the chicken in the seasoned flour and reserve any excess dredging mixture.

3 In a large skillet, melt the butter in the oil over medium-high heat until hot but not smoking. Add the chicken and sauté until golden all over, about 3 minutes per side. Remove the chicken to a plate.

4 Add the reserved dredging mixture to the drippings in the skillet and cook it, stirring constantly, until it is a light golden color, 2 to 3 minutes. Add ¼ cup of the cider and stir until the sauce is smooth. Stir in another ½ cup cider and check the consistency of the sauce. If you would prefer a thinner sauce, add up to ½ cup more cider.

5 Bring the sauce to a boil over medium-high heat. Return the chicken to the skillet and add the diced apple and the raisins. Cover, reduce the heat to medium-low and simmer for 5 minutes. Turn the chicken over and simmer, covered, until the chicken is tender and opaque throughout, about 5 minutes longer. Remove the chicken to a plate.

Step 5

6 Stir the cream into the sauce in the pan. To serve, top each chicken breast with some of the sauce, diced apple and raisins.

TIME-SAVERS

■ *Do-ahead: The dredging mixture (Step 2) can be made ahead. The chicken can be sautéed (Step 3) and the sauce made (Step 4) an hour or so ahead. Proceed with the rest of the recipe just before serving.*

Values are approximate per serving: Calories: 384 Protein: 34 gm Fat: 13 gm
Carbohydrates: 34 gm Cholesterol: 93 mg Sodium: 403 mg

Step 6

Stovetop Arroz con Pollo

▼

The modest cousin of a paella, arroz con pollo—rice with chicken—eschews the expensive shellfish and elaborate spicing of its rich relative. This humble example of Latin home cooking is an unfailingly appealing combination of rice, chicken, vegetables, garlic and seasonings. A satisfying dinner in a skillet, arroz con pollo arrives on the table in under an hour with minimal cleanup afterward.

Working time: 20 minutes
Total time: 50 minutes

4 Servings

- 1 medium onion
- 1 pound skinless, boneless chicken breast
- 3 tablespoons olive or other vegetable oil
- 3 cloves garlic, minced or crushed through a press
- 1 large green bell pepper
- 2 tablespoons chopped pimiento, drained (optional)
- 3 plum tomatoes or 4 whole canned tomatoes, well drained

- 1 cup raw rice
- 1 tablespoon paprika
- 1½ teaspoons thyme
- ¼ teaspoon black pepper
- 2 cups chicken broth
- ¼ cup dry white wine or chicken broth
- ½ teaspoon salt
- Pinch of cayenne pepper
- 1 bay leaf
- 1 cup frozen peas

Step 2

1 Coarsely chop the onion. Cut the chicken into 1-inch pieces.

2 In a large skillet, warm 2 tablespoons of the oil over medium-high heat until hot but not smoking. Add the garlic, onion and chicken, and sauté until the onion begins to brown, about 10 minutes.

3 Meanwhile, cut the bell pepper into thin strips. Mince the pimiento (if using). Chop the tomatoes into chunks.

4 Remove the onion and chicken to a plate and set aside. Add the remaining 1 tablespoon oil to the skillet and warm until hot but not smoking. Add the rice, paprika, thyme and black pepper, and cook, stirring, until the rice is lightly coated with the oil, about 1 minute.

Step 4

5 Add the chicken broth, wine, tomatoes, salt, cayenne and bay leaf. Bring the mixture to a boil over medium-high heat.

6 When the broth has come to a boil, add the bell pepper and pimiento, and return to a boil. Reduce the heat to low, cover and simmer until the rice is tender, about 20 minutes.

7 Stir in the peas. Return the chicken and onion mixture to the skillet and cook until the chicken is cooked through, about 3 minutes. Remove the bay leaf before serving.

TIME-SAVERS

■ *Do-ahead: The vegetables and chicken can be cut up ahead. The whole dish can be made ahead and gently reheated.*

Values are approximate per serving: Calories: 456 Protein: 34 gm Fat: 13 gm
Carbohydrates: 49 gm Cholesterol: 66 mg Sodium: 890 mg

Step 6

Cajun-Style Grilled Chicken Breasts

▼

*Cajun cooking has swept the country, bringing its intriguing flavor combinations
to tables far from its Louisiana origins. Spice blends are a staple of the Cajun kitchen;
they are rubbed on meat and fish and stirred into vegetables and soups.
Garlic and onion powders are a common ingredient in these flavoring blends,
as they combine easily with other ground spices.*

Working time: 5 minutes
Total time: 20 minutes

Cajun-Style
Grilled Chicken Breasts

4 Servings

4 boneless chicken breast halves, with skin on (about 1½ pounds total)
⅓ cup lemon juice
2 tablespoons garlic powder

2 tablespoons onion powder
1 teaspoon oregano
1 teaspoon thyme
2 teaspoons black pepper
½ teaspoon cayenne pepper

1 Preheat the broiler or start the charcoal. If broiling, line a broiler pan with foil.

2 Place the chicken in a shallow container. Pour the lemon juice over the chicken, turning it over to completely coat with the juice.

Step 2

3 On a plate, combine the garlic powder, onion powder, oregano, thyme, black pepper and cayenne. Dredge the chicken in the spice mixture.

4 Place the chicken skin-side down on the broiler pan or grill and cook 4 inches from the heat for 4 minutes.

5 Turn the chicken over and grill or broil for 4 minutes longer, or until golden brown and the juices run clear.

Step 3

Values are approximate per serving: Calories: 263 Protein: 36 gm Fat: 9 gm
Carbohydrates: 8 gm Cholesterol: 97 mg Sodium: 90 mg

Step 5

27

Oregano-Garlic Chicken Breasts

▼

All of the ingredients for this easy herbed chicken dish are probably in your kitchen right now—except, perhaps, the chives. Although you can purchase fresh chives by the bunch, if you buy a potted chive plant (sold at some supermarkets), you can always have this subtle seasoning on hand. Instead of mincing them with a knife, use a pair of sharp scissors to snip the chives directly into the measuring cup.

Working time: 15 minutes
Total time: 35 minutes

Oregano-Garlic Chicken Breasts

4 Servings

¼ cup lemon juice
5 cloves garlic, minced or crushed
   through a press
1½ teaspoons oregano
¼ teaspoon pepper
4 skinless, boneless chicken breast
   halves (about 1¼ pounds total)
¼ cup minced fresh chives or
   scallion greens

1 medium onion
¼ cup cornstarch
1 tablespoon butter
1 tablespoon olive or other
   vegetable oil
¾ cup chicken broth
2½ teaspoons grated lemon zest
   (optional)
Pinch of sugar

1 In a shallow 11 x 7-inch baking dish, combine the lemon juice, garlic, ¾ teaspoon of the oregano and the pepper. Add the chicken, turn to coat well with the seasonings and set aside to marinate for 10 minutes.

2 Meanwhile, chop the chives (or scallion greens). Cut the onion into thin wedges. Place the cornstarch on a plate or in a shallow bowl.

3 Remove the chicken from the marinade, reserving the marinade. Dredge the chicken lightly in the cornstarch; reserve the excess cornstarch.

Step 3

4 In a large skillet, warm the butter in the oil over medium-high heat until the butter is melted. Place the chicken in the skillet and cook for 5 minutes on each side. Remove the chicken to a plate and cover loosely to keep warm.

5 Add the onion to the skillet and stir-fry until it begins to soften, 1 to 2 minutes. In a small bowl, blend the chicken broth with the reserved cornstarch. Add the broth mixture, reserved marinade, remaining ¾ teaspoon oregano, 2 tablespoons of the chives, the lemon zest (if using) and the sugar to the skillet, and bring to a boil.

Step 5

6 Return the chicken (and any juices that have accumulated on the plate) to the skillet and cook for 2 to 3 minutes, or until the chicken is cooked through.

7 Serve the chicken topped with the onion and sauce and sprinkled with the remaining 2 tablespoons chives.

TIME-SAVERS

■ **Do-ahead:** *The chicken can be marinated ahead of time.*

Values are approximate per serving: Calories: 265 Protein: 34 gm Fat: 8 gm
Carbohydrates: 12 gm Cholesterol: 90 mg Sodium: 312 mg

Step 6

Piquant Lemon Chicken Salad

▼

Carrots, scallions, green bell peppers and cherry tomatoes make this chicken salad a colorful all-in-one main dish. The recipe calls for steaming skinless, boneless chicken (it takes about 10 minutes); however, there's no reason not to use leftover chicken or turkey, or even roasted chicken from the supermarket or deli. Just remove the skin and any visible fat before adding the chicken to the vegetable mixture.

Working time: 20 minutes
Total time: 40 minutes

4 Servings

1 pound skinless, boneless chicken breast	**¼ teaspoon cayenne pepper**
¼ cup plain yogurt	**3 quarter-size slices (¼ inch thick) fresh ginger, unpeeled**
2 tablespoons mayonnaise	**¼ cup (packed) parsley sprigs (optional)**
¼ cup lemon juice	
2 teaspoons grated lemon zest (optional)	**1 large carrot**
	4 scallions
1½ teaspoons ground coriander	**1 large green bell pepper**
½ teaspoon salt	**1 pint cherry tomatoes**
¼ teaspoon black pepper	

Step 1

1 Place the chicken in a vegetable steamer over boiling water and steam until cooked through, about 12 minutes. Remove the chicken to a plate and cover loosely to keep warm.

2 Meanwhile, in a salad bowl, combine the yogurt, mayonnaise, lemon juice, lemon zest (if using), coriander, salt, black and cayenne peppers.

3 In a food processor, mince the ginger and parsley (if using). Add the mixture to the salad bowl.

4 In the same processor work bowl, finely chop the carrot and scallions, and add them to the salad bowl.

Step 4

5 Cut the bell pepper into thin strips. Halve the cherry tomatoes. Add the bell pepper and tomatoes to the salad bowl.

6 When the chicken is cool enough to handle, shred it and add it to the vegetables in the bowl. Toss the ingredients to coat with the dressing.

TIME-SAVERS

■ *Microwave tip:* Instead of steaming the chicken, place it in a shallow microwave-safe baking dish, cover loosely and cook at 100% for 5 to 6 minutes, or until cooked through.

■ *Do-ahead:* The chicken can be cooked, the dressing (Step 2) made and the carrot, scallions and bell pepper cut up ahead.

Step 6

Values are approximate per serving: Calories: 219 Protein: 28 gm Fat: 7 gm
Carbohydrates: 9 gm Cholesterol: 71 mg Sodium: 414 mg

Hushpuppy Chicken Breasts with Pepper-Corn Salad

▼

While frying up their catch, the story goes, Southern fishermen dropped bits of cornmeal batter into the skillet of hot fat and threw the resulting "hushpuppies" to their hungry hounds to quiet them. In homage to those fritters, these chicken breasts are coated with cornmeal and fried until crisp on the outside and tender on the inside.

Working time: 15 minutes
Total time: 25 minutes

Hushpuppy Chicken Breasts with Pepper-Corn Salad

4 Servings

4 skinless, boneless chicken breast halves (about 1¼ pounds total)
3 tablespoons yellow cornmeal
2 tablespoons flour
1 teaspoon salt
½ teaspoon black pepper
Pinch of cayenne pepper
1 tablespoon butter
1 tablespoon olive or other vegetable oil

3 tablespoons cider vinegar
2 teaspoons Dijon mustard
¼ teaspoon sugar
1 package (10 ounces) frozen corn, thawed and drained on paper towels
3 scallions
1 medium red bell pepper
¼ cup chopped parsley (optional)

Step 1

1 If desired, pound the chicken breasts to an even thickness of about ½ inch: Place the chicken between two sheets of plastic wrap and use a rolling pin or meat pounder.

2 In a plastic or paper bag, combine the cornmeal, flour, salt, black pepper and cayenne, and shake to mix. Add the chicken and shake to coat lightly.

3 In a large skillet, warm the butter in the oil over medium-high heat until the butter is melted. Add the chicken and cook until browned all over and cooked through, about 6 minutes per side.

Step 2

4 Meanwhile, in a medium bowl, combine the vinegar, mustard and sugar. Add the corn and toss to combine.

5 Coarsely chop the scallions and bell pepper and add them to the corn. Add 2 tablespoons of the parsley (if using) and toss to combine.

6 Serve the chicken garnished with the remaining 2 tablespoons parsley (if using) and with the pepper-corn salad on the side.

TIME-SAVERS

■ *Microwave tip: To thaw the corn, remove it from its package, place it on a microwave-safe plate and cook at 100% for 3 minutes.*

■ *Do-ahead: The pepper-corn salad (Steps 4 and 5) can be made in advance.*

Step 3

Values are approximate per serving: Calories: 330   Protein: 36 gm   Fat: 9 gm
Carbohydrates: 27 gm   Cholesterol: 90 mg   Sodium: 751 mg

Broiled Chicken with Tomato Butter

▼

The tomato butter that coats these broiled chicken breasts is more tomato than butter: It's made with intensely flavorful sun-dried tomatoes. The tomatoes are sometimes packed in oil, but this recipe calls for the type that are sold dry. If you can only find oil-packed tomatoes, drain them and pat with paper towels to remove as much oil as possible. (You can use the oil in vinaigrettes—just a little will add lots of flavor.)

Working time: 10 minutes
Total time: 30 minutes

Broiled Chicken with Tomato Butter

4 Servings

3 sun-dried tomatoes, not oil-
   packed
½ cup boiling water
2 scallions
2 tablespoons butter, at room
   temperature
2 teaspoons grated lemon zest
   (optional)

Pinch of dry mustard
Pinch of pepper, preferably white
Pinch of red pepper flakes
¼ cup lemon juice
4 skinless, boneless chicken breast
   halves (about 1¼ pounds total)

Step 1

1 In a small bowl, combine the sun-dried tomatoes and the boiling water. Let stand until the tomatoes are plumped and softened, about 5 minutes. Drain the tomatoes well.

2 In a food processor, chop the sun-dried tomatoes and the scallions. Add the butter, lemon zest (if using), mustard, pepper and red pepper flakes, and pulse to combine. Remove half of the tomato butter to a small skillet or saucepan and set aside. Scrape the remaining tomato butter onto a sheet of waxed paper and mold into a rough log shape. Roll the butter up in the waxed paper and twist the ends to seal. Refrigerate the butter until serving time.

3 Preheat the broiler. Line a broiler pan with foil.

4 Place the lemon juice in a medium bowl. Add the chicken and toss to coat. Warm the tomato butter in the skillet until just melted.

5 Arrange the chicken on the broiler pan. Lightly brush the chicken with the melted tomato butter. Broil 4 inches from the heat for 6 minutes.

Step 2

6 Turn the chicken over and broil for 6 minutes longer, or until golden brown and cooked through.

7 Cut the cold tomato butter into 8 slices and place 2 slices on each serving of the hot chicken.

TIME-SAVERS

■ *Do-ahead: The tomato butter (Steps 1 and 2) can be made well ahead. Refrigerate the entire amount, then remove half of it from the refrigerator to melt in Step 4. The chicken can be marinated in the lemon juice several hours ahead of time.*

Step 5

Values are approximate per serving: Calories: 218 Protein: 33 gm Fat: 8 gm
Carbohydrates: 3 gm Cholesterol: 98 mg Sodium: 157 mg

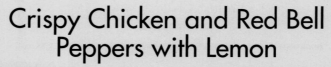

Crispy Chicken and Red Bell Peppers with Lemon

Boneless chicken breasts don't take long to cook, but for an even speedier entrée—like this fried chicken smothered in a sauce of red bell peppers and lemon—flatten them to a half-inch thickness. Place the chicken breasts on a work surface, cover with plastic wrap and rap gently with a rolling pin (or a meat pounder if you have one). If you choose to omit this procedure, be sure to add a little extra cooking time in Step 3.

Working time: 25 minutes
Total time: 35 minutes

Crispy Chicken and Red Bell Peppers with Lemon

4 Servings

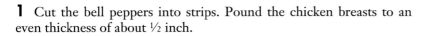

2 large red bell peppers	½ teaspoon salt
4 skinless, boneless chicken breast halves (about 1¼ pounds total)	¼ teaspoon black pepper
	¼ cup vegetable oil
1 egg	1 cup chicken broth
3 tablespoons flour	¼ cup lemon juice
2 tablespoons cornstarch	2 teaspoons grated lemon zest
1½ teaspoons basil	(optional)

Step 1

1 Cut the bell peppers into strips. Pound the chicken breasts to an even thickness of about ½ inch.

2 In a small bowl, lightly beat the egg. Stir in the flour, 1 tablespoon of the cornstarch, ½ teaspoon of the basil, the salt and black pepper, and beat until a smooth batter is formed. Lightly coat the chicken in the batter.

3 In a large skillet, warm the oil over medium-high heat until hot but not smoking. Add the chicken and cook until dark golden all over and cooked through, about 5 minutes per side. Drain on paper towels.

Step 2

4 Pour all but a thin film of oil out of the skillet. In a small bowl, combine the remaining 1 tablespoon cornstarch with the remaining 1 teaspoon basil and the chicken broth.

5 Add the broth mixture, bell pepper slices, lemon juice and lemon zest (if using) to the skillet. Bring to a boil over medium heat, stirring constantly, and cook until just thickened, about 2 minutes.

6 Slice the chicken and serve topped with the peppers and pan juices.

TIME-SAVERS

■ ***Do-ahead:*** *The bell peppers can be cut up ahead. The chicken can be pounded ahead; leave it between the sheets of plastic wrap and refrigerate.*

Step 3

Values are approximate per serving: Calories: 296 Protein: 36 gm Fat: 10 gm
Carbohydrates: 13 gm Cholesterol: 135 mg Sodium: 633 mg

Orange Chicken with Oriental Noodles

▼

The same colorfully packaged ramen noodles that make a speedy mug of soup for lunch are the basis for this quick dinner dish: The almost-instant noodles are tossed with a chicken and mandarin orange stir-fry. In this recipe, the seasoning packet that comes with the ramen is used only in the noodle cooking water, thus adding flavor without overloading the dish with sodium.

Working time: 20 minutes
Total time: 25 minutes

Orange Chicken with Oriental Noodles

6 Servings

1 pound skinless, boneless chicken breast
1 tablespoon cornstarch
¼ teaspoon pepper
1 tablespoon Oriental sesame oil
3 cups shredded cabbage (about ½ pound)
4 scallions
4 quarter-size slices (¼ inch thick) fresh ginger, unpeeled
2 packages (3½ ounces each) instant ramen noodles

2 tablespoons vegetable oil
3 cloves garlic, minced or crushed through a press
1 can (8 ounces) sliced water chestnuts, drained
1 can (11 ounces) mandarin oranges, drained
3 tablespoons reduced-sodium or regular soy sauce

Step 2

1 Cut the chicken across the grain into ¼-inch-thick strips.

2 In a plastic or paper bag, combine the cornstarch and pepper, and shake to mix. Add the chicken and shake to coat lightly. Remove the chicken to a bowl, add the sesame oil and toss to coat.

3 Shred the cabbage. Cut the scallions into 1-inch sections. Mince the ginger.

4 In a large saucepan, bring 1½ quarts of water and the seasoning packets from the ramen to a boil.

5 Meanwhile, in a large skillet, warm 1 tablespoon of the vegetable oil over medium-high heat until hot but not smoking. Add the chicken and stir-fry until the chicken is opaque, 3 to 4 minutes.

6 Remove the chicken to a plate and cover loosely to keep warm. Add the remaining 1 tablespoon vegetable oil, the cabbage, ginger, garlic and water chestnuts to the skillet and cook, stirring, until the cabbage is wilted, about 3 minutes.

Step 6

7 Meanwhile, add the ramen noodles (breaking them up a bit) to the boiling water and cook until al dente, about 3 minutes. Drain well.

8 Return the chicken (and any juices that have accumulated on the plate) to the skillet. Add the scallions, noodles, mandarin oranges and soy sauce. Toss to distribute the seasonings and ingredients.

Values are approximate per serving: Calories: 362 Protein: 23 gm Fat: 14 gm
Carbohydrates: 37 gm Cholesterol: 44 mg Sodium: 568 mg

Step 8

Curry-Broiled Chicken with Raisin Chutney

▼

The curry powder and chutney in this chicken dinner are both Indian in inspiration, but the dish incorporates a few Oriental notes as well: The chicken is brushed with a curry paste that contains soy sauce and sesame oil, and the raisin chutney—which is delicious and easy to make—is spiced with candied ginger. Complement the tangy chicken and chutney with a simple avocado-and-pepper salad.

Working time: 15 minutes
Total time: 25 minutes

Curry-Broiled Chicken with Raisin Chutney

4 Servings

1 tablespoon curry powder
1 tablespoon reduced-sodium soy sauce
2 tablespoons vegetable oil
2 teaspoons Oriental sesame oil
½ teaspoon granulated sugar
¼ teaspoon black pepper
½ teaspoon red pepper flakes
4 boneless chicken breast halves, with skin (about 1¼ pounds total)
1 small onion

1 tablespoon candied ginger or 2 quarter-size slices (¼ inch thick) fresh ginger, unpeeled
1 cup raisins
3 tablespoons lemon juice
2 tablespoons cider vinegar
3 tablespoons brown sugar
1 clove garlic, minced or crushed through a press
2 teaspoons grated lemon zest (optional)

1 Preheat the broiler. Line a broiler pan with foil.

2 In a small bowl, combine the curry powder, soy sauce, vegetable oil, sesame oil, granulated sugar, black pepper and ¼ teaspoon of the red pepper flakes.

Step 2

3 Place the chicken on the prepared broiler pan, skin-side down, and broil 4 inches from the heat for 4 minutes.

4 Turn the chicken over, brush with the curry paste and broil until the chicken is golden brown and cooked through, 7 to 9 minutes. If portions of the chicken begin to char, cover them with foil.

5 Meanwhile, finely chop the onion and candied (or fresh) ginger.

6 In a small saucepan, combine the onion, ginger, raisins, lemon juice, vinegar, brown sugar, garlic, lemon zest (if using) and remaining ¼ teaspoon red pepper flakes. Bring the mixture to a boil over medium-high heat, stirring. Reduce the heat to low, cover and simmer for 2 minutes.

Step 5

7 Transfer the raisin mixture to a food processor and process to a purée.

8 Serve the chicken with the chutney on the side.

TIME-SAVERS

■ *Do-ahead: The curry paste (Step 2) and raisin chutney (Steps 5 through 7) can be made ahead. The chicken can be broiled ahead and served at room temperature.*

Step 6

Values are approximate per serving: Calories: 436 Protein: 31 gm Fat: 17 gm
Carbohydrates: 43 gm Cholesterol: 81 mg Sodium: 230 mg

Chicken Paprika with Ziti

▼

Chicken in a rosy sour cream-paprika sauce is one of Hungary's most famous dishes. In the original, a cut-up chicken simmers for at least half an hour, but in this adaptation, strips of chicken breast are sautéed in just minutes. Any brand of paprika will do for this recipe, but for an extra touch of authenticity, look for a bright-red tin of sweet Hungarian paprika, available in many supermarkets.

Working time: 25 minutes
Total time: 30 minutes

Chicken Paprika with Ziti

4 Servings

4 skinless, boneless chicken breast
   halves (about 1¼ pounds total)
4 scallions
½ pound small mushrooms
2 tablespoons flour
2 tablespoons paprika
¾ teaspoon salt
¼ teaspoon pepper
2 tablespoons butter

3 tablespoons olive oil
3 cloves garlic, minced or crushed
   through a press
½ pound ziti
½ cup sour cream
¼ cup plain yogurt
1 cup canned tomatoes, with their
   juice
½ cup chicken broth

1 Bring a large pot of water to a boil.

2 Meanwhile, cut the chicken across the grain into ¼-inch-thick slices. Coarsely chop the scallions. Halve the mushrooms if they are large. In a medium bowl, combine the flour, paprika, salt and pepper.

Step 2

3 In a large skillet, warm 1 tablespoon of the butter in 1 tablespoon of the oil over medium-high heat until the butter is melted. Add the scallions and garlic and cook until the scallions are translucent, about 3 minutes.

4 Dredge the chicken slices in the flour mixture and reserve the excess. Add the chicken to the skillet and sauté until cooked through, about 5 minutes. Remove the chicken and set aside.

5 Add the pasta to the boiling water and cook until al dente, 9 to 11 minutes, or according to package directions.

6 Meanwhile, add the remaining 1 tablespoon butter and 2 tablespoons oil to the skillet. Add the mushrooms and cook, stirring occasionally, for about 5 minutes.

Step 4

7 In a small bowl, combine the sour cream and yogurt, and stir in the reserved flour mixture.

8 Add the tomatoes and their juice to the skillet. Stir in the chicken broth and sour cream mixture. Return the chicken to the skillet and cook over medium heat until heated through, about 2 minutes. Drain the pasta and serve topped with the chicken, mushrooms and sauce.

TIME-SAVERS

■ *Do-ahead: The chicken and sauce can be made ahead through Step 8; but do not add the sour cream-yogurt mixture until just before serving.*

Values are approximate per serving: Calories: 639 Protein: 45 gm Fat: 26 gm
Carbohydrates: 56 gm Cholesterol: 111 mg Sodium: 817 mg

Step 8

Sliced Chicken and Tomatoes with Lemon-Herb Vinaigrette

▼

Bottled salad dressing often doubles as a marinade for meat or poultry. Here, a quick homemade vinaigrette is used to baste broiled chicken and to dress juicy, ripe tomatoes as well. If you happen to have a garden (or a generous neighbor), beefsteak tomatoes and fresh-picked basil would make this dinner even better. Serve the chicken hot from the oven, at room temperature or chilled.

Working time: 10 minutes
Total time: 25 minutes

Sliced Chicken and Tomatoes with Lemon-Herb Vinaigrette

4 Servings

2 cloves garlic
⅓ cup fresh basil leaves or
   2 teaspoons dried
1½ teaspoons fresh thyme leaves
   or ½ teaspoon dried
2 teaspoons grated lemon zest
   (optional)

¼ cup lemon juice
¼ cup olive or other vegetable oil
4 skinless, boneless chicken breast
   halves (about 1¼ pounds total)
3 medium plum tomatoes

1 Preheat the broiler. Line a broiler pan with foil.

2 In a food processor, mince the garlic. Add the basil and thyme and mince. Add the lemon zest (if using), lemon juice and olive oil, and pulse until blended. Measure out 3 tablespoons of the vinaigrette to use as a basting mixture for the chicken.

3 Place the chicken on the broiler pan and brush with 1 tablespoon of the reserved basting mixture. Broil the chicken 4 inches from the heat until it begins to brown, about 10 minutes.

4 Meanwhile, slice the tomatoes crosswise. Place the tomatoes in a shallow bowl and pour the vinaigrette remaining in the food processor over them; set aside.

5 Turn the chicken over and brush with the remaining 2 tablespoons reserved basting mixture. Broil 4 inches from the heat until the chicken is cooked through and browned on the second side, about 6 minutes.

6 To serve, slice the chicken across the grain on the diagonal. Serve with the sliced tomatoes and spoon some of the excess vinaigrette on top.

TIME-SAVERS

■ *Do-ahead: The vinaigrette can be made well in advance and the chicken can be broiled ahead and served at room temperature or chilled.*

Values are approximate per serving: Calories: 289 Protein: 33 gm Fat: 15 gm
Carbohydrates: 3 gm Cholesterol: 82 mg Sodium: 98 mg

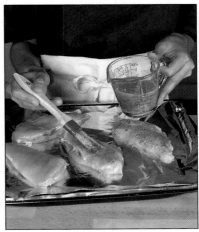

Step 3

Step 4

Step 6

Mediterranean Chicken Breasts with Yellow Rice

▼

Chorizo is a sausage of Latin origin, and both the Spanish and Mexican types are sold in this country. The Spanish version—used in this recipe—is a firm, dry sausage made of smoked pork; Mexican chorizo is commonly filled with fresh pork. Chorizo is sold in Latin markets and some supermarkets. The sausage is seasoned with chilies, paprika and herbs, so it makes a substantial flavor contribution to this skillet chicken dish.

Working time: 40 minutes
Total time: 55 minutes

Mediterranean Chicken Breasts with Yellow Rice

4 Servings

5 plum tomatoes or 6 whole canned tomatoes, well drained
2 medium onions
1 large green bell pepper
3 tablespoons flour
½ teaspoon black pepper
4 skinless, boneless chicken breast halves (about 1¼ pounds total)
2 tablespoons plus 1 teaspoon olive or other vegetable oil
5 cloves garlic, minced

¼ pound chorizo sausage
1 cup raw rice
2 cups chicken broth
½ cup water
¼ cup chopped pimiento (optional)
¼ teaspoon saffron or turmeric
1 tablespoon butter
1 cup dry white wine or chicken broth
¼ teaspoon sugar
1 bay leaf

Step 3

1 Coarsely chop the tomatoes. Thinly slice the onions. Cut the bell pepper into bite-size pieces. In a bowl, combine the flour and black pepper; dredge the chicken lightly in the flour, reserving the excess.

2 In a large skillet, warm 1 tablespoon of the oil over medium-high heat. Add 3 of the garlic cloves and the onions, and stir-fry until the onions are golden, about 5 minutes. Add the bell pepper and cook until softened, about 3 minutes. Remove the vegetables to a plate.

3 Add 1 tablespoon of the oil to the skillet. Add the chicken and cook until browned all over, about 5 minutes per side. Remove the chicken to a plate and cover loosely to keep warm.

4 Meanwhile, remove the papery outer coating from the sausage and cut the sausage into ¼-inch dice. In a medium saucepan, warm the remaining 1 teaspoon oil over medium-high heat until hot but not smoking. Add the sausage and cook, stirring, for 3 minutes. Add the 2 remaining cloves of garlic and the rice and cook, stirring, until the rice is lightly coated with oil, about 1 minute. Add 1½ cups of the chicken broth, the water, pimiento (if using) and saffron (or turmeric). Bring to a boil, reduce the heat to medium-low, cover and simmer until the rice is tender, about 20 minutes.

Step 4

5 While the rice simmers, return the cooked vegetables to the skillet. Add the butter and sprinkle with 1 tablespoon of the reserved dredging mixture. Cook, stirring, until the flour is no longer visible, about 30 seconds. Add the tomatoes, wine, remaining ½ cup chicken broth, the sugar and bay leaf, and bring the mixture to a boil. Return the chicken (and any accumulated juices) to the skillet, reduce the heat to low, cover and simmer until the chicken is cooked through, about 15 minutes. Discard the bay leaf and serve the chicken over the rice.

Values are approximate per serving: Calories: 619   Protein: 46 gm   Fat: 25 gm
Carbohydrates: 51 gm   Cholesterol: 90 mg   Sodium: 627 mg

Step 5

Honey-Orange Chicken

▼

The combination of honey and orange juice concentrate makes a wonderful sweet-tart glaze for sautéed chicken breasts. For a simple variation on the theme, make the glaze with frozen tangerine or apple juice concentrate. Or use maple syrup in place of the honey. Serve the chicken with steamed white rice and a green salad dressed with a lemon vinaigrette.

Working time: 20 minutes
Total time: 30 minutes

Honey-Orange Chicken

4 Servings

2 tablespoons cornstarch
½ teaspoon salt
⅛ teaspoon pepper
4 skinless, boneless chicken breast
  halves (about 1¼ pounds total)
2 tablespoons butter
½ cup chicken broth

2 tablespoons frozen orange juice
  concentrate
1 teaspoon Dijon mustard
½ teaspoon honey
2 tablespoons chopped parsley
  (optional)
Orange slices (optional)

1 In a plastic bag or small paper bag, combine the cornstarch, salt and pepper and shake to mix. Add the chicken and shake to coat the chicken lightly. Remove the chicken and reserve the excess cornstarch mixture.

2 In a large skillet, melt 1 tablespoon of the butter over medium heat until hot but not smoking. Add the chicken and brown on one side, about 5 minutes.

Step 3

3 Add the remaining 1 tablespoon butter, turn the chicken and brown well on the second side, about 5 minutes longer. Transfer the chicken to a plate and set aside.

4 Dissolve the reserved cornstarch mixture in the chicken broth.

5 Whisk the broth, orange juice concentrate, mustard and honey into the juices in the skillet. Bring the mixture to a boil over medium heat, stirring constantly.

Step 5

6 Add the chicken, reduce the heat to medium-low and cover the skillet. Cook until the chicken is tender and opaque throughout, 5 to 8 minutes.

7 Divide the chicken and sauce among 4 plates. Sprinkle with parsley and garnish with oranges slices, if desired.

TIME-SAVERS

■ ***Do-ahead:*** *The orange juice-broth mixture (Step 5) can be made ahead.*

Step 6

Values are approximate per serving: Calories: 244 Protein: 33 gm Fat: 8 gm
Carbohydrates: 8 gm Cholesterol: 98 mg Sodium: 588 mg

Southern Fried Chicken Strips with Honey Mustard

▼

You can't improve on old-fashioned fried chicken—or can you? Using narrow strips of chicken breast, which cook in minutes, is one appealing change; another is skinning the chicken and using a minimum of oil for a meal that is lower in fat. The delectable honey-mustard dipping sauce is another reason to try this recipe. For a different texture, try using coarse (whole-grain) mustard in the sauce.

Working time: 10 minutes
Total time: 15 minutes

Southern Fried Chicken Strips with Honey Mustard

4 Servings

4 skinless, boneless chicken breast
  halves (about 1¼ pounds total)
⅓ cup flour
2 tablespoons chopped parsley
  (optional)
1 teaspoon paprika
½ teaspoon salt
¼ teaspoon black pepper

Pinch of cayenne pepper
2 tablespoons plus 1 teaspoon
  vegetable oil
¼ cup Dijon or whole-grain
  mustard
1½ teaspoons honey
1 teaspoon cider vinegar

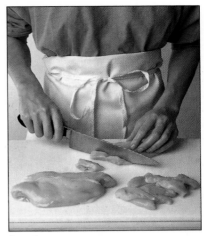
Step 1

1 Cut the chicken across the grain into ½-inch-wide strips.

2 In a plastic or paper bag, combine the flour, parsley (if using), paprika, salt, black pepper and cayenne. Add the chicken strips and shake to coat lightly.

3 In a large skillet, preferably nonstick, warm 2 tablespoons of the oil over medium-high heat until hot but not smoking. Add the chicken strips in one layer and cook, turning frequently, until cooked through and golden, about 7 minutes. Drain the chicken on paper towels.

4 In a small bowl, combine the mustard, honey and vinegar with the remaining 1 teaspoon oil.

5 Serve the chicken with the honey mustard on the side.

Step 2

TIME-SAVERS

■ *Do-ahead: The honey mustard (Step 4) can be made ahead. If the honey you have is crystallized or hard to pour, place the jar (without cap) in the microwave for 30 to 45 seconds at 100%.*

Step 3

Values are approximate per serving: Calories: 292   Protein: 34 gm   Fat: 11 gm
Carbohydrates: 13 gm   Cholesterol: 82 mg   Sodium: 816 mg

Oriental Chicken and Rice Salad

The tantalizing seasonings in this warm salad will make it a popular choice at your next buffet—or at your family dinner table. It's packed with strips of spicy broiled chicken and colorful vegetables, and tossed with a sesame-soy-citrus dressing. Feel free to vary the salad according to what's available: Use brown instead of white rice, or substitute different vegetables, such as peppers, corn, asparagus or green beans.

Working time: 30 minutes
Total time: 45 minutes

Oriental Chicken and Rice Salad

6 Servings

6 quarter-size slices (¼ inch thick) fresh ginger, unpeeled
2 cups chicken broth
¼ teaspoon red pepper flakes
1 cup raw rice
2 cloves garlic, minced or crushed through a press
6 tablespoons Oriental sesame oil
4 skinless, boneless chicken breast halves (about 1¼ pounds total)
3 medium carrots
¼ pound mushrooms

¼ pound fresh or frozen snow peas
4 scallions
¼ cup (packed) cilantro sprigs (optional)
¼ cup orange juice
3 tablespoons rice wine vinegar or cider vinegar
2 tablespoons reduced-sodium soy sauce
1 tablespoon grated orange zest (optional)
¼ teaspoon pepper

Step 4

1 Mince the ginger. Preheat the broiler. Line a broiler pan with foil.

2 In a medium saucepan, bring the chicken broth, half the ginger and the red pepper flakes to a boil over medium-high heat, covered. Add the rice, reduce the heat to medium-low, cover and simmer until the rice is tender and all the liquid is absorbed, about 20 minutes. When the rice is done, set it aside, uncovered, to cool slightly.

3 Meanwhile, in a small bowl, combine the remaining ginger with the garlic and 1 tablespoon of the sesame oil.

4 Place the chicken breasts on the broiler pan and brush the tops with half of the ginger-garlic mixture. Broil the chicken 4 inches from the heat for 6 minutes. Turn the chicken over, brush with the remaining ginger-garlic mixture and broil until the chicken is cooked through, about 7 minutes.

Step 5

5 Meanwhile, thinly slice the carrots on the diagonal. Slice the mushrooms. Slice the snow peas lengthwise into slivers. Finely chop the scallions and cilantro (if using).

6 In a large salad bowl, combine the orange juice, vinegar, soy sauce, orange zest (if using), pepper and the remaining 5 tablespoons sesame oil.

7 When the chicken is cool enough to handle, slice it across the grain into ¼-inch-wide strips.

8 Add the chicken (and any juices from the broiler pan), vegetables, cilantro and the rice to the salad bowl. Toss to combine all the ingredients with the dressing. Serve warm.

Step 8

Values are approximate per serving: Calories: 389 Protein: 27 gm Fat: 16 gm
Carbohydrates: 34 gm Cholesterol: 55 mg Sodium: 608 mg

Herbed
Country Chicken Stew

▼

This creamy country-style chicken stew is enriched and thickened with a butter-and-flour mixture called "beurre manié." The flour and butter are thoroughly combined (using your fingers is the most efficient way to do this) to form a paste. Pieces of the beurre manié are then pinched off and stirred into the stew one at a time. This method produces a rich, smooth sauce.

Working time: 20 minutes
Total time: 45 minutes

Herbed
Country Chicken Stew

4 Servings

1 medium onion
2½ cups chicken broth
3 cloves garlic, minced or crushed
    through a press
1 teaspoon basil
1 teaspoon thyme
½ teaspoon oregano
¼ teaspoon pepper
1 bay leaf
3 medium carrots

2 ribs celery
1 pound small red potatoes,
    unpeeled
1¼ pounds skinless, boneless
    chicken breast
3 tablespoons butter
3 tablespoons flour
4 tablespoons chopped parsley
    (optional)

Step 3

1 Cut the onion into thin wedges.

2 In a large saucepan, bring the chicken broth, onion wedges, garlic, basil, thyme, oregano, pepper and bay leaf to a boil over medium-high heat.

3 Meanwhile, cut the carrots and celery into 1-inch lengths. Cut the potatoes into ¾-inch chunks.

4 Add the vegetables to the boiling broth and let the broth return to a boil. Reduce the heat to low, cover and simmer until the potatoes are tender, about 20 minutes.

5 Meanwhile, cut the chicken into ¾-inch chunks. In a small bowl, thoroughly blend the butter and flour to make a smooth paste.

Step 5

6 Add the chicken to the broth. Stir in 2 tablespoons of the parsley (if using). Pinch off several pieces of the butter-flour mixture at a time, add them to the simmering broth and stir well. Repeat until all of the mixture has been incorporated. Cook until the sauce is thickened and the chicken is cooked through, 5 to 7 minutes.

7 Remove the bay leaf. Serve the stew garnished with the remaining chopped parsley (if using).

TIME-SAVERS

■ ***Do-ahead:*** *The whole stew can be made ahead and reheated.*

Step 6

Values are approximate per serving: Calories: 403 Protein: 39 gm Fat: 12 gm
Carbohydrates: 35 gm Cholesterol: 106 mg Sodium: 843 mg

Cajun Chicken Kebabs with Spicy Fruit Salad

▼

The basting sauce for these tangy kebabs has no fewer than eighteen ingredients, but it hardly matters since nearly all of them go straight into the pot with no advance preparation. The recipe yields three cups of sauce, but less than one cup is needed for the kebabs; save the extra to use another time on chicken thighs, pork chops or ham steak.

Working time: 40 minutes
Total time: 1 hour

Cajun Chicken Kebabs
with Spicy Fruit Salad

4 Servings

1 cup **water**
⅓ cup **Worcestershire sauce**
¼ cup **cider vinegar**
⅓ cup **brown sugar**
2 tablespoons **instant coffee**
¼ teaspoon **hot pepper sauce**
4 cloves **garlic,** minced or crushed through a press
2¼ teaspoons **black pepper**
2 teaspoons **paprika**
1 teaspoon **rosemary**
1 teaspoon **white pepper**
1½ teaspoons **oregano**
1½ teaspoons **thyme**
¼ teaspoon **cayenne pepper**

¾ teaspoon **salt**
2 **bay leaves**
1 cup **ketchup**
⅓ cup **vegetable oil**
4 skinless, boneless **chicken breast halves** (about 1¼ pounds total)
2 medium **red onions**
2 **oranges**
1 large fresh **peach** or 1 cup frozen unsweetened peaches, thawed
1 tablespoon **olive oil**
1 tablespoon **lime juice**
1 teaspoon grated **lime zest** (optional)
4 **lettuce leaves** (optional)

Step 3

1 In a medium saucepan, combine the water, Worcestershire sauce, vinegar, sugar, coffee, hot pepper sauce, garlic, 2 teaspoons of the black pepper, the paprika, rosemary, white pepper, oregano, thyme, cayenne, ½ teaspoon of the salt and the bay leaves. Stir in the ketchup and vegetable oil. Bring the mixture to a boil over medium-high heat, stirring frequently. Reduce the heat to low, cover and simmer for 10 minutes.

2 Meanwhile, preheat the broiler or start the charcoal. If broiling, line a broiler pan with foil.

3 Cut the chicken into 1-inch chunks. Cut the onion into ½-inch-thick wedges. Alternating, thread the chicken and onion onto 8 skewers.

Step 4

4 Pour about ⅔ cup of the basting sauce into a bowl (store the remainder for another use, or pass at the table if desired). Brush the kebabs with half the basting sauce (if broiling, place the kebabs on the broiling pan). Grill or broil 4 inches from the heat for 8 minutes. Turn the skewers over, brush with the remaining basting sauce and grill or broil until the chicken is cooked through, about 5 minutes.

5 Meanwhile, peel the oranges. Cut the oranges and the peach into ½-inch chunks. Place them in a bowl and add the olive oil, lime juice, lime zest (if using) and remaining ¼ teaspoon each salt and black pepper.

6 Serve the kebabs with the fruit salad (in a lettuce leaf, if desired).

Values are approximate per serving: Calories: 346   Protein: 34 gm   Fat: 11 gm
Carbohydrates: 27 gm   Cholesterol: 88 mg   Sodium: 354 mg

Step 5

Fruit-Glazed Cornish Game Hens

▼

Nothing could be easier—or look more elegant—than these fruit-glazed Cornish game hens. Experiment with different flavors, such as apricot jam, cherry preserves, currant jelly or orange marmalade. Halved game hens make good-sized single servings. If possible, have your butcher split the hens; if not, use a heavy chef's knife or cleaver to divide each bird in two. If you prefer, quartered chicken could be substituted for the hens.

Working time: 15 minutes
Total time: 30 minutes

Fruit-Glazed
Cornish Game Hens

4 Servings

2 Cornish game hens (about 2½ pounds total), split
1 tablespoon olive or other vegetable oil
1 teaspoon salt
½ teaspoon pepper
⅓ cup fruit jam or jelly

1 Preheat the broiler. Line a broiler pan with foil.

2 If the Cornish hens are not already split, with a heavy knife, cut through the hens at the backbone. Turn the hens skin-side down and cut through the white membrane on either side of the breastbone. Bend the breasts backward until the breastbone breaks, then pull out the breastbone and the attached cartilage. Cut the hen in half.

3 In a small bowl, combine the oil, salt and pepper.

4 Rub the Cornish hen halves all over with the seasoned oil and place them, skin-side up, on the broiler pan.

5 Broil the hens 4 inches from the heat for 15 minutes.

6 Meanwhile, in a small saucepan over low heat, melt the jam (or jelly), about 4 minutes.

7 Brush the hens with the jam and broil for 3 to 5 minutes longer, or until the hens are cooked through and glazed. Watch carefully to keep the jam from charring.

TIME-SAVERS

■ *Microwave tip: To melt the jam, place it in a glass measuring cup, cover with waxed paper and cook at 100% for 1 minute.*

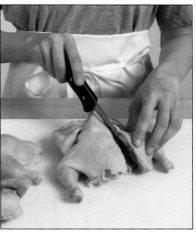

Step 2

Step 2

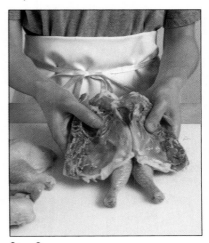

Step 2

Values are approximate per serving: Calories: 401 Protein: 34 gm Fat: 20 gm
Carbohydrates: 19 gm Cholesterol: 110 mg Sodium: 656 mg

Turkey Scallopini with Bell Peppers and Mushrooms

▼

The increased availability of turkey parts, such as the cutlets used here, has proved a boon for health-conscious cooks. Turkey is even lower in fat and cholesterol than chicken. If your supermarket does not carry cutlets, you can make this dish with uncooked turkey breast sliced and pounded ¼ inch thick. Serve the scallopini and vegetables with steamed rice and pour some of the pan juices over it.

Working time: 20 minutes
Total time: 20 minutes

Turkey Scallopini with Bell Peppers and Mushrooms

4 Servings

2 tablespoons flour
¾ teaspoon oregano
½ teaspoon salt
¼ teaspoon black pepper
4 turkey cutlets (about 1 pound total)
1 tablespoon olive or other vegetable oil

¼ pound mushrooms
1 medium red bell pepper
1 medium yellow or green bell pepper
½ cup chicken broth
3 tablespoons chopped parsley (optional)

Step 2

1 In a plastic or paper bag, combine the flour, ½ teaspoon of the oregano and the salt and black pepper. Add the turkey cutlets and lightly dredge them in the seasoned flour.

2 In a large skillet, preferably nonstick, warm the oil over medium-high heat until hot but not smoking. Add the turkey and cook until light golden on both sides, 3 to 4 minutes per side.

3 Meanwhile, slice the mushrooms ¼ inch thick. Cut the peppers into ¼-inch-wide strips.

4 Remove the turkey from the skillet and cover loosely to keep warm. Add the bell peppers, mushrooms, chicken broth and remaining ¼ teaspoon oregano to the skillet. Reduce the heat to medium, cover and simmer for 3 minutes.

5 Return the turkey to the pan. Increase the heat to medium-high, cover and cook until the turkey is heated through, about 2 minutes.

Step 3

6 Serve the turkey with the vegetables and some of the pan juices. Sprinkle with parsley if desired.

TIME-SAVERS

■ **Do-ahead:** *The bell peppers and mushrooms can be cut up ahead of time.*

Values are approximate per serving: Calories: 195   Protein: 28 gm   Fat: 6 gm   Carbohydrates: 7 gm   Cholesterol: 70 mg   Sodium: 477 mg

Step 5

Marinated Broiled Turkey

▼

Marinating thin turkey scallops in a yogurt and lemon juice mixture allows the Indian-inspired spices to penetrate the meat. Let the turkey marinate overnight, if possible, for maximum flavor. To keep clean-up to a minimum, place the turkey and marinade in a heavy-duty plastic bag; seal the bag and turn it a few times to coat the turkey, then place it in the refrigerator.

Working time: 15 minutes
Total time: 3 hours 25 minutes

Marinated Broiled Turkey

8 Servings

3 scallions
1 cup plain yogurt
¼ cup lemon juice
4 cloves garlic, minced or crushed
    through a press
¼ cup chopped parsley (optional)
1 tablespoon Dijon mustard
2 teaspoons grated lemon zest
    (optional)

2 teaspoons cumin
2 teaspoons coriander
½ teaspoon salt
¼ teaspoon black pepper
¼ teaspoon cayenne pepper
1 skinless, boneless turkey
    breast half (about 2¾ pounds)

Step 2

1 Coarsely chop the scallions.

2 In a medium bowl, combine the chopped scallions, yogurt, lemon juice, garlic, parsley (if using), mustard, lemon zest (if using), cumin, coriander, salt, black pepper and cayenne.

3 Slice the turkey across the grain into ¼-inch-thick scallops.

4 Toss the turkey with the marinade, cover and refrigerate for at least 3 hours, or overnight. If possible, toss the turkey in the marinade occasionally.

5 Preheat the broiler. Line a broiler pan with foil.

6 Arrange the turkey scallops in one layer on the broiler pan. Broil the turkey 4 inches from the heat until golden and cooked through, 10 to 12 minutes.

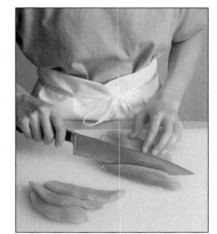
Step 3

TIME-SAVERS

■ *Do-ahead: The turkey is meant to be marinated ahead, but it can also be broiled ahead and served cold or at room temperature.*

Step 4

Values are approximate per serving: Calories: 206 Protein: 38 gm Fat: 3 gm
Carbohydrates: 4 gm Cholesterol: 98 mg Sodium: 320 mg

Gingered Turkey Kebabs

▼

*For these kebabs, long, thin strips of turkey are "woven" around chunks of
zucchini, bell pepper squares and whole cherry tomatoes. The kebabs are then brushed
with a gingery sweet-and-sour basting mixture and broiled. Pita bread and a fresh
cabbage salad are good companions for the kebabs. For portable picnic sandwiches,
slide the turkey and vegetables off the skewers into pita pockets.*

Working time: 15 minutes
Total time: 25 minutes

Gingered Turkey Kebabs

4 Servings

¾ **pound turkey scallopini**
3 **quarter-size slices (¼ inch thick) fresh ginger, unpeeled**
2 **garlic cloves, minced or crushed through a press**
¼ **cup reduced-sodium soy sauce**
1 **tablespoon Oriental sesame oil**
2 **teaspoons cider vinegar**

½ **teaspoon honey**
¼ **teaspoon pepper, preferably white**
1 **large zucchini (about ½ pound)**
1 **large yellow bell pepper**
24 **cherry tomatoes**
1 **teaspoon sesame seeds**

Step 1

1 Cut the scallopini lengthwise into 1-inch-wide strips. Mince the ginger.

2 In a shallow dish, combine the ginger, garlic, soy sauce, sesame oil, vinegar, honey and pepper. Add the turkey strips to the marinade and stir to coat them thoroughly.

3 Preheat the broiler. Line a broiler pan with foil.

4 Halve the zucchini lengthwise, then cut crosswise into 1-inch chunks. Cut the bell pepper into 1-inch squares.

Step 2

5 Dividing the ingredients evenly among 12 skewers, weave the strips of turkey around the cherry tomatoes, zucchini and bell pepper.

6 Place the skewers on the broiler pan and brush them with any remaining marinade. Sprinkle them with sesame seeds and broil 4 inches from the heat for 3 minutes.

7 Turn the kebabs over and broil until the turkey is cooked through, about 3 minutes longer.

TIME-SAVERS

■ **Do-ahead:** *The turkey can be marinated and the vegetables cut up ahead.*

Step 5

Values are approximate per serving: Calories: 173   Protein: 23 gm   Fat: 5 gm
Carbohydrates: 9 gm   Cholesterol: 53 mg   Sodium: 665 mg

Ham and Turkey Jambalaya

▼

*In an authentic New Orleans jambalaya, the ham used would be tasso, a highly
seasoned smoked ham that is a regional specialty. Although tasso is not widely
available, you might want to try making this jambalaya with another smoked ham
such as Black Forest, which is available at many supermarket deli counters.
Of course any type of lean ham—boiled or baked—will do just fine.*

Working time: 35 minutes
Total time: 35 minutes

Ham and Turkey Jambalaya

4 Servings

¼ pound bacon (4 to 6 slices)
1 medium onion
1 cup raw rice
1 can (28 ounces) whole tomatoes, with their juice
1 cup chicken broth
½ teaspoon thyme
¼ teaspoon black pepper

1 bay leaf
1½ cups cubed (½ inch) cooked turkey (about ½ pound)
1½ cups cubed (½ inch) lean ham (about ½ pound)
1 medium red bell pepper
¼ cup chopped parsley (optional)

Step 2

1 In a flameproof casserole or large skillet, cook the bacon over medium heat until crisp, about 10 minutes. Reserving the fat in the pan, drain the bacon on papers towels; crumble and set aside.

2 Meanwhile, coarsely chop the onion. Add the onion and the rice to the pan and cook, stirring constantly, for 2 minutes.

3 Increase the heat to medium-high and add the tomatoes and their juice, the broth, thyme, black pepper and bay leaf. Bring the mixture to a boil, breaking up the tomatoes with a spoon. Reduce the heat to medium-low, cover the pan, and simmer for 15 minutes.

Step 3

4 Meanwhile, cube the turkey and ham. Cut the bell pepper into thin slivers.

5 Stir the turkey, ham and bell pepper into the jambalaya. Cover and cook, stirring occasionally, until the pepper is limp, about 5 minutes.

6 Serve sprinkled with crumbled bacon and parsley if desired.

TIME-SAVERS

■ ***Microwave tip:*** *Although you will sacrifice some of the flavor that the bacon fat imparts to this dish, you can cook the bacon in the microwave on paper towels at 100% for 3 to 4 minutes. In Step 2, use about 3 tablespoons of olive or other vegetable oil for sautéing the onion and rice.*

■ ***Do-ahead:*** *The onion, turkey, ham and bell pepper can all be cut up ahead of time. The bacon can be cooked and crumbled ahead of time (be sure to save the bacon drippings for sautéing the onion). The whole dish can be made ahead and reheated gently in the oven or microwave.*

Step 4

Values are approximate per serving: Calories: 556 Protein: 36 gm Fat: 23 gm
Carbohydrates: 50 gm Cholesterol: 89 mg Sodium: 1625 mg

Turkey-Mushroom Chowder

▼

*Here is a delicious turkey chowder chock-full of mushrooms, rice, vegetables
and turkey. Although it takes less than an hour to make, you can cut the cooking
time even further by using leftover or storebought roast turkey. You'll
need about ¾ pound, or roughly three ½-inch slices. Cut the cooked turkey into
cubes and add them at the end, when you pour in the milk.*

Working time: 25 minutes
Total time: 50 minutes

Turkey-Mushroom Chowder

4 Servings

3 cups chicken broth
½ cup water
1 pound skinless, boneless turkey
  breast
1½ teaspoons oregano
¼ teaspoon pepper
3 cloves garlic
1 medium onion

1 medium carrot
¾ pound mushrooms
1 tablespoon olive or other
  vegetable oil
2 tablespoons butter
½ cup raw rice
3 tablespoons flour
1 cup milk

1 In a medium saucepan, bring the chicken broth and water to a boil over high heat.

2 Meanwhile, cut the turkey into 8 equal pieces to shorten the cooking time.

Step 2

3 Add the turkey pieces, oregano and pepper to the boiling broth. Let the broth return to a boil, then reduce the heat to medium-low, cover and simmer for 15 minutes. Remove the turkey to a plate and cover loosely to keep warm. Set the pan of broth aside.

4 Meanwhile, in a food processor, mince the garlic. Add the onion and coarsely chop. Remove and set aside.

5 In the same processor work bowl, coarsely chop the carrot; set aside. In two batches, coarsely chop the mushrooms.

6 In another medium saucepan, warm the oil over medium-high heat until hot but not smoking. Add the garlic and onion and cook until the onion has softened slightly, about 3 minutes.

7 Add the butter, rice, carrot and mushrooms, and cook, stirring, to coat the ingredients with the butter, about 3 minutes.

Step 5

8 Stir in the flour and cook, stirring, until the flour is no longer visible, about 30 seconds. Add the reserved broth and bring the mixture to a boil. Reduce the heat to medium-low, cover and simmer until the rice is tender, about 20 minutes.

9 Meanwhile, cut the turkey into bite-size pieces. When the rice is cooked, return the chowder to a boil over medium-high heat. Add the turkey and milk, and cook until heated through, about 2 minutes.

Values are approximate per serving: Calories: 418 Protein: 36 gm Fat: 15 gm
Carbohydrates: 35 gm Cholesterol: 94 mg Sodium: 915 mg

Step 9

Make-Ahead
Turkey Newburg

▼

To bring lobster Newburg within your weekday budget, try this variation, made with turkey, ham and a flavorful eggless sauce. All of the components are prepared ahead so that the dish can be assembled in only 30 minutes—about the time it takes to cook rice or noodles to go with it. Shaking the sauce ingredients in a jar to combine them is a useful trick: Try it the next time you need to blend flour and liquid for making gravy.

Working time: 30 minutes
Total time: 30 minutes

6 Servings

1 cup chicken broth
½ cup dry sherry
3 tablespoons flour
1 teaspoon brown sugar
1¾ pounds skinless, boneless
turkey breast
½ pound ham, unsliced

2 tablespoons olive or other
vegetable oil
1½ teaspoons rosemary, crumbled
¼ teaspoon pepper
1 tablespoon butter
1 pound small mushrooms

1 In a small bowl or screw-top jar, combine the chicken broth, 6 tablespoons of the sherry, the flour and ½ teaspoon of the sugar. Stir or shake to blend well. Cover and refrigerate until ready to cook the dish.

2 Cut the turkey into 1-inch chunks. Cut the ham lengthwise into two pieces. Cut each piece crosswise into slices about ¼ inch thick.

Step 4

3 In a medium bowl, combine the turkey, ham, the remaining 2 tablespoons sherry, ½ teaspoon sugar, 1 tablespoon of the oil, the rosemary and pepper. Toss to coat well, cover the bowl and refrigerate until ready to cook the dish (up to 1 or 2 days, but for at least 30 minutes). Stir the ingredients occasionally if possible to be sure they are marinating evenly.

4 To assemble the dish: In a large skillet, warm the butter in the remaining 1 tablespoon oil over medium-high heat until the butter is melted. Add the mushrooms and sauté until the mushrooms begin to wilt, about 5 minutes.

5 Add the turkey-ham mixture (including the marinade) and cook, stirring frequently, until the meat is nearly cooked through, 8 to 10 minutes.

Step 5

6 Stir or shake the chicken broth mixture to recombine and add to the skillet. Bring the mixture to a boil, stirring constantly, and cook until the sauce has thickened and the meat is cooked through, 2 to 3 minutes.

TIME-SAVERS

■ ***Do-ahead:*** *The broth mixture (Step 1) and the turkey-ham mixture (Steps 2 and 3) can be prepared a day or two ahead.*

Values are approximate per serving: Calories: 326 Protein: 42 gm Fat: 12 gm
Carbohydrates: 10 gm Cholesterol: 110 mg Sodium: 845 mg

Step 6

Barbecue-Roasted Turkey Breast

▼

Now that fresh turkey is available year 'round, it makes an ideal choice for a weekend barbecue. If you have a grill with a cover and a controllable heat source, you can experiment with cooking the turkey outdoors. Or, you can follow the directions given here for oven-roasting. Because this recipe is for a boneless breast half, the cooking time is far shorter than that for a conventional roast turkey.

Working time: 15 minutes
Total time: 2 hours

Barbecue-Roasted Turkey Breast

6 Servings

1 medium onion	**1 tablespoon Worcestershire sauce**
⅔ cup ketchup	**3 tablespoons brown sugar**
2 tablespoons tomato paste	**2 teaspoons dry mustard**
2 tablespoons butter	**1 boneless turkey breast half**
2 tablespoons soy sauce	**(about 3½ pounds)**
2 tablespoons vinegar	

1 Preheat the oven to 425°. Line a roasting pan with foil.

2 Make the barbecue sauce: Coarsely chop the onion. In a small saucepan, combine the onion, ketchup, tomato paste, butter, soy sauce, vinegar, Worcestershire sauce, sugar and mustard. Bring to a boil over medium-high heat, stirring until well blended. Remove the pan from the heat and set aside.

Step 2

3 Place the turkey breast on the prepared roasting pan and brush the turkey with one-fourth of the barbecue sauce. Roast the turkey for 15 minutes.

4 Remove the turkey from the oven and reduce the oven temperature to 325°. Brush the turkey with most of the remaining sauce and roast it, basting it periodically with the remaining sauce, until the turkey registers 170° on a meat thermometer, about 1 hour and 45 minutes longer.

5 Let the turkey stand for 5 to 10 minutes before slicing and serving. Bring any leftover basting sauce to a boil and serve it on the side.

Step 3

TIME-SAVERS

■ *Microwave tip: In a medium microwave-safe bowl, combine the chopped onion and the butter, cover and cook at 100% for 30 seconds to 1 minute, or until the butter is melted. Stir in the remaining barbecue sauce ingredients. Place the turkey in a shallow microwave-safe baking dish and tent with waxed paper. Cook at 50%, rotating the dish occasionally, for 35 to 45 minutes, or until the turkey registers 170° on a meat thermometer. About halfway through the cooking time, brush the turkey with the barbecue sauce. Let stand 5 minutes before slicing; reheat the remaining sauce and serve it on the side.*

■ *Do-ahead: The barbecue sauce can be made well ahead of time. In fact, the whole dish can be made ahead and the turkey served at room temperature or cold.*

Step 4

Values are approximate per serving: Calories: 492 Protein: 60 gm Fat: 19 gm
Carbohydrates: 18 gm Cholesterol: 160 mg Sodium: 900 mg

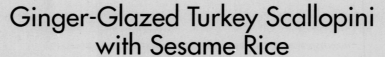

Ginger-Glazed Turkey Scallopini with Sesame Rice

▼

These thin turkey cutlets are pan-cooked in a cornstarch-thickened broth infused with ginger, garlic, honey and soy sauce. The highly flavorful but low-calorie sauce that glazes the cutlets is served with the turkey and the accompanying sesame rice. For a complementary salad course, toast a few extra tablespoons of sesame seeds and sprinkle them over vinaigrette-dressed greens.

Working time: 20 minutes
Total time: 40 minutes

Ginger-Glazed Turkey Scallopini with Sesame Rice

4 Servings

3 tablespoons flour
¼ teaspoon pepper
4 turkey scallopini (about ¾ pound total)
1 tablespoon olive or other vegetable oil
2 cups low-sodium chicken broth
1 cup water
1 cup raw rice

5 quarter-size slices (¼ inch thick) fresh ginger, unpeeled
⅓ cup cilantro sprigs (optional)
1 tablespoon reduced-sodium soy sauce
2 cloves garlic, minced or crushed through a press
1 tablespoon honey
1 tablespoon sesame seeds

1 In a shallow bowl, combine the flour and the pepper. Lightly dredge the turkey in the seasoned flour, reserving any excess.

2 In a large nonstick skillet, warm the oil over medium-high heat until hot but not smoking. Add the turkey and cook until golden brown all over, about 3 minutes per side. Remove the turkey to a plate and cover loosely to keep warm.

3 In a medium saucepan, bring 1 cup of the chicken broth and the water to a boil. Add the rice, reduce the heat to medium-low, cover and simmer until the rice is tender and all the liquid is absorbed, about 20 minutes.

4 Meanwhile, finely chop the ginger and cilantro (if using).

5 In a small bowl, blend the remaining 1 cup chicken broth with the reserved dredging mixture. Add the broth to the skillet along with the soy sauce and bring to a boil. Add the ginger, 3 tablespoons of the cilantro (if using), the garlic and honey. Reduce the heat to low, cover and simmer for 10 minutes.

6 Return the turkey (and any juices that have accumulated on the plate) to the skillet. Cover with some of the sauce, re-cover the pan and continue to simmer for another 5 minutes.

7 Meanwhile, in a small ungreased skillet, toast the sesame seeds over medium heat, shaking the pan frequently, about 7 minutes.

8 When the rice is done, stir in the toasted sesame seeds and the remaining cilantro (if using). Serve the turkey cutlets with the rice and some of the sauce.

Step 2

Step 5

Step 8

Values are approximate per serving: Calories: 368 Protein: 26 gm Fat: 7 gm
Carbohydrates: 48 gm Cholesterol: 53 mg Sodium: 237 mg

Mustard Sirloin Steak with Herbed Potatoes (page 91)

CHAPTER 2
MEAT

London Broil with Caramelized Onions

▼

When onions are gently cooked with a bit of sugar, they undergo a wonderful transformation, turning delectably sweet and golden. They're an appetizing accompaniment to meat, and in the time it takes to broil a steak, you can caramelize a skilletful of onions for a delicious topping. Even family members who don't normally fancy onions will take to them in this new guise.

Working time: 15 minutes
Total time: 30 minutes

London Broil with Caramelized Onions

6 Servings

4 medium onions
2 tablespoons butter
1 tablespoon olive or other
  vegetable oil
3 cloves garlic, minced or crushed
  through a press
1½ pounds London broil

2 teaspoons sugar
¼ cup beef broth
2 tablespoons sherry or
  chicken broth
¼ teaspoon salt
¼ teaspoon pepper

1 Preheat the broiler. Line a broiler pan with foil.

2 Slice the onions.

Step 2

3 In a medium skillet, warm the butter in the oil over medium-high heat until the butter is melted. Add the onions and garlic, and cook, stirring, until the onion begins to brown, about 5 minutes.

4 Broil the steak 4 inches from heat for 8 minutes on one side. Turn the steak over and broil for 7 minutes for rare, 10 minutes for medium-rare, 11 to 12 minutes for medium.

5 Meanwhile, add the sugar to the onions and cook 5 minutes longer.

6 Add the beef broth and sherry (or chicken broth) to the skillet and bring the liquid to a boil over medium-high heat. Reduce the heat to low and cook, uncovered, until ready to slice the steak, about 15 minutes, stirring occasionally. Season with the salt and pepper.

Step 6

7 Let the steak rest for about 5 minutes, then slice it across the grain and on the diagonal. Serve the steak with the caramelized onions on the side.

TIME-SAVERS

■ ***Do-ahead:*** *The onions can be caramelized ahead of time and reheated gently before serving.*

Values are approximate per serving: Calories: 271   Protein: 23 gm   Fat: 17 gm
Carbohydrates: 6 gm   Cholesterol: 67 mg   Sodium: 233 mg

Step 7

Ginger Orange Beef

▼

Orange zest and fresh ginger heighten the flavors of the carrots, green beans, scallions and water chestnuts used in this low-calorie stir-fry. The proportion of vegetables to meat in this simple dish render it not only low-fat but high in carbohydrates as well. And serving it with rice, which adds only 100 calories per half-cup portion, makes the balance of complex carbohydrates, protein and fat in the meal even more favorable.

Working time: 20 minutes
Total time: 30 minutes

Ginger Orange Beef

4 Servings

¼ pound flank steak
1 tablespoon cornstarch
1 tablespoon reduced-sodium
  soy sauce
2 drops hot pepper sauce
½ pound fresh green beans or
  1 package (10 ounces) frozen cut
  green beans, thawed
2 medium carrots
2 scallions

3 quarter-size slices (¼ inch thick)
  fresh ginger, unpeeled
1 tablespoon grated orange zest
1 tablespoon vegetable oil
⅔ cup beef broth
2 cloves garlic, minced or crushed
  through a press
1 can (8 ounces) sliced water
  chestnuts, drained
1 tablespoon water

Step 1

1 Cut the flank steak with the grain into 2-inch-wide strips. Cut the strips across the grain into ¼-inch-thick slices.

2 In a medium bowl, combine 1 teaspoon of the cornstarch with the soy sauce and hot pepper sauce. Add the steak strips and toss to coat well.

3 Cut the fresh green beans into 2-inch lengths. Cut the carrots into thin slices. Coarsely chop the scallions. Mince the ginger. Grate the orange zest.

Step 3

4 In a large nonstick skillet, warm the oil over medium-high heat until hot but not smoking. Add the steak strips and stir-fry until the meat is browned but still slightly pink inside. Remove the meat to a plate and cover loosely to keep warm.

5 Add the beef broth, garlic, ginger and orange zest to the skillet and bring to a boil over medium-high heat. Add the beans, carrots, scallions and water chestnuts. Return the mixture to a boil. Reduce the heat to medium-low, cover and cook for 4 minutes.

6 Meanwhile, in a small bowl, combine the remaining 2 teaspoons cornstarch with the water.

7 Bring the mixture in the skillet back to a boil over medium-high heat and stir in the cornstarch mixture. Return the steak strips (and any juices that have accumulated on the plate) to the skillet and cook, stirring, until the meat is cooked through and the sauce is slightly thickened, about 4 minutes.

Step 7

TIME-SAVERS

■ **Do-ahead:** *The steak and vegetables can be cut up ahead.*

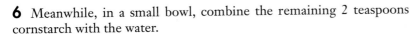

Values are approximate per serving: Calories: 159 Protein: 8 gm Fat: 6 gm
Carbohydrates: 18 gm Cholesterol: 14 mg Sodium: 332 mg

Mediterranean Pot Roast

▼

*Long, slow cooking brings out the best in the beef and vegetables in this dish.
The chuck roast becomes meltingly tender, and the potatoes, zucchini, bell peppers and
mushrooms soak up the delicious broth, flavored with wine, garlic and herbs.
If you can make the pot roast a day ahead, so much the better; when refrigerated,
any fat will congeal on top, so you can easily remove it before reheating.*

Working time: 15 minutes
Total time: 3 hours

10 Servings

¼ **cup flour**
1½ **teaspoons salt**
¼ **teaspoon black pepper**
4-pound chuck roast, well trimmed
3 **tablespoons olive or other**
  vegetable oil
2 **medium onions**
4 **cloves garlic, minced or crushed**
  through a press
2 **cans (16 ounces each) crushed**
  tomatoes

2 **cups red wine**
1½ **teaspoons thyme**
1 **bay leaf**
1¾ **pounds small red potatoes**
2 **medium red bell peppers**
1 **large zucchini**
½ **pound small mushrooms**
¼ **cup chopped parsley**
  (optional)

Step 2

1 On a plate, combine the flour, salt and black pepper. Lightly dredge the roast in the seasoned flour. Reserve the excess dredging mixture.

2 In a flameproof casserole or Dutch oven, warm 2 tablespoons of the oil over medium-high heat until hot but not smoking. Add the roast and cook until browned on all sides, about 10 minutes.

3 Meanwhile, very coarsely chop the onions.

4 Remove the roast from the pan. Add the remaining 1 tablespoon oil, the onions and the garlic. Sauté until the onions begin to brown, about 5 minutes.

5 Add the reserved dredging mixture to the pan and stir until the fat absorbs the flour. Add the tomatoes, wine, thyme and bay leaf, and bring the mixture a boil. Return the roast to the casserole and bring the liquid to a boil. Reduce the heat to medium-low, cover and simmer for 2 hours, turning the roast from time to time.

Step 7

6 Meanwhile, halve the potatoes. Cut the bell peppers into strips. Halve the zucchini lengthwise and cut it into 1-inch lengths.

7 When the roast has cooked for 2 hours, add the potatoes, bell peppers and whole mushrooms to the casserole. Re-cover and cook for 30 minutes.

8 Add the zucchini and cook for 5 minutes longer. Remove the bay leaf. Stir in the parsley (if using) just before serving.

Step 8

Values are approximate per serving: Calories: 323 Protein: 30 gm Fat: 11 gm
Carbohydrates: 26 gm Cholesterol: 74 mg Sodium: 571 mg

Beef and Barley Soup

▼

You might expect a recipe for beef and barley soup to begin with directions for making beef stock from bones, and end with hours of simmering "on the back of the stove." This soup makes no such demands on time and energy: You start with ready-made broth and boneless stew beef, and the preparations are simple. After the ingredients go into the pot, the soup simmers unattended for less than an hour.

Working time: 10 minutes
Total time: 1 hour

Beef and Barley Soup

6 Servings

1 can (14 ounces) whole tomatoes, with their juice
3 cups beef broth
½ cup water
¼ cup pearl barley
2 cloves garlic, minced or crushed through a press
1 teaspoon sugar

¾ teaspoon thyme
¼ teaspoon pepper
1 bay leaf
¾ pound lean stew beef
2 large or 3 medium carrots
½ pound small mushrooms
1 cup frozen pearl onions

1 In a large saucepan, combine the tomatoes and their juice, the broth, water, barley, garlic, sugar, thyme, pepper and bay leaf. Bring the liquid to a boil over medium-high heat, breaking up the tomatoes with a spoon.

2 Meanwhile, cut the beef into ¾- to 1-inch cubes. Cut the carrots into large dice. Halve or quarter any large mushrooms.

3 When the soup has come to a boil, add the beef, carrots, mushrooms and pearl onions. Bring the soup back to a boil, reduce the heat to medium-low, cover and simmer until the barley is tender, about 55 minutes.

4 Remove the bay leaf and serve the soup hot.

TIME-SAVERS

■ **Do-ahead:** *The whole soup can be made ahead.*

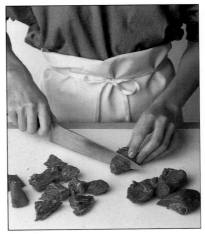

Step 2

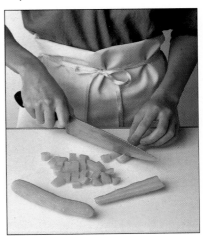

Step 2

Step 3

Values are approximate per serving: Calories: 189 Protein: 15 gm Fat: 6 gm
Carbohydrates: 19 gm Cholesterol: 37 mg Sodium: 582 mg

Oven-Roasted Steak-and-Scallion Kebabs with Potatoes

▼

Kebabs probably require the least effort of any barbecue food—they're easy to serve, no carving is required, and they can just as easily be cooked indoors, in the broiler. The potatoes served with these steak kebabs are deliciously buttery and crusty. If your broiler is too small to cook the kebabs and potatoes at the same time, finish the potatoes under the broiler first, then cover them with foil to keep warm while you broil the meat.

Working time: 30 minutes
Total time: 45 minutes

Oven-Roasted Steak-and-Scallion Kebabs with Potatoes

4 Servings

4 tablespoons butter
1 pound small red potatoes
2 tablespoons fresh tarragon or 1 teaspoon dried
¼ cup dry red wine or beef broth
2 tablespoons Dijon mustard
1 tablespoon olive or other vegetable oil

½ teaspoon dry mustard
1 clove garlic, minced or crushed through a press
¼ teaspoon pepper
1 pound sirloin steak, well trimmed
1 bunch scallions (6 to 8)

Step 3

1 Preheat the oven to 425°. Line a broiler pan with foil.

2 In a small skillet, melt 2 tablespoons of the butter over medium heat. Remove from the heat.

3 Cut the potatoes into quarters and place them on the broiler pan. Drizzle the melted butter over the potatoes and toss them to coat evenly. Roast the potatoes in the oven until beginning to brown, about 20 minutes.

4 Meanwhile, mince the tarragon. In a small saucepan, combine the tarragon, wine, Dijon mustard, olive oil, dry mustard, garlic and pepper, and stir to combine.

5 Cut the steak into 1½-inch cubes. Cut the scallions into 1½-inch lengths. Alternating them, thread the steak cubes and scallion pieces onto skewers.

6 When the potatoes have roasted for 20 minutes, remove them from the oven and preheat the broiler.

Step 5

7 Move the potatoes to one side of the broiler pan and place the skewers on the pan. Brush the meat and scallions with some of the tarragon-mustard mixture and broil 4 inches from the heat for 5 minutes. Turn the kebabs over, brush with more tarragon-mustard mixture and broil for 7 minutes longer, or until the meat is medium-rare.

8 Meanwhile, bring the remaining tarragon-mustard mixture to a boil over medium heat. Reduce the heat to low and simmer for 10 minutes. Stir in the remaining 2 tablespoons butter. When the kebabs are done, pour any pan juices from the broiler pan into the sauce. Serve the sauce on the side.

Values are approximate per serving: Calories: 391   Protein: 27 gm   Fat: 21 gm
Carbohydrates: 24 gm   Cholesterol: 100 mg   Sodium: 419 mg

Step 7

Quick Beef Paprika Stew over Egg Noodles

▼

This is no everyday beef stew, but it is fast and easy enough to make for a weekday dinner. Its special-occasion feeling comes from two features that give the dish something of the flavor of beef Stroganoff: a golden bed of egg noodles beneath the beef and a dollop of sour cream on top. Accompany this main dish with a crisp salad tossed with a light, tangy dressing.

Working time: 25 minutes
Total time: 40 minutes

Quick Beef Paprika Stew
over Egg Noodles

4 Servings

1 medium onion
1 large red bell pepper
1 pound stewing beef
⅓ cup flour
2 tablespoons paprika
¼ teaspoon salt
¼ teaspoon black pepper
2 tablespoons olive or other
  vegetable oil

3 cloves garlic, minced or crushed
  through a press
1 can (14½ ounces) stewed
  tomatoes, with their juice
¼ cup beef broth
2 teaspoons Worcestershire sauce
½ pound egg noodles
1 tablespoon butter
⅓ cup sour cream

Step 1

1 Cut the onion into thin slices. Cut the bell pepper into bite-size pieces. Cut the beef into ¾-inch chunks.

2 In a plastic or paper bag, combine the flour, paprika, salt and black pepper, and shake to mix. Add the beef and shake to coat lightly. Remove the beef and reserve the excess seasoned flour.

3 In a large skillet, warm 1 tablespoon of the oil over medium-high heat until hot but not smoking. Add the onion and garlic and cook until the mixture begins to brown, about 3 minutes; remove to a plate and set aside.

4 Bring a large pot of water to a boil.

5 Meanwhile, add the remaining 1 tablespoon oil to the skillet. Add the beef and sauté until browned all over, about 5 minutes.

Step 5

6 Return the onion mixture to the skillet along with the reserved dredging mixture and cook, stirring, until the flour is no longer visible, about 30 seconds.

7 Add the stewed tomatoes and their juice, the beef broth and Worcestershire sauce, and bring to a boil over medium-high heat. Add the bell pepper, reduce the heat to low, cover and simmer while you cook the noodles.

8 Add the noodles to the boiling water and cook until al dente, 10 to 12 minutes, or according to package directions.

9 Drain the noodles and toss them with the butter. Serve the noodles topped with the stew and a heaping tablespoon of sour cream.

Step 7

Values are approximate per serving: Calories: 606   Protein: 34 gm   Fat: 25 gm
Carbohydrates: 62 gm   Cholesterol: 144 mg   Sodium: 617 mg

Mustard Sirloin Steak with Herbed Potatoes

▼

In this steak-and-potatoes dinner, thick sirloin steaks are basted with a two-mustard mixture that's flavored with garlic, pepper and tarragon. The herb-buttered potatoes (left unpeeled in the interests of efficiency and additional dietary fiber) are broiled alongside the steak after a brief precooking. For a change, try a different herb: Oregano and basil are two possibilities.

Working time: 10 minutes
Total time: 40 minutes

Mustard Sirloin Steak with Herbed Potatoes

4 Servings

1 pound small red potatoes, unpeeled
2 tablespoons red wine vinegar
4 cloves garlic, minced or crushed through a press
3 tablespoons Dijon mustard
1 teaspoon dry mustard
½ teaspoon cracked pepper
1½ teaspoons tarragon
¾ teaspoon salt
2 tablespoons butter
¼ cup chopped parsley (optional)
¼ teaspoon ground pepper
2 medium sirloin steaks (about 1½ pounds total)

Step 4

1 Bring a medium saucepan of water to a boil.

2 Meanwhile, halve the potatoes. Add them to the boiling water and return the water to a boil; reduce the heat to medium-low, cover and cook for 10 minutes.

3 Preheat the broiler. Line a broiler pan with foil.

4 In a small bowl, combine the vinegar, half of the minced garlic, the Dijon mustard, dry mustard, cracked pepper, 1 teaspoon of the tarragon and ½ teaspoon of the salt.

5 Melt the butter on the stovetop or in the microwave. In a medium bowl, combine the melted butter, 2 tablespoons of the parsley (if using), the remaining minced garlic, ½ teaspoon tarragon, ¼ teaspoon salt and the ground pepper.

Step 6

6 Place the steaks on the broiler pan and brush with half the mustard mixture. Drain the potatoes and toss them with the herb butter. Arrange the potatoes around the steaks and broil 4 inches from the heat for 7 minutes.

7 Turn the steaks and potatoes over. Brush the steaks with the remaining mustard mixture. Broil for 7 minutes longer for rare; 9 minutes for medium-rare; 11 minutes for medium. Let the steaks rest 5 minutes before slicing across the grain. Serve with the potatoes and some of the pan juices. Garnish with the remaining parsley, if desired.

TIME-SAVERS

■ *Microwave tip: Instead of boiling the potatoes as directed in Step 2, place them and ¼ cup water in a 2-quart microwave-safe casserole. Cover and cook at 100% for 5 minutes, or until just tender. Proceed with the rest of the recipe as directed.*

Values are approximate per serving: Calories: 462   Protein: 35 gm   Fat: 25 gm
Carbohydrates: 24 gm   Cholesterol: 119 mg   Sodium: 890 mg

Step 6

Tex-Mex Beef Skillet

Super quick stir-frying lets you make a one-pan meal in minimal time.
Though stir-frying is an Oriental technique, it works perfectly well with the staples
and seasonings of other cuisines. Here, the flavors are Mexican: flank steak strips,
garlic, onion, bell pepper and black beans are spiced with chili powder. A yellow pepper
makes the dish prettier, but a red pepper or a second green one will be fine.

Working time: 25 minutes
Total time: 30 minutes

Tex-Mex Beef Skillet

4 Servings

1 pound flank steak	3 tablespoons flour
1 medium onion	3 tablespoons chili powder
1 large yellow bell pepper	¼ teaspoon black pepper
1 large green bell pepper	⅔ cup beef broth
1 can (15 ounces) black beans	⅓ cup water
2 tablespoons vegetable oil	2 teaspoons Worcestershire sauce
2 cloves garlic, minced or crushed through a press	½ teaspoon oregano
	¼ teaspoon salt

1 Cut the steak with the grain into two strips about 2 inches wide. Then cut each strip across the grain into ¼-inch-thick slices.

Step 1

2 Coarsely chop the onion. Dice the bell peppers. Drain the beans in a colander, rinse under cold running water and drain well.

3 In a large skillet, warm 1 tablespoon of the oil over medium-high heat until hot but not smoking. Add the onion and garlic and stir-fry until the onion is golden, about 5 minutes. Remove the garlic-onion mixture from the skillet and set aside.

4 In a plastic or paper bag, combine the flour, chili powder and black pepper, and shake to mix. Add the beef and shake to coat lightly. Remove the beef and reserve the excess seasoned flour.

5 Add the remaining 1 tablespoon oil to the skillet and warm over medium-high heat until hot but not smoking. Add the beef to the skillet and stir-fry until the meat is browned but still slightly pink in the center, about 5 minutes.

Step 5

6 Stir 1 tablespoon of the reserved dredging mixture into the skillet and cook, stirring, until the flour is no longer visible, about 1 minute.

7 Return the garlic-onion mixture to the skillet. Add the bell peppers, beans, beef broth, water, Worcestershire sauce, oregano and salt. Bring the mixture to a boil and cook, stirring, until the peppers are tender and the liquid thickens slightly, 2 to 3 minutes.

TIME-SAVERS

■ **Do-ahead:** *The meat and vegetables can be cut up ahead.*

Values are approximate per serving: Calories: 399 Protein: 32 gm Fat: 17 gm
Carbohydrates: 31 gm Cholesterol: 57 mg Sodium: 851 mg

Step 7

Meat-and-Potatoes Loaf

▼

This hearty supper is cooked in a baking dish instead of a loaf pan, but that's just the beginning of the delicious difference between this and an ordinary meat loaf. A mixture of ground beef and veal, made zesty with barbecue sauce, is layered with shredded potatoes and chopped vegetables; the top layer of potatoes, dusted with Parmesan, turns crunchy and golden as it bakes.

Working time: 25 minutes
Total time: 1 hour 25 minutes

Meat-and-Potatoes Loaf

6 Servings

5 medium carrots	2 tablespoons tomato paste
1 large yellow or red bell pepper	1 tablespoon brown sugar
3 tablespoons butter	1 teaspoon basil
5 medium scallions	¾ teaspoon salt
½ pound lean ground beef	1 teaspoon black pepper
½ pound ground veal	1¼ pounds red potatoes, unpeeled
⅔ cup bottled barbecue sauce	1 tablespoon flour
¾ cup fine unseasoned	1 egg
breadcrumbs	⅓ cup grated Parmesan cheese

1 Preheat the oven to 425°. Butter a shallow 2-quart baking dish.

2 Cut the carrots into 1-inch lengths. Cut the bell pepper into large pieces. In a medium saucepan, bring 2 inches of water to a boil. Add the carrots and bell pepper and return to a boil. Reduce the heat to low, cover and simmer until the carrots are tender, about 7 minutes.

3 Meanwhile, melt the butter on the stovetop or in the microwave. Mince the scallions. In a medium bowl, combine the beef, veal, barbecue sauce, scallions and ½ cup of the breadcrumbs. Set aside.

Step 3

4 Drain the carrots and bell pepper and place them in a food processor. Add the tomato paste, 1 tablespoon of the melted butter, the brown sugar, remaining ¼ cup bread crumbs, the basil, ½ teaspoon of the salt and ¼ teaspoon of the black pepper. Process to just combine.

5 In the same processor work bowl, shred the potatoes. Transfer to a medium bowl and toss with the flour. In a small bowl, beat the egg with the remaining 2 tablespoons melted butter, ¼ teaspoon salt and ¾ teaspoon black pepper. Add to the potatoes and toss to combine.

Step 6

6 Spread half of the potatoes in the bottom of the baking dish. Spread the carrot-pepper mixture on top. Spread the meat mixture on top of the carrot layer. Spread the remaining potatoes on top.

7 Sprinkle the Parmesan cheese on top and bake for 1 hour, or until the meat is cooked through and the potato topping is golden brown.

TIME-SAVERS

■ *Microwave tip: Assemble the casserole as directed, but in a shallow microwave-safe baking dish. Cover loosely with waxed paper and cook at 100% for 5 minutes, then at 50% for 15 minutes, rotating the dish once. If desired, brown the top under the broiler.*

Values are approximate per serving: Calories: 461   Protein: 22 gm   Fat: 20 gm
Carbohydrates: 48 gm   Cholesterol: 116 mg   Sodium: 1054 mg

Step 7

Easy Beef-Tomato Curry

▼

Strips of lean flank steak cook quickly in this pungently spicy dish, which combines the indispensable Chinese stir-frying technique with Indian-inspired curry seasonings. Despite the brief cooking time, the flavors are beautifully blended, as if the ingredients had simmered together for hours. For a side salad, try sliced cucumbers with a yogurt-mint dressing.

Working time: 25 minutes
Total time: 35 minutes

Easy Beef-Tomato Curry

4 Servings

1 cup raw rice
1 pound flank steak
1 pound fresh plum tomatoes or
    1 can (16 ounces) whole
    tomatoes, drained
1 medium onion
1 large green bell pepper
3 quarter-size slices (¼ inch thick)
    fresh ginger, unpeeled

2 tablespoons vegetable oil
3 cloves garlic, minced or crushed
    through a press
¼ cup curry powder
¼ cup beef broth
3 tablespoons reduced-sodium or
    regular soy sauce
2 teaspoons cornstarch
¼ teaspoon black pepper

Step 2

1 In a medium saucepan, bring 2 cups of water to a boil over medium-high heat. Add the rice, reduce the heat to low, cover and simmer until the rice is done, about 20 minutes.

2 Meanwhile, cut the steak with the grain into 2-inch-wide strips. Then cut each strip across the grain into ¼-inch-thick slices.

3 Quarter the tomatoes. Cut the onion into wedges. Cut the bell pepper into ¾-inch squares. Finely chop the ginger.

4 In a large skillet, warm 1 tablespoon of the oil over medium-high heat until hot but not smoking. Add the onion, ginger and garlic, and sauté until the onion begins to brown, about 3 minutes.

5 Add the steak strips and 2 tablespoons of the curry powder and stir-fry until the beef is still slightly pink in the middle, about 3 minutes. Remove the onion, garlic and beef to a plate and set aside.

Step 5

6 Add the remaining 1 tablespoon oil, 2 tablespoons curry powder and the tomatoes to the skillet. Cook, stirring, for 1 minute. Add the bell pepper and stir-fry until it is crisp-tender, about 3 minutes.

7 Meanwhile, in a small bowl, stir together the beef broth, soy sauce, cornstarch and black pepper.

8 Return the onion, garlic and beef to the skillet. Stir in the broth mixture and bring the liquid to a boil. Cook, stirring constantly, until the beef and vegetables are tender and the sauce is slightly thickened, about 2 minutes. Serve the curry over the cooked rice.

TIME-SAVERS

■ *Do-ahead: The beef and vegetables can be cut up ahead. The whole curry mixture can be made ahead, reheated and served over freshly cooked rice.*

Values are approximate per serving: Calories: 506 Protein: 29 gm Fat: 21 gm
Carbohydrates: 52 gm Cholesterol: 59 mg Sodium: 599 mg

Step 6

Super Chunky Hash

Although it is traditionally composed of leftovers, a well-made hash requires no apologies. In this hearty version (which bears no resemblance to canned hash), cubes of potato and carrot are steamed until crisp-tender and the sauce is vibrant with garlic, Worcestershire sauce and cayenne pepper. Generous chunks of roast beef make it a substantial meal; but you could use steak, chicken, turkey or corned beef instead.

Working time: 20 minutes
Total time: 35 minutes

Super Chunky Hash

4 Servings•

- **1 pound small red potatoes, unpeeled**
- **2 medium carrots**
- **1 pound roast beef, unsliced**
- **1 bunch scallions (6 to 8)**
- **2 ribs celery**
- **2 tablespoons butter**
- **2 tablespoons olive or other vegetable oil**
- **3 cloves garlic, minced or crushed through a press**
- **¼ cup ketchup**
- **2 tablespoons Worcestershire sauce**
- **1½ teaspoons thyme**
- **¼ teaspoon black pepper**
- **Pinch of cayenne pepper**
- **¼ cup chopped parsley (optional)**

1 Cut the potatoes into 1-inch cubes. Cut the carrots into ½-inch dice.

2 Steam the potatoes and carrots in a vegetable steamer until the vegetables are tender, about 15 minutes.

Step 3

3 Meanwhile, cut the roast beef into ¾-inch cubes. Coarsely chop the scallions and celery.

4 In a large skillet, warm 1 tablespoon of the butter in 1 tablespoon of the oil over medium-high heat until the butter is melted. Add the scallions and garlic and cook for 2 to 3 minutes. Remove the scallions and set aside.

5 Add the remaining 1 tablespoon each butter and oil. Add the potatoes, carrots, roast beef and celery, and cook, stirring frequently, until the potatoes are golden, about 7 minutes.

Step 5

6 Add the ketchup, Worcestershire sauce, thyme, black and cayenne peppers, and cook for 1 to 2 minutes to meld the flavors. Return the scallions to the pan and stir to blend. Stir in parsley (if using) just before serving.

TIME-SAVERS

■ *Do-ahead: The potatoes and carrots can be steamed ahead of time. The hash can be made ahead and gently reheated (add a bit of water to the pan if all of the liquid has been absorbed).*

Values are approximate per serving: Calories: 468 Protein: 37 gm Fat: 21 gm
Carbohydrates: 33 gm Cholesterol: 107 mg Sodium: 436 mg

Step 6

Light Beef Stew with Asparagus

▼

All the hearty ingredients that go into a standard beef stew are here, along with the luxurious bonus of fresh asparagus. The stew is served over rice, which makes it an especially satisfying meal. If you can't find low-sodium beef broth and wish to keep the dish relatively low in sodium, dilute ¾ cup of regular broth with an equal amount of water. This will not affect the fat content of the dish, which is notably low.

Working time: 25 minutes
Total time: 50 minutes

Light Beef Stew with Asparagus

6 Servings

- ¾ **pound top round steak, well trimmed**
- 1 **pound small red potatoes, unpeeled**
- 3 **medium carrots**
- ½ **pound asparagus**
- 1 **bunch scallions (6 to 8)**
- ¼ **cup flour**
- ¼ **teaspoon pepper**
- 1 **tablespoon olive or other vegetable oil**
- 2 **cups water**
- 1 **cup raw rice**
- 1½ **cups low-sodium beef broth**
- 2 **garlic cloves, minced or crushed through a press**
- 1½ **teaspoons thyme**
- 1 **bay leaf**

Step 1

1 Cut the steak, potatoes and carrots into 1-inch chunks. Trim the asparagus and cut into 1-inch lengths. Coarsely chop the scallions.

2 In a shallow bowl, combine the flour and pepper. Dredge the beef lightly in the seasoned flour, reserving the excess.

3 In a large nonstick skillet, warm the oil over medium-high heat until hot but not smoking. Add the beef and cook, stirring frequently, until the meat is browned, about 9 minutes.

4 In a medium saucepan, bring the water to a boil. Add the rice, reduce the heat to medium-low, cover and simmer until the rice is tender and all the liquid is absorbed, about 20 minutes.

5 Meanwhile, add the reserved seasoned flour to the skillet and stir until the flour is no longer visible, about 1 minute. Stir in the beef broth. Add the potatoes, carrots, garlic, thyme and bay leaf. Bring the stew to a boil, reduce the heat to low, cover and simmer until the potatoes are tender, 15 to 20 minutes.

Step 3

6 Discard the bay leaf. Return the stew to a boil over medium-high heat. Add the asparagus and scallions, and cook until the asparagus is just tender, about 5 minutes.

7 Serve the stew over the rice.

TIME-SAVERS

■ ***Do-ahead:*** *The meat and vegetables can be cut up in advance; or the whole stew can be made ahead and reheated.*

Step 5

Values are approximate per serving: Calories: 315 Protein: 19 gm Fat: 5 gm
Carbohydrates: 49 gm Cholesterol: 32 mg Sodium: 53 mg

Skirt Steak with Black Bean Chili Sauce

▼

Skirt steak, the cut of beef traditionally used for fajitas, is thin, and can be less than tender if not properly cooked. Here, it is brushed with a lime juice and olive oil marinade (the steak could also be marinated in this mixture) and broiled just until medium-rare to keep it juicy and tender. Serve the sauce-topped beef with a fresh corn salad and hot, buttered corn muffins.

Working time: 25 minutes
Total time: 25 minutes

Skirt Steak with Black Bean Chili Sauce

4 Servings

1 can (15 ounces) black beans
1 medium onion
1 cup canned stewed tomatoes,
  with their juice
1 tablespoon cornstarch
1 tablespoon butter
3 cloves garlic, minced or crushed
  through a press

3 tablespoons lime juice
2 tablespoons chili powder
2 teaspoons paprika
½ teaspoon salt
⅛ teaspoon cayenne pepper
1 tablespoon olive or other
  vegetable oil
1 skirt steak (about 1 pound)

1 Preheat the broiler. Line a broiler pan with foil.

2 Drain the beans in a colander, rinse under cold water and drain well. Coarsely chop the onion. Drain the stewed tomatoes in a strainer set over a small bowl. Stir the cornstarch into the tomato liquid.

Step 2

3 In a medium skillet, warm the butter over medium-high heat until it is melted. Add the onion and garlic and cook, stirring, until the onion is translucent, about 5 minutes.

4 Add the black beans, stewed tomatoes, the cornstarch-tomato mixture, 1½ tablespoons of the lime juice, 1 tablespoon of the chili powder, 1 teaspoon of the paprika, the salt and cayenne. Bring to a boil over medium-high heat and cook, stirring, until slightly thickened, 1 to 2 minutes. Keep warm while you broil the steak.

5 In a small bowl, combine the oil, the remaining 1½ tablespoons lime juice, 1 tablespoon chili powder and 1 teaspoon paprika.

Step 4

6 Place the steak on the broiler pan. Brush with half of the basting mixture and broil 4 inches from the heat for 3 minutes. Turn the steak over, brush with the remaining basting mixture and broil for 3 minutes longer, until medium-rare. Let the steak rest for 5 minutes before slicing across the grain on the diagonal. Top with chili sauce.

TIME-SAVERS

■ *Microwave tip: To make the sauce: In a medium microwave-safe bowl, combine the butter, onion and garlic. Cover and cook at 100% for 3 minutes, or until the onion is tender. Stir in the tomatoes, cornstarch-tomato mixture, beans, 1½ tablespoons lime juice, 1 tablespoon chili powder, 1 teaspoon paprika, the salt and cayenne. Cover with waxed paper and cook at 100% for 6 minutes, stirring once.*

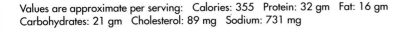
Step 6

Values are approximate per serving: Calories: 355   Protein: 32 gm   Fat: 16 gm
Carbohydrates: 21 gm   Cholesterol: 89 mg   Sodium: 731 mg

Microwave Baked Potato Stroganoff

▼

One of the most rewarding things a microwave can do is bake a potato in a fraction of the time a conventional oven takes. This recipe for a potato stuffed with beef Stroganoff takes advantage of this splendid feature, and also provides a way to use leftover roast beef—although it's so good and simple you might want to make it even when you don't have leftovers. Serve the potato with sliced plum tomatoes and cucumbers.

Working time: 25 minutes
Total time: 25 minutes

4 Servings

4 medium baking potatoes (about
   2 pounds)
3 cups cubed roast beef (about
   ¾ pound)
¼ pound mushrooms
1 medium onion
2 tablespoons butter
¼ cup beef broth

1 tablespoon paprika (optional)
½ teaspoon salt
⅛ teaspoon pepper
¾ cup sour cream
2 scallions, chopped, for garnish
   (optional)
¼ cup grated Cheddar cheese, for
   garnish (optional)

1 With a sharp knife, cut 1 or 2 short slits in the potatoes to act as steam vents. Place the potatoes end to end (but not touching) in a circle in the microwave and cook at 100% for 15 to 20 minutes, or until tender.

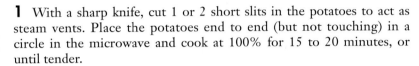

Step 2

2 Meanwhile, cut the roast beef into ½-inch cubes. Cut the mushrooms into ¼-inch-thick slices. Coarsely chop the onion.

3 In a medium skillet, melt the butter over medium-high heat until hot but not smoking. Add the onion and sauté until golden, about 5 minutes.

4 Add the mushrooms and sauté until they are well coated with butter, 1 to 2 minutes.

5 Add the beef broth, paprika, salt and pepper. Reduce the heat to medium-low, cover and simmer until the mushrooms are just tender, 2 to 3 minutes.

6 Stir in the roast beef and the sour cream and remove the skillet from the heat.

Step 4

7 Cut open the baked potatoes and place them on plates. Spoon the Stroganoff mixture over them and sprinkle with scallions and Cheddar, if desired.

TIME-SAVERS

■ *Do-ahead: The Stroganoff mixture can be prepared (Steps 2 through 5) ahead of time. Bring back to a simmer before adding the roast beef and sour cream.*

Values are approximate per serving: Calories: 495 Protein: 32 gm Fat: 22 gm
Carbohydrates: 43 gm Cholesterol: 103 mg Sodium: 480 mg

Step 6

Italian-Style Veal Stew

▼

Tomatoes, bell peppers, olives and red wine give this veal stew an Italian flair. Although the recipe calls for stuffed olives, pitted green olives can be used instead. Or, if your deli carries more exotic types of olives, try another brine-cured variety, such as Calamata or picholine. If you're watching your sodium intake, omit the salt from this recipe, rinse and drain the olives before adding them to the stew and choose no-salt-added tomatoes.

Working time: 25 minutes
Total time: 50 minutes

Italian-Style Veal Stew

4 Servings

1½ pounds stew veal
¼ cup flour
½ teaspoon salt
½ teaspoon pepper
1 tablespoon butter
1 tablespoon olive or other vegetable oil
2 medium carrots

1 large green bell pepper
¼ pound small mushrooms
1 can (14½ ounces) stewed tomatoes, with their juice
1 cup dry red wine or beef broth
1½ teaspoons thyme
1 bay leaf
½ cup stuffed green olives

Step 4

1 If the pieces of veal are large, cut them into 1½-inch chunks.

2 In a plastic or paper bag, combine the flour, salt and pepper, and shake to mix. Add the veal and shake to coat lightly. Remove the veal and reserve the excess seasoned flour.

3 In a large skillet, warm the butter in the oil over medium-high heat until the butter is melted. Add the veal and cook until browned all over, about 10 minutes.

4 Meanwhile, cut the carrots into ½-inch-thick slices. Cut the bell pepper into thin strips. Halve the mushrooms.

Step 5

5 Stir the reserved dredging mixture into the skillet and cook, stirring, until the flour is no longer visible, about 30 seconds. Add the stewed tomatoes and their juice, the wine or broth, thyme and bay leaf. Bring the mixture to a boil over medium-high heat. Add the carrots and mushrooms, and return to a boil. Reduce the heat to low, cover and simmer until the veal is tender, about 20 minutes.

6 Add the bell pepper and olives, and simmer until the flavors have blended and the pepper is tender, about 8 minutes.

7 Remove the bay leaf before serving.

TIME-SAVERS

■ **Do-ahead:** *The whole stew can be made ahead and reheated.*

Step 6

Values are approximate per serving: Calories: 352 Protein: 38 gm Fat: 13 gm
Carbohydrates: 21 gm Cholesterol: 151 mg Sodium: 1131 mg

Layered Ham and Potato Casserole

▼

Creamy scalloped potatoes are the starting point for this dish—but the addition of ham and broccoli turns them into a hearty dinner casserole. Red potatoes work well in this casserole because they hold their shape when cooked. For an easy variation, substitute cooked chicken or turkey for the ham and add some grated Cheddar to the ingredients that are tossed together before baking.

Working time: 20 minutes
Total time: 1 hour 35 minutes

Layered Ham and Potato Casserole

6 Servings

1 medium red onion	**2 cups milk**
1 medium stalk broccoli	**2 tablespoons Dijon mustard**
½ pound lean ham, unsliced	**1 teaspoon salt**
6 medium red potatoes, unpeeled	**½ teaspoon pepper**
(about 1 pound)	**2 tablespoons butter**
⅔ cup flour	

1 Preheat the oven to 350°. Grease a shallow 1½-quart baking dish.

2 Coarsely chop the onion and broccoli. Cut the ham into ½-inch cubes.

3 In a food processor fitted with a slicing blade, cut the potatoes into ¼-inch-thick slices.

Step 3

4 In a large bowl, combine the potatoes, onion, broccoli, ham and flour. Toss to distribute the ingredients evenly. Spread the mixture in the prepared baking dish.

5 In a small bowl, beat the milk, mustard, salt and pepper together. Pour the milk mixture over the vegetables and ham in the baking dish. Dot with the butter.

6 Cover the dish with foil and bake for 30 minutes. Uncover and bake for 45 minutes longer, or until the top is browned and the potatoes are tender.

Step 4

TIME-SAVERS

■ *Microwave tip:* *In a 1-quart microwave-safe container, combine the milk, mustard, salt, pepper and butter. Cook at 50% for 7 minutes. Prepare the potatoes, onion, broccoli and ham as directed above and toss the ingredients with the flour. Layer these ingredients in a microwave-safe casserole and pour the hot milk mixture over them. Loosely cover the casserole and elevate it off the oven floor by placing it on an inverted glass pie plate or several custard cups. Cook at 100% for 20 minutes, rotating and stirring twice during the cooking time.*

■ *Do-ahead:* *The onion, broccoli and ham can all be cut up ahead of time. Of course the entire dish can be made ahead of time and reheated.*

Values are approximate per serving: Calories: 263   Protein: 14 gm   Fat: 9 gm
Carbohydrates: 31 gm   Cholesterol: 40 mg   Sodium: 1149 mg

Step 5

Garlic-Studded Pork Loin with Potatoes and Peppers

The French technique of cutting slits in lamb and inserting slivers of garlic into them to enhance the meat's flavor works equally well with pork. Here, a tart basting sauce made with apple juice concentrate and mustard contrasts well with the subtle but meaty flavor of the pork. Although today's pork is quite lean, it still has a richness that makes it a satisfying as well as a low-calorie entrée.

Working time: 25 minutes
Total time: 1 hour 30 minutes

Garlic-Studded Pork Loin with Potatoes and Peppers

8 Servings

⅓ cup apple juice concentrate
3 tablespoons Dijon mustard
1 tablespoon cumin
¼ teaspoon salt
¼ teaspoon black pepper
6 cloves garlic
1 small boneless pork loin (about 1¾ pounds)

1 cup low-sodium or regular chicken broth
1 pound small red potatoes, unpeeled
1 large yellow or green bell pepper

Step 3

1 Preheat the oven to 425°.

2 In a small bowl, combine the apple juice concentrate, mustard, cumin, salt and black pepper.

3 Peel the garlic and cut each clove lengthwise into thirds. With a sharp knife, make 18 slits randomly in the pork loin. Tuck a piece of garlic into each slit.

4 Place the pork loin in a small roasting pan and brush the pork with half of the apple-mustard mixture. Pour ½ cup of chicken broth into the bottom of the pan. Roast the pork loin for 30 minutes.

5 Meanwhile, halve the potatoes. Cut the bell pepper lengthwise into thin strips.

Step 3

6 Reduce the oven temperature to 350°. Brush the pork with the remaining apple-mustard mixture and roast until it is cooked through, about 20 minutes longer.

7 Meanwhile, steam the potatoes in a vegetable steamer until almost done, about 15 minutes. Add the bell pepper to the steamer and continue steaming until the potatoes and pepper are tender, about 5 minutes. Place the vegetables in a serving bowl.

8 Remove the pork from the roasting pan and let it rest for 5 minutes before slicing. Add the remaining ½ cup broth to the roasting pan and set over medium-low heat. Stir to incorporate any browned bits clinging to the pan. Pour the pan juices over the vegetables and toss to coat. Slice the pork and serve the vegetables on the side.

TIME-SAVERS

■ **Do-ahead:** *The basting mixture (Step 2) can be made ahead.*

Step 8

Values are approximate per serving: Calories: 240   Protein: 22 gm   Fat: 8 gm
Carbohydrates: 18 gm   Cholesterol: 60 mg   Sodium: 316 mg

German-Style Pork Chops with Mushrooms

When beer is used in cooking, almost all the alcohol evaporates, leaving behind
an elusive, smoky flavor that is particularly complementary to pork. Any kind of
beer—light or dark, fizzy or flat—will do for this recipe. Buttered broad noodles are a
natural accompaniment for a German dish; boiled new potatoes are another possibility.
If you're in a hurry, just serve some thickly sliced rye bread with the chops.

Working time: 15 minutes
Total time: 35 minutes

German-Style Pork Chops with Mushrooms

4 Servings

1 medium onion
½ pound small mushrooms
¼ cup flour
1½ teaspoons thyme
½ teaspoon salt
¼ teaspoon pepper
4 center-cut loin pork chops (½ inch thick), well trimmed

1 tablespoon olive or other vegetable oil
2 cloves garlic, minced or crushed through a press
½ cup dark beer
½ cup chicken broth

1 Coarsely chop the onion. If the mushrooms are small, leave them whole; otherwise, halve or quarter them.

2 In a plastic or paper bag, combine the flour, ½ teaspoon of the thyme, the salt and pepper, and shake to mix. Add the pork chops and shake to coat lightly. Remove the chops and reserve the excess seasoned flour.

3 In a large skillet, warm the oil over medium-high heat until hot but not smoking. Add the pork chops and cook until well browned, about 7 minutes per side. Remove the pork chops to a plate and cover loosely to keep warm.

4 In the same skillet, cook the onion, mushrooms and garlic over medium-high heat, stirring, for 1 minute. Add 1 tablespoon of the reserved seasoned flour and cook, stirring, until the flour is no longer visible, about 1 minute.

5 Stir in the beer, chicken broth and remaining 1 teaspoon thyme, and bring to a boil over medium-high heat.

6 Return the pork chops (and any juices that have accumulated on the plate) to the skillet and return the mixture to a boil. Reduce the heat to low, cover and simmer for 8 minutes, turning the chops over halfway through.

7 Uncover the skillet and cook until the sauce has thickened slightly and the chops are cooked through, about 2 minutes.

Values are approximate per serving: Calories: 274 Protein: 28 gm Fat: 12 gm
Carbohydrates: 12 gm Cholesterol: 72 mg Sodium: 477 mg

Step 3

Step 4

Step 6

Southwestern Pork and Pepper Stew

▼

Pork stew is a favorite dish in Mexico and the American Southwest; this version is made with a variety of colorful vegetables. The southwestern flavor comes from mild green chilies, cilantro and cayenne pepper. This stew is only moderately spicy, so adjust the cayenne pepper up or down according to taste. Serve the stew with corn muffins or cornbread.

Working time: 25 minutes
Total time: 1 hour 35 minutes

Southwestern Pork and Pepper Stew

6 Servings

1 pound pork shoulder
1 bunch scallions (6 to 8)
2 tablespoons flour
¼ teaspoon black pepper
2 tablespoons olive or other
   vegetable oil
4 cloves garlic, minced or crushed
   through a press
1 can (16 ounces) crushed tomatoes
   with their juice
3 cups beef broth

½ cup water
3 cans (4 ounces each) chopped
   mild green chilies, drained
1 teaspoon oregano
¼ teaspoon cayenne pepper
1 medium red bell pepper
1 medium green bell pepper
1 large (or two small) all-purpose
   potato(es)
1 package (10 ounces) frozen corn
¼ cup chopped cilantro (optional)

Step 2

1 Cut the pork into 1-inch chunks. Coarsely chop the scallions.

2 In a shallow bowl, combine the flour and black pepper. Lightly dredge the pork in the seasoned flour.

3 In a large skillet, warm the oil over medium-high heat until hot but not smoking. Add the pork and sauté, stirring, until the pork is browned all over, about 6 minutes.

4 Add the scallions and garlic and cook until the scallions are softened, about 3 minutes.

5 Stir in the tomatoes and their juice, the broth, water and green chilies. Bring the liquid to a boil and add the oregano and cayenne. Reduce the heat to medium-low, cover and simmer for 1 hour.

Step 5

6 Meanwhile, cut the red and green bell peppers into bite-size pieces. Peel the potato and cut it into small cubes.

7 Add the bell peppers, potato and corn to the skillet. Bring the stew to a boil over medium-high heat. Reduce the heat to medium-low, cover and simmer until the potatoes are tender, about 15 minutes.

8 Serve the stew sprinkled with cilantro if desired.

TIME-SAVERS

■ *Do-ahead: Stews are perfectly designed to be made ahead and often taste much better after being reheated. If you need to break the stew-making into stages, prepare the recipe through Step 5 and cook it for only 30 minutes. Then, when you're ready to continue, bring the stew back to a boil, cook for another 30 minutes and proceed with Steps 6 through 8.*

Values are approximate per serving: Calories: 285 Protein: 20 gm Fat: 12 gm
Carbohydrates: 27 gm Cholesterol: 51 mg Sodium: 945 mg

Step 6

Confetti Rice
Casserole with Ham

▼

Reminiscent of the sort of dish your grandmother might have taken to a potluck supper, this appealing mix of rice, vegetables, ham and cheese is as delicious the next day as it is on the night you serve it for dinner. If you're lucky enough to have leftovers for lunch, pack individual portions into food storage containers. You can eat the dish cold, or reheat it in a microwave.

Working time: 15 minutes
Total time: 1 hour 5 minutes

Confetti Rice
Casserole with Ham

6 Servings

1 cup chicken broth	¼ teaspoon pepper
1 cup milk	1 bunch scallions (6 to 8)
¾ cup raw rice	½ pound ham, unsliced
1 package (10 ounces) frozen corn	1 cup shredded Cheddar cheese
1 package (10 ounces) frozen peas	¼ cup chopped parsley (optional)
2 tablespoons flour	1 package (3 ounces) cream cheese,
1 teaspoon oregano	at room temperature

1 Preheat the oven to 425°. Butter a 13 x 9-inch baking dish.

2 In a medium saucepan, bring the chicken broth and milk to a boil over medium heat. Add the rice and cook for 10 minutes.

3 Meanwhile, place the corn and peas in a large mixing bowl and break them up to separate. Stir in the flour, oregano and pepper.

Step 3

4 Coarsely chop the scallions. Cut the ham into ½-inch cubes. Add the scallions and ham to the vegetables in the bowl. Add the Cheddar cheese and and parsley (if using), and stir to blend.

5 In a small bowl, beat the cream cheese to soften it. Measure out about ⅓ cup of the hot milk-broth mixture from the saucepan, and stir it into the cream cheese until smooth. Stir the softened cream cheese into the vegetable-ham mixture. Then stir in the remaining rice and cooking liquid.

Step 4

6 Turn the mixture into the prepared baking dish and cover tightly with foil. Bake for 35 to 40 minutes, or until the rice is tender. Stir several times for more even cooking.

TIME-SAVERS

■ **Do-ahead:** *The casserole can be assembled ahead and baked just before serving.*

Step 5

Values are approximate per serving: Calories: 401   Protein: 20 gm   Fat: 18 gm
Carbohydrates: 42 gm   Cholesterol: 63 mg   Sodium: 898 mg

Honey-Glazed Pork Tenderloin

▼

Lean, center-cut pork tenderloin is all meat and no waste, so 1½ pounds will serve six. The sweet and spicy glaze couldn't be easier: it mixes in seconds in a food processor. And, if desired, you can make another batch of the glaze, with or without the scallions, to pass as a sauce. Serve the grilled pork with a variety of grilled vegetables.

Working time: 10 minutes
Total time: 55 minutes

Honey-Glazed Pork Tenderloin

6 Servings

3 scallions
1 quarter-size slice (¼ inch thick) fresh ginger, unpeeled
2 cloves garlic
¼ cup frozen apple juice concentrate

2 tablespoons reduced-sodium or regular soy sauce
2 tablespoons honey
¼ teaspoon pepper
1½ pounds lean center-cut pork tenderloin

Step 2

1 Preheat the broiler or start the charcoal. If broiling, line a broiler pan with foil.

2 Make the glaze: In a food processor, mince the scallions, ginger and garlic. Scrape into a small bowl and stir in the apple juice concentrate, soy sauce, honey and pepper.

3 Brush the pork with some of the glaze. If broiling, place the tenderloin on the broiler pan before brushing with the glaze.

4 Broil or grill the pork 4 inches from the heat until golden, 30 to 40 minutes. While it is broiling, turn it every 7 minutes or so and brush with more glaze.

5 To serve, cut the tenderloin into thin slices.

Step 2

TIME-SAVERS

■ ***Microwave tip:*** *Prepare the pork loin as described above. Place it in a microwave-safe baking dish and cook at 100% for 8 minutes per pound.*

■ ***Do-ahead:*** *The glaze (Step 2) can be made ahead.*

Step 3

Values are approximate per serving: Calories: 175 Protein: 24 gm Fat: 3 gm
Carbohydrates: 12 gm Cholesterol: 74 mg Sodium: 259 mg

Apple-Braised Pork Chops with Red Cabbage

▼

You may not think of pork chops as low-calorie fare, but if you choose center-cut loin chops and trim them of all visible fat, this dish will be as lean as it is luscious. The combination of pork, apples and red cabbage is typically German, and the caraway seeds add a special (and traditional) flavor. However, if you do not care for the taste of caraway seeds, the dish will be fine without them.

Working time: 20 minutes
Total time: 30 minutes

Apple-Braised Pork Chops with Red Cabbage

4 Servings

1 small Granny Smith or other tart
  green apple
1 small onion
¼ pound red cabbage
2 tablespoons cornstarch
½ teaspoon salt
½ teaspoon pepper
4 lean center-cut loin pork chops
  (cut ¼ inch thick, about ¾
  pound total), well trimmed

1 tablespoon vegetable oil
½ cup apple juice
1 tablespoon cider vinegar
½ teaspoon caraway seeds,
  lightly crushed
½ teaspoon sugar

Step 1

1 Core the apple but leave it unpeeled. In a food processor with a shredding blade, shred the apple, onion and cabbage.

2 In a shallow bowl, combine the cornstarch with ¼ teaspoon of the salt and ¼ teaspoon of the pepper. Dredge the pork lightly in the seasoned cornstarch, reserving the excess.

3 In a large nonstick skillet, warm the oil over medium-high heat until hot but not smoking. Add the pork chops and cook for 5 minutes per side.

4 Slowly add the apple juice and bring the liquid back to a boil. Reduce the heat to medium-low, cover and simmer for 5 minutes. Remove the pork chops to a plate and cover loosely to keep warm.

Step 4

5 Meanwhile, in a small bowl, stir together the excess cornstarch mixture and the vinegar. Set aside.

6 Add the shredded apple, onion and cabbage to the skillet. Increase the heat to medium-high and bring the mixture to a boil.

7 Add the caraway seeds, sugar, the remaining ¼ teaspoon salt and ¼ teaspoon pepper, and the cornstarch-vinegar mixture. Stir the mixture until it has thickened slightly. Reduce the heat to medium-low, cover and simmer, stirring occasionally, until the cabbage is just tender, about 5 minutes. Taste for seasoning and add more salt, if necessary.

8 Serve the pork chops topped with some of the cabbage and apple.

TIME-SAVERS

■ *Do-ahead: The apple, onion and cabbage can be shredded ahead.*

Step 6

Values are approximate per serving: Calories: 222 Protein: 18 gm Fat: 9 gm
Carbohydrates: 16 gm Cholesterol: 50 mg Sodium: 331 mg

Spicy Lamb Sauté

▼

Bow-tie noodles topped with lamb, vegetables and a gingery-hot sauce is a delicious variation on the spaghetti-with-meat-sauce theme. The strips of lamb, bell pepper and green beans are stir-fried in a mixture that includes vinegar, soy sauce, ginger and red pepper flakes. If your family doesn't care for lamb, try this recipe with lean beef or pork instead. If you make it with pork, substitute chicken broth for the beef broth.

Working time: 30 minutes
Total time: 30 minutes

Spicy Lamb Sauté

4 Servings

1 large red bell pepper
3 quarter-size slices (¼ inch thick) fresh ginger, unpeeled
1 pound lean boneless lamb (leg or loin)
¼ cup cornstarch
2 tablespoons olive or other vegetable oil
½ pound bow-tie pasta
3 cloves garlic, minced or crushed through a press

1 package (10 ounces) frozen green beans
⅔ cup beef broth
2 tablespoons reduced-sodium or regular soy sauce
1 tablespoon red wine vinegar or cider vinegar
½ teaspoon sugar
¼ teaspoon red pepper flakes

1 Bring a large pot of water to a boil.

2 Meanwhile, cut the bell pepper into ¾-inch squares. Finely chop the ginger.

Step 3

3 Cut the lamb with the grain into 2-inch-wide strips. Cut the strips across the grain into ¼-inch-thick slices. Toss the lamb strips with 2 tablespoons of the cornstarch.

4 In a large skillet, warm 1 tablespoon of the oil over medium-high heat until hot but not smoking. Add the lamb and stir-fry until the lamb begins to brown, about 4 minutes. Remove the lamb to a plate and cover loosely to keep warm.

5 Add the pasta to the boiling water and cook until al dente, 7 to 9 minutes, or according to package directions.

6 Meanwhile, add the remaining 1 tablespoon oil to the skillet. Add the ginger and garlic and stir-fry until the garlic begins to brown, 1 to 2 minutes.

Step 4

7 Add the bell pepper, green beans, ⅓ cup of the beef broth, the soy sauce, vinegar, sugar and red pepper flakes, and bring to a boil.

8 Meanwhile, blend the remaining ⅓ cup beef broth and 2 tablespoons cornstarch. When the mixture in the skillet has come to a boil, add the lamb (and any juices that have accumulated on the plate) and the cornstarch mixture. Return the mixture to a boil, stirring constantly until thickened, 2 to 3 minutes.

9 Drain the noodles and serve topped with the lamb mixture.

Values are approximate per serving: Calories: 488 Protein: 33 gm Fat: 13 gm Carbohydrates: 58 gm Cholesterol: 73 mg Sodium: 516 mg

Step 7

Easy Irish Stew

Just the thing for a blustery winter day, Irish stew is chockablock with chunks
of lamb, potatoes and carrots in a thick savory sauce. Serve some crusty bread alongside
so nobody misses a drop. If you prefer, use two sliced medium onions instead of
the pearl onions called for here. And, of course, the stew can just as easily be made with
beef if your family doesn't care for the taste of lamb.

Working time: 10 minutes
Total time: 40 minutes

Easy Irish Stew

6 Servings

- 1 pound lamb stew meat
- 1 pound small red potatoes, unpeeled
- 3 large carrots
- 2¾ cups beef broth
- ¼ cup tomato paste
- 3 cloves garlic, minced or crushed through a press
- 1 bay leaf
- ¼ teaspoon pepper
- 1 cup frozen pearl onions
- 2 tablespoons cornstarch
- 1 cup frozen peas

Step 1

1 If the lamb is in large chunks, cut into bite-size pieces. Quarter the potatoes (or cut them into bite-size pieces if they are large). Cut the carrots into 2-inch sections.

2 In a large saucepan, combine 2½ cups of the broth, the tomato paste, garlic, bay leaf and pepper. Add the pearl onions and bring the mixture to a boil over medium-high heat.

3 Add the lamb, potatoes and carrots and return to a boil. Reduce the heat to medium-low, cover and simmer until the vegetables are tender, about 20 minutes.

Step 2

4 In a small bowl, combine the remaining ¼ cup broth with the cornstarch. Increase the heat under the stew to medium-high and return to a boil. Stir in the cornstarch mixture and peas, and cook, stirring constantly, until the stew thickens, about 1 minute.

5 Remove the bay leaf and serve.

TIME-SAVERS

■ **Do-ahead:** *The whole stew can be made ahead and reheated.*

Step 4

Values are approximate per serving: Calories: 246 Protein: 20 gm Fat: 5 gm
Carbohydrates: 30 gm Cholesterol: 49 mg Sodium: 568 mg

Garlic Roasted Leg of Lamb with Summer Vegetables

▼

Leg of lamb is a festive offering for a holiday gathering or special dinner party. Here, the lamb, fragrant with garlic and rosemary, is served surrounded by colorful vegetables. This cut is expensive, but a 6-pound leg of lamb will serve eight to ten people. And any leftover lamb is a welcome bonus: Use it in sandwiches or make a quick curry to serve over rice.

Working time: 15 minutes
Total time: 1 hour 40 minutes

Garlic Roasted Leg of Lamb with Summer Vegetables

8 Servings

8 large cloves garlic
1 leg of lamb (about 6 pounds)
2 tablespoons olive or other vegetable oil
1½ teaspoons rosemary, crumbled
1 teaspoon sage
2 teaspoons thyme
¾ teaspoon pepper

1 large yellow squash (about ½ pound)
1 large zucchini (about ½ pound)
4 large plum tomatoes
1 teaspoon salt
2 tablespoons chopped parsley (optional)

1 Preheat the oven to 450°. Line a large roasting pan with foil and place a rack in the pan.

2 Cut 6 of the garlic cloves lengthwise into 3 or 4 slices. With a small sharp knife, make slits all over the leg of lamb and stuff each slit with a slice of garlic.

Step 2

3 In a small bowl, combine 1 tablespoon of the oil, the rosemary, sage, 1 teaspoon of the thyme and ½ teaspoon of the pepper. Rub the lamb all over with the herbed oil.

4 Place the lamb on the rack in the roasting pan and place the pan in the oven. Roast the lamb for 30 minutes.

5 Meanwhile, halve the yellow squash and zucchini lengthwise and then cut crosswise into ½-inch half-rounds. Cut the tomatoes into quarters. Mince the remaining 2 cloves of garlic (or crush them through a press).

6 In a medium bowl, combine the garlic, ½ teaspoon of the salt, the remaining 1 tablespoon oil, 1 teaspoon thyme, ¼ teaspoon pepper and the parsley (if using). Add the vegetables and toss to coat. Set aside, covered.

Step 6

7 Reduce the oven temperature to 350° and roast the lamb for 15 minutes.

8 Add the vegetables to the roasting pan and roast until the vegetables are tender and the lamb is medium-rare, about 30 minutes. Roast an additional 10 minutes for medium and 20 to 25 minutes for well-done.

9 Sprinkle the remaining ½ teaspoon of salt over the lamb and let stand for 15 minutes before carving. Serve the lamb with the roasted vegetables.

Values are approximate per serving: Calories: 365   Protein: 47 gm   Fat: 16 gm
Carbohydrates: 5 gm   Cholesterol: 145 mg   Sodium: 391 mg

Step 8

Lemon-Garlic Shrimp with Parslied Rice (page 157)

CHAPTER 3
SEAFOOD

Swordfish with Spicy Tropical Sauce

▼

Whether for a family supper or a company dinner, it's hard to go wrong with meaty swordfish steaks. Here, they are topped with a tangy sauce that is both sweet and spicy—a blend of crushed pineapple and orange, tomato, garlic and hot pepper flakes. Serve the swordfish with either plain rice or rice that has been cooked with a pinch of cayenne pepper and some shredded unsweetened coconut.

Working time: 15 minutes
Total time: 40 minutes

Swordfish with Spicy Tropical Sauce

4 Servings

1 orange
1 small red onion
2 tablespoons chopped scallion greens
1 can (8 ounces) crushed pineapple, packed in juice
3 tablespoons tomato paste
3 cloves garlic, minced or crushed through a press

2 teaspoons cornstarch
¾ teaspoon sugar
½ teaspoon salt
¼ teaspoon hot pepper flakes
Pinch of cayenne pepper
2 large swordfish steaks (1 inch thick, about 1½ pounds total)

Step 1

1 Peel the orange, removing all the bitter white pith, and coarsely chop. Coarsely chop the onion. Chop the scallion greens.

2 In a medium saucepan, combine the orange, onion, scallion greens, pineapple and its juice, tomato paste, garlic, cornstarch, sugar, salt, hot pepper flakes and cayenne. Bring to a boil over medium heat, stirring frequently. Cook, uncovered, for 10 minutes, stirring occasionally.

3 Reduce the heat to low and simmer, uncovered, until thickened, about 10 minutes.

Step 3

4 Meanwhile, preheat the broiler. Line a broiler pan with foil and lightly grease the foil.

5 Cut the swordfish steaks in half to make 4 portions. Place the swordfish steaks on the broiler pan. Top each steak with one-fourth of the tropical sauce and broil 4 inches from the heat for 12 minutes, or until the fish just flakes when tested with a fork.

TIME-SAVERS

■ *Do-ahead: The tropical sauce can be made well ahead.*

Values are approximate per serving: Calories: 260 Protein: 31 gm Fat: 6 gm
Carbohydrates: 19 gm Cholesterol: 59 mg Sodium: 508 mg

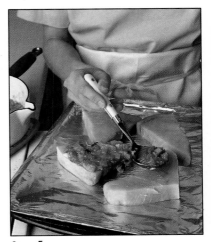
Step 5

Corn-Fried Snapper with Spicy Pineapple Salsa

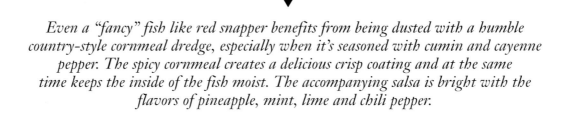

▼

Even a "fancy" fish like red snapper benefits from being dusted with a humble country-style cornmeal dredge, especially when it's seasoned with cumin and cayenne pepper. The spicy cornmeal creates a delicious crisp coating and at the same time keeps the inside of the fish moist. The accompanying salsa is bright with the flavors of pineapple, mint, lime and chili pepper.

Working time: 20 minutes
Total time: 20 minutes

Corn-Fried Snapper with Spicy Pineapple Salsa

4 Servings

⅓ cup cornmeal

2 tablespoons chopped parsley (optional)

1 teaspoon cumin

¾ teaspoon salt

¼ teaspoon cayenne pepper

1 egg white

4 red snapper or any firm-fleshed white fish fillets (about 1¼ pounds total)

1 tablespoon butter

2 tablespoons plus 1 teaspoon olive or other vegetable oil

1 plum tomato

1 fresh or pickled jalapeño pepper

2 tablespoons chopped fresh mint or 1 teaspoon dried

1 can (8 ounces) crushed pineapple, packed in juice, drained

2 teaspoons lime juice

1 teaspoon grated lime zest (optional)

Step 2

1 In a shallow bowl, combine the cornmeal, parsley (if using), cumin, ½ teaspoon of the salt, and the cayenne. In another shallow bowl, lightly beat the egg white.

2 Dip the fish in the egg white and then in the cornmeal mixture.

3 In a large nonstick skillet, warm the butter in 2 tablespoons of the oil over medium-high heat until the butter is melted. Add the fish and cook until it just flakes when tested with a fork and is golden brown on both sides, 3 to 4 minutes per side.

Step 3

4 Meanwhile, mince the tomato. Seed and mince the jalapeño. Chop the fresh mint.

5 In a small bowl, combine the tomato, jalapeño, mint, drained pineapple, lime juice, lime zest (if using) and remaining 1 teaspoon olive oil and ¼ teaspoon salt.

6 Serve the fish topped with the pineapple salsa.

TIME-SAVERS

■ *Do-ahead: The cornmeal dredge (Step 1) and pineapple salsa (Step 5) can be made ahead.*

Step 5

Values are approximate per serving: Calories: 316 Protein: 31 gm Fat: 13 gm
Carbohydrates: 18 gm Cholesterol: 60 mg Sodium: 549 mg

Broiled Fillets with Garlic Butter and Mustard Breadcrumbs

▼

It's a good rule of thumb to always toss a lemon into your shopping cart when buying fish for dinner, as so many fish recipes—including this one—call for lemon juice or zest. Even if you're simply broiling, baking or poaching the fish, a squeeze of lemon adds an incomparable fresh flavor. If, however, you are out of lemons when you prepare this dish, substitute 3 tablespoons of bottled or frozen lemon juice and omit the zest.

Working time: 15 minutes
Total time: 20 minutes

Broiled Fillets with Garlic Butter and Mustard Breadcrumbs

4 Servings

2 tablespoons butter
2 tablespoons olive or other vegetable oil
3 cloves garlic, minced or crushed through a press
1 lemon
4 small fillets of firm-fleshed white fish, such as scrod (about 1½ pounds total)

2 tablespoons Dijon mustard
¼ cup chopped parsley (optional)
1 teaspoon oregano
¼ teaspoon salt
¼ teaspoon pepper
¼ cup fine unseasoned breadcrumbs

Step 3

1 Preheat the broiler.

2 In a large broilerproof skillet, warm the butter in the oil over medium heat until the butter is melted. Add the garlic and cook, stirring occasionally, until the garlic is fragrant and light golden, about 3 minutes.

3 Meanwhile, grate the zest from the lemon. Halve the lemon and set aside.

4 Measure out 2 tablespoons of the garlic butter and set aside in a small bowl. Increase the heat under the skillet to medium-high. Add the fish and cook until golden brown on the bottom, about 4 minutes. Remove the skillet from the heat.

5 Meanwhile, in a small bowl, combine the lemon zest, mustard, 2 tablespoons of the parsley (if using), the oregano, salt and pepper.

Step 6

6 Squeeze the juice from the lemon halves over the fish in the skillet. Spread the mustard mixture over the fish and then dust with the breadcrumbs. Drizzle the reserved garlic butter on top.

7 Place the skillet under the broiler and broil 4 inches from the heat until the top is golden and the fish just flakes when tested with a fork, about 3 minutes.

8 Serve sprinkled with the remaining parsley.

TIME-SAVERS

■ **Do-ahead:** *The garlic butter (Step 2) and mustard mixture (Step 5) can be made ahead.*

Values are approximate per serving: Calories: 291 Protein: 31 gm Fat: 14 gm
Carbohydrates: 7 gm Cholesterol: 89 mg Sodium: 557 mg

Step 6

Tuna Burgers

▼

If you like tuna salad, you will like these tuna burgers. All the ingredients of a tuna salad sandwich—minus the mayo—are coarsely chopped together in a food processor, mixed with an egg to bind them and then formed into patties and pan-fried. Serve the tuna burgers on hamburger buns and accompany them with potato salad and pickles. You can substitute canned salmon for the tuna.

Working time: 20 minutes
Total time: 20 minutes

Tuna Burgers

4 Servings

- 1 small red onion
- 1 stalk celery
- 2 cans (6½ ounces each) water-pack solid white tuna, well drained
- 1 egg
- 3 slices whole wheat or white bread, torn into pieces

- 2 tablespoons butter
- 2 teaspoons Dijon mustard
- ¼ teaspoon cayenne pepper
- ¼ teaspoon black pepper
- About ¼ cup flour, for dredging
- 2 tablespoons olive or other vegetable oil

Step 3

1 Cut the onion and celery into rough quarters. Place them in a food processor and, pulsing the machine on and off, process until coarsely chopped.

2 Add the tuna and process briefly to break it up.

3 Add the egg, bread, butter, mustard, cayenne and black pepper and process until just blended.

4 Place the flour in a shallow bowl. Lightly flour your hands and shape the tuna mixture into four patties about 4 inches across. Dredge the patties lightly in the flour.

Step 4

5 In a large skillet, preferably nonstick, warm the oil over medium-high heat until hot but not smoking. Add the patties and cook until browned, about 3 minutes on each side. Serve hot.

TIME-SAVERS

■ *Do-ahead: The burger mixture can be prepared ahead of time, but do not dust the patties with flour until you're ready to fry them.*

Step 5

Values are approximate per serving: Calories: 326 Protein: 27 gm Fat: 17 gm
Carbohydrates: 16 gm Cholesterol: 121 mg Sodium: 588 mg

Creole-Style Scallops and Rice

▼

Seafood and rice is a favorite Louisiana combination. Here, the rice is cooked in a skillet in a zesty blend of vegetable juice cocktail, lime juice, hot pepper sauce and cayenne. For extra peppery punch, use spicy-hot vegetable juice cocktail. Scallops are delicate, and if cooked too long, they'll toughen. In this recipe, the scallops are virtually steamed in the pan of cooked rice, so there's little danger of overcooking them.

Working time: 20 minutes
Total time: 45 minutes

Creole-Style Scallops and Rice

4 Servings

3 cloves garlic
1 large onion
2 ribs celery
¼ cup (packed) parsley sprigs (optional)
1 large green bell pepper
1 tablespoon olive or other vegetable oil
1¾ cups vegetable juice cocktail
1 tablespoon lime juice

1 tablespoon tomato paste
1 teaspoon grated lime zest (optional)
4 drops of hot pepper sauce
1½ teaspoons basil
½ teaspoon black pepper
Pinch of cayenne pepper
1 cup raw rice
¾ pound bay or sea scallops

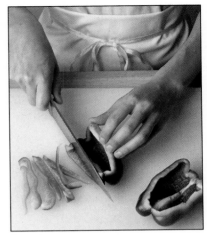

Step 1

1 In a food processor, mince the garlic. Add the onion and coarsely chop; remove and set aside. In the same processor work bowl, one at a time, coarsely chop the celery and parsley (if using). By hand, cut the bell pepper into thin strips.

2 In a large nonstick skillet, warm the oil over medium-high heat until hot but not smoking. Add the garlic-onion mixture and stir-fry until the onion just begins to brown, about 4 minutes.

3 Add the celery, 2 tablespoons of the parsley (if using), the bell pepper, vegetable juice cocktail, lime juice, tomato paste, lime zest (if using), hot pepper sauce, basil, black pepper and cayenne. Add the rice and bring to a boil. Reduce the heat to low, cover and simmer until the rice is not quite tender, 15 to 20 minutes.

Step 3

4 Meanwhile, if using sea scallops, cut them into quarters.

5 When the rice is cooked, stir in the scallops and remaining 2 tablespoons parsley (if using). Re-cover and cook until the scallops are cooked through, 3 to 5 minutes.

Values are approximate per serving: Calories: 328 Protein: 20 gm Fat: 5 gm
Carbohydrates: 51 gm Cholesterol: 28 mg Sodium: 526 mg

Step 5

Crispy Baked Flounder
with Sweet-and-Sour Sauce

▼

Not only does this breaded baked flounder make a delicious low-calorie dinner entrée, it also makes a wonderful sandwich. Spread some of the creamy sweet-and-sour sauce on a hard roll and top with the baked fish and some crisp lettuce. The sandwich can be made with fish hot from the oven or at room temperature. Serve the flounder—either in or out of a sandwich—with steamed carrots and green beans.

Working time: 15 minutes
Total time: 30 minutes

Crispy Baked Flounder
with Sweet-and-Sour Sauce

4 Servings

½ cup plain yogurt
1 tablespoon apricot jam or orange marmalade
2 teaspoons Dijon mustard
1 teaspoon cider vinegar
1 tablespoon chopped parsley (optional)
1 egg
2 tablespoons milk

¾ cup fine, unseasoned breadcrumbs
¼ cup grated Parmesan cheese (about 1 ounce)
½ teaspoon salt
¼ teaspoon pepper
1½ pounds flounder fillets (about ½ inch thick)

Step 1

1 Make the sweet-and-sour sauce: In a medium bowl, combine the yogurt, apricot jam, mustard, vinegar and parsley (if using). Stir to blend.

2 Preheat the oven to 400°. Line a baking sheet with foil and lightly grease the foil.

3 In a shallow bowl, beat the egg and milk together. In another shallow bowl or platter, combine the breadcrumbs, Parmesan, salt and pepper.

4 Dip the fish first into the egg mixture and then into the breadcrumb mixture, coating well on both sides.

5 Place the fish on the prepared baking sheet in a single layer. Bake, uncovered, for 10 to 12 minutes, or until the fish is opaque and flakes easily with a fork.

6 Serve the fish hot with the sweet-and-sour sauce on the side.

Step 3

TIME-SAVERS

■ ***Do-ahead:*** *The sweet-and-sour sauce can be made ahead. The fish can also be breaded ahead of time and then frozen.*

Values are approximate per serving: Calories: 320 Protein: 41 gm Fat: 7 gm
Carbohydrates: 20 gm Cholesterol: 159 mg Sodium: 798 mg

Step 4

Lemon-Basil Scallops with Green Beans

▼

This light seafood dish is simple enough for every day and elegant enough for entertaining. And it is so delicious that neither your family nor guests will suspect they're eating a low-calorie dish. Serve the scallops with rice or French bread and perhaps a tossed salad. And if you're having company, dress the meal up with a glass of white wine and a light dessert of sorbet or fruit.

Working time: 15 minutes
Total time: 20 minutes

Lemon-Basil Scallops with Green Beans

4 Servings

1 small red onion
½ pound fresh green beans or
    1 package (10 ounces) frozen cut
    green beans
½ pound sea scallops
½ cup low-sodium or regular
    chicken broth
1 tablespoon lemon juice
2 teaspoons cornstarch

1 tablespoon grated lemon zest
    (optional)
½ teaspoon basil
¼ teaspoon pepper
1 tablespoon olive or other
    vegetable oil
2 cloves garlic, minced or crushed
    through a press

Step 1

1 Cut the onion into thin wedges. Cut the fresh green beans into 2-inch lengths. Halve any unusually large scallops.

2 In a small bowl, combine the broth, lemon juice, cornstarch, lemon zest (if using), basil and pepper.

3 In a medium skillet, warm the oil over medium-high heat until hot but not smoking. Add the onion and garlic and sauté for 1 minute. Add the scallops and cook until they are almost completely opaque, about 4 minutes.

4 Add the green beans. Stir the broth mixture to reblend the cornstarch and add it to the skillet. Bring the liquid to a boil, stirring constantly. Reduce the heat to medium-low, cover and simmer until the beans are crisp-tender and the scallops are cooked through, about 4 minutes.

Step 3

TIME-SAVERS

■ **Do-ahead:** *The vegetables can be cut up ahead.*

Step 4

Values are approximate per serving: Calories: 113 Protein: 11 gm Fat: 4 gm
Carbohydrates: 8 gm Cholesterol: 19 mg Sodium: 103 mg

Light Seafood Newburg

▼

This lightened version of a classic seafood Newburg is made without the usual heavy cream and egg yolks. And although the sherry adds an authentic flavor to the dish, it could certainly be left out. If you are watching calories, serve the Newburg over plain noodles or steamed rice; otherwise, for an elegant touch, serve it in puff pastry shells. Frozen shells are widely available; follow the package directions for baking them.

Working time: 30 minutes
Total time: 30 minutes

144

Light Seafood Newburg

4 Servings

½ pound large or medium shrimp
½ pound sea scallops
4 scallions
1 cup chicken broth
3 tablespoons sherry, dry white
wine or chicken broth
Pinch of cayenne pepper

2 cloves garlic, minced or crushed
through a press
3 tablespoons butter
¼ cup flour
½ cup milk
1 can (6 ounces) lump crabmeat,
drained

Step 1

1 Shell and devein the shrimp. Halve any unusually large scallops. Coarsely chop the scallion whites and greens separately.

2 In a medium covered saucepan, bring the chicken broth, sherry, cayenne, garlic and scallion whites to a boil over medium-high heat .

3 Add the shrimp and scallops, and return to a boil, stirring. When the mixture has returned to a boil, remove the shrimp, scallops and scallions with a slotted spoon; cover loosely and set aside.

4 In a large saucepan, warm the butter over medium heat until melted. Stir in the flour and cook, stirring, until the flour is no longer visible, about 1 minute.

5 Slowly stir in the broth, whisking until smooth. Blend in the milk.

Step 3

6 Return the shrimp, scallops and scallion whites to the sauce. Gently stir in the crabmeat and add the scallion greens. Cook, stirring gently, until the seafood is cooked through, about 3 minutes.

TIME-SAVERS

■ *Microwave tip: Prepare the shrimp, scallops and scallions as instructed in Step 1. In a 2-quart microwave-safe casserole, combine ½ cup of the chicken broth with the sherry, cayenne, garlic and scallion whites. Cover and cook at 100% for 2 minutes, or until the liquid comes to a boil. Add the shrimp and scallops, re-cover and cook at 50% for 3 minutes. With a slotted spoon, remove the seafood and scallions and set aside. Add the butter to the casserole. Blend the flour with the remaining ½ cup chicken broth and stir into the casserole. Stir in only ¼ cup of milk. Cook, uncovered, at 100%, stirring once, for 3 minutes, or until the sauce is thickened. Stir in the shrimp, scallops, crabmeat and scallion whites and greens. Cook, uncovered, at 100% for 3 minutes, or until the seafood is cooked through.*

■ *Do-ahead: The shrimp can be shelled and deveined ahead. The dish can be made ahead through Step 5; before serving, bring the sauce slowly back to a simmer and add the seafood, scallions and crabmeat and cook to heat through.*

Step 6

Values are approximate per serving: Calories: 283 Protein: 31 gm Fat: 12 gm
Carbohydrates: 12 gm Cholesterol: 155 mg Sodium: 653 mg

Flounder Rolls Stuffed with Cheese and Spinach

▼

Rolled, stuffed fish fillets often appear in classic French cooking. Some recipes call for the fillets to be formed into small, tight rolls called "turbans," or shaped in small round molds. Here, flounder fillets are loosely rolled around a filling of spinach, cottage cheese, tangy feta cheese, onion and garlic. The stuffed fillets are then baked in butter and lemon juice. For an unusual side dish, try cornmeal-coated, fried green tomatoes.

Working time: 15 minutes
Total time: 35 minutes

Flounder Rolls Stuffed with Cheese and Spinach

4 Servings

3 cloves garlic
1 small onion
Half of a 10-ounce package frozen chopped spinach, thawed
½ cup cottage cheese
½ cup crumbled feta (about 2 ounces) or 2 ounces cream cheese
1 egg
2 teaspoons grated lemon zest (optional)

3 tablespoons flour
1 teaspoon oregano
¼ teaspoon pepper
4 flounder or sole fillets (about 1 pound total)
¼ cup lemon juice
4 teaspoons butter

Step 5

1 Preheat the oven to 350°. Butter an 11 x 7-inch baking dish.

2 In a food processor, mince the garlic. Add the onion and finely chop.

3 Thaw the spinach in the microwave and then squeeze it as dry as possible in several thicknesses of paper towel.

4 In a medium bowl, combine the garlic-onion mixture, the spinach, cottage cheese, feta, egg, lemon zest (if using), flour, oregano and pepper.

5 Place the fillets on a work surface. Dividing evenly, spread each fillet with the filling. Loosely roll up the fillets and place them seam-side down in the prepared baking dish.

6 Pour the lemon juice over the fish and dot each roll with 1 teaspoon of the butter. Bake the fish for 20 minutes, or until the fish just flakes when tested with a fork. About halfway through the baking, spoon some of the melted butter and lemon juice over the fish.

Step 5

TIME-SAVERS

■ *Microwave tip: Prepare the recipe as directed, using an unbuttered microwave-safe baking dish. Cover with plastic wrap and cook at 100% until the fish just flakes when tested with a fork and the filling is heated through, about 7 minutes, rotating the dish once halfway through.*

■ *Do-ahead: The filling (Steps 2 through 4) can be made, or the fish stuffed and rolled, in advance; in either case, the filling or stuffed fish must be refrigerated until time to complete the dish.*

Step 6

Values are approximate per serving: Calories: 247   Protein: 26 gm   Fat: 5 gm
Carbohydrates: 23 gm   Cholesterol: 42 mg   Sodium: 218 mg

Tex-Mex Steamed Halibut

▼

A vegetable steamer can be used for much more than just vegetables. Either a flat Chinese bamboo steamer or the folding metal variety, set in a wide pan, can hold fish steaks or fillets. If you don't have a steamer, you can use a small cake-cooling rack set in a skillet. To make it easier to remove the fish steaks and shredded cabbage called for here, line the steamer with large whole cabbage leaves or Romaine lettuce leaves.

Working time: 20 minutes
Total time: 25 minutes

Tex-Mex
Steamed Halibut

4 Servings

2 small halibut steaks (about 1¼ pounds total)
2 cups shredded cabbage (about ¼ pound)
1 large yellow or red bell pepper
1 medium red onion
2 limes

1½ tablespoons butter
1 teaspoon chili powder
¾ teaspoon cumin
¼ teaspoon salt
¼ teaspoon black pepper
Pinch of cayenne pepper
8 corn tortillas (5½-inch diameter)

1 Cut the halibut steaks in half to make 4 equal serving portions. Shred the cabbage. Cut the bell pepper and onion into thin rings.

2 Line a flat vegetable steamer or steamer insert with the shredded cabbage, bell pepper and onion. Bring the water in the steamer to a boil and steam the vegetables for about 1 minute.

Step 2

3 Meanwhile, grate the zest from one of the limes. Cut both limes into quarters.

4 Melt the butter on the stovetop or in the microwave. In a small bowl, combine the melted butter, lime zest, chili powder, cumin, salt, black pepper and cayenne.

5 Remove the steamer from the heat. Place the fish steaks on top of the steamed vegetables. Brush the fish with the seasoned butter. Re-cover and steam until the fish just flakes when tested with a fork, about 4 minutes.

Step 5

6 Meanwhile, warm the tortillas in the oven or a toaster oven (wrapped in foil) or in the microwave (wrapped in a moist paper towel).

7 Dividing evenly, serve the fish with the steamed vegetables. Using one-quarter lime per portion, squeeze the lime juice over the fish. Serve with one lime wedge and two warm tortillas per person.

TIME-SAVERS

■ *Microwave tip: To make the lime easier to juice, cook it at 100% for 45 seconds.*

■ *Do-ahead: The vegetables can be cut up and the seasoned butter (Step 4) made ahead.*

Values are approximate per serving: Calories: 362   Protein: 35 gm   Fat: 10 gm
Carbohydrates: 34 gm   Cholesterol: 57 mg   Sodium: 376 mg

Step 7

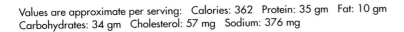

Shrimp Curry with Coconut-Almond Rice

▼

A refreshing drink and some sweet chutney, such as Major Grey's, are all you need to serve with this colorful entrée. Coconut in the rice adds an authentic flavor, as this dish would traditionally be made with coconut milk in the sauce. If desired, bring out the flavors of the almonds and coconut by toasting them in a dry skillet for a few minutes, shaking the pan and stirring frequently.

Working time: 40 minutes
Total time: 50 minutes

Shrimp Curry with Coconut-Almond Rice

4 Servings

1 pound large or medium shrimp
3 cloves garlic
1 medium onion
¼ cup packed cilantro sprigs (optional)
1 large green bell pepper
2¾ cups chicken broth
1 cup raw rice

2 tablespoons olive oil
3 tablespoons curry powder
1 tablespoon flour
½ cup milk
⅓ cup sweetened shredded coconut
¼ cup sliced almonds

1 Shell and devein the shrimp.

2 In a food processor, mince the garlic. Add the onion and coarsely chop. Remove the garlic-onion mixture. In the same work bowl, chop the cilantro (if using). Cut the bell pepper into 1-inch pieces.

3 In a medium saucepan, bring 2 cups of the chicken broth to a boil over medium-high heat. Add the rice, reduce the heat to low, cover and cook until the rice is tender, 15 to 20 minutes.

4 Meanwhile, in a large skillet, warm 1 tablespoon of the oil over medium-high heat until hot but not smoking. Add the garlic-onion mixture and cook until the onion begins to brown, about 3 minutes.

5 Add the remaining 1 tablespoon oil, the shrimp and bell pepper and stir-fry for 2 minutes.

6 Stir in the curry powder and flour and cook, stirring, until the flour and curry powder are completely incorporated.

7 Stir in the remaining ¾ cup chicken broth, the milk and cilantro (if using), and bring to a boil over medium-high heat. Reduce the heat to medium-low, cover and simmer until the shrimp are cooked through and the bell pepper is tender, about 2 minutes.

8 When the rice is done, stir in the coconut and almonds.

TIME-SAVERS

■ ***Microwave tip:*** *To toast the almonds and coconut, toss them together and place them in a pie plate. Cook at 70% for 6 minutes, or until light brown, tossing twice.*

■ ***Do-ahead:*** *The shrimp can be shelled and deveined, the vegetables cut up, and the almonds and coconut toasted ahead*

Values are approximate per serving: Calories: 466 Protein: 28 gm Fat: 16 gm
Carbohydrates: 52 gm Cholesterol: 144 mg Sodium: 838 mg

Step 5

Step 6

Step 7

Italian-Style Fish Fillets

▼

Mild-flavored haddock is a perfect fish to cook in an herbed tomato sauce, but other firm-fleshed white fish—such as cod, pollock or whiting—would also be good. Choose steaks, or thick fillets, so you can cut the fish into 1-inch cubes. The fish pieces will cook quickly, so be careful not to overcook them: The fish is done when the touch of a fork will barely flake it; the fish should not fall apart.

Working time: 20 minutes
Total time: 35 minutes

4 Servings

1 bunch scallions (6 to 8)
2 tablespoons olive or other vegetable oil
3 cloves garlic, minced or crushed through a press
1 cup crushed tomatoes
1 tablespoon tomato paste

1 teaspoon basil
¼ teaspoon pepper
1 large yellow squash
1½ pounds haddock or other firm-fleshed white fish
¼ cup chopped parsley (optional)

Step 3

1 Coarsely chop the scallions.

2 In a large skillet, warm the oil over medium-high heat until hot but not smoking. Add the scallions and garlic and cook, stirring occasionally, until the garlic begins to brown, about 5 minutes.

3 Add the crushed tomatoes, tomato paste, basil and pepper and bring to a boil. Reduce the heat to medium-low, cover and simmer for 10 minutes.

4 Meanwhile, slice the squash into rounds. Add the squash to the tomato sauce and simmer for 5 minutes longer.

Step 4

5 Meanwhile, cut the fish into 1-inch pieces. Add the fish to the simmering sauce (increase the heat if necessary to be sure the sauce continues to simmer), cover and cook until the fish is still firm but flakes easily when tested with a fork, about 10 minutes.

6 Stir in the parsley (if using) and serve hot.

TIME-SAVERS

■ *Microwave tip: Reduce the oil to 1 tablespoon. In a 3-quart microwave-safe casserole, combine the oil, scallions, garlic, tomatoes, tomato paste, basil and pepper. Cover and cook at 100% for 5 minutes. Add the sliced squash and cook at 50% for 5 minutes. Add the fish and cook at 50% for 10 minutes, or until the fish is tender.*

■ *Do-ahead: The sauce can be made ahead through Step 3. The squash and fish can be cut up ahead.*

Step 5

Values are approximate per serving: Calories: 242   Protein: 34 gm   Fat: 8 gm
Carbohydrates: 8 gm   Cholesterol: 97 mg   Sodium: 154 mg

Tuna-Rice Salad with Lemon-Pepper Dressing

▼

When potato salad palls, try rice salad, its slightly lighter cousin. This combination of tuna, rice and vegetables with a tangy herbed dressing makes an appealing light supper dish; leave out the tuna and it could be a side dish with broiled or barbecued chicken. For a picnic or a party lunch, serve the tuna-rice salad in edible cups made from hollowed-out tomatoes or bell peppers.

Working time: 10 minutes
Total time: 30 minutes

Tuna-Rice Salad with Lemon-Pepper Dressing

6 Servings

- 1 cup low-sodium or regular chicken broth
- 1 cup water
- 1 cup raw rice
- 2 cloves garlic, minced or crushed through a press
- 1 large yellow or green bell pepper
- 1 pint cherry tomatoes
- 4 scallions
- ¼ cup chopped fresh dill or 2 teaspoons dried

- ⅓ cup lemon juice
- ¼ cup olive or other vegetable oil
- 1 tablespoon Dijon mustard
- ½ teaspoon black pepper
- ¼ teaspoon salt
- 1 can (6½ ounces) water-packed tuna, drained
- 1 small head Boston or iceberg lettuce, separated into leaves

Step 1

1 In a medium saucepan, bring the chicken broth and water to a boil. Add the rice and garlic, reduce the heat to low, cover and simmer until the rice is tender and all the liquid is absorbed, about 20 minutes. When the rice is done, remove it from the heat and turn it into a large bowl to cool slightly; fluff the rice with a fork or spoon to separate the grains and speed the cooling.

2 Meanwhile, cut the bell pepper into bite-size pieces. Halve the cherry tomatoes. Coarsely chop the scallions and dill.

3 Make the lemon-pepper dressing: In a small bowl, combine the lemon juice, olive oil, mustard, black pepper and salt.

Step 2

4 When the rice has cooled slightly, add the bell pepper, tomatoes, scallions, dill, tuna and lemon-pepper dressing. Toss lightly to combine.

5 Serve the rice salad mounded in lettuce leaves.

TIME-SAVERS

■ ***Microwave tip:*** *Although it does not save any time to cook rice in the microwave, it is a way to free up a burner; and, in the summer, it can help keep the kitchen a bit cooler. To cook rice, combine the broth, 1 cup hot water, the rice and minced garlic in a shallow, 2-quart microwave-safe casserole. Cover and cook at 100% for 8 minutes, or until the liquid comes to a boil. Then cook at 50% for 12 minutes, or until the rice is tender.*

■ ***Do-ahead:*** *The rice can be cooked and the lemon-pepper dressing (Step 3) made ahead. The whole dish can be made ahead and served at room temperature or slightly chilled (do not place the salad in the lettuce leaves until ready to serve).*

Step 4

Values are approximate per serving: Calories: 258 Protein: 12 gm Fat: 10 gm
Carbohydrates: 30 gm Cholesterol: 12 mg Sodium: 282 mg

Lemon-Garlic Shrimp with Parslied Rice

▼

The rice for this scampi-like shrimp dish is cooked in chicken broth to give it extra flavor and richness. If you have access to fresh herbs, try a little chopped dill, basil or chives in the rice instead of the parsley. Although the recipe calls for large shrimp, you can also use medium shrimp, which will be less expensive but will take longer to shell and devein.

Working time: 30 minutes
Total time: 30 minutes

Lemon-Garlic Shrimp
with Parslied Rice

4 Servings

2 cups chicken broth
1 cup raw rice
1 pound large shrimp
1 bunch scallions (6 to 8)
2 tablespoons butter
2 tablespoons olive or other
   vegetable oil
5 cloves garlic, minced or crushed
   through a press

3 tablespoons lemon juice
¼ teaspoon pepper
½ cup grated Parmesan cheese
   (about 2 ounces)
2 tablespoons chopped parsley
Lemon slices, for garnish (optional)

Step 3

1 In a medium saucepan, bring the broth to a boil over medium-high heat. Add the rice, reduce the heat to low, cover and simmer until the rice is done, about 20 minutes.

2 Meanwhile, shell and devein the shrimp. Coarsely chop the scallions.

3 In a large skillet, warm the butter and oil over medium heat until they are hot but not smoking. Add the scallions and garlic, and cook, stirring, until the scallions are softened and beginning to brown, about 3 minutes.

4 Add the shrimp and cook for 4 minutes.

5 Stir in the lemon juice and pepper, and cook until the shrimp turn pink, about 4 minutes longer.

Step 5

6 Stir the Parmesan and parsley into the cooked rice, then transfer the rice to a serving platter. Spoon the shrimp mixture on top of the rice and serve, garnished with lemon slices, if desired.

TIME-SAVERS

■ ***Do-ahead:*** *The scallions can be chopped and the shrimp shelled and deveined ahead of time.*

Step 6

Values are approximate per serving: Calories: 473 Protein: 30 gm Fat: 20 gm
Carbohydrates: 43 gm Cholesterol: 166 mg Sodium: 953 mg

Quick Cioppino
with Parsley Toasts

▼

Cioppino is said to have originated among Italian and Portuguese fisherman working out of San Francisco. It's a typical "catch of the day" recipe, adaptable to what is best in the market. In this case, striped bass and crabmeat are the choices, but cioppino can also be made with sea bass, red snapper, halibut, shrimp, scallops, mussels and even lobster. Herbed toasts accompany the soup, but you could serve garlic bread instead.

Working time: 45 minutes
Total time: 45 minutes

Quick Cioppino
with Parsley Toasts

6 Servings

4 parsley sprigs
5 cloves garlic, minced or crushed
   through a press
1 large onion
1 large green bell pepper
½ pound mushrooms
4 fresh plum tomatoes or 6 canned
   whole tomatoes, well drained
3 teaspoons olive oil
3 tablespoons butter
1 cup bottled clam juice or chicken
   broth

1 cup chicken broth
⅔ cup dry red wine
2 tablespoons tomato paste
Pinch of sugar
¾ teaspoon black pepper
1 medium loaf Italian bread
½ pound striped bass fillet or other
   firm-fleshed white fish
1 can (6 ounces) lump crabmeat,
   drained

Step 5

1 In a food processor, mince the parsley; remove and set aside. In the same work bowl, mince the garlic. Add the onion and coarsely chop; remove and set aside. One at a time, coarsely chop the bell pepper and mushrooms. By hand, coarsely chop the tomatoes.

2 In a large skillet, warm 2 teaspoons of the oil over medium-high heat until hot but not smoking. Add the garlic-onion mixture, and stir-fry until the onion begins to brown, about 5 minutes.

3 Add the remaining 1 teaspoon oil, 1 tablespoon of the butter, the bell pepper and mushrooms, and cook, stirring, until the pepper begins to soften, about 3 minutes.

4 Add the chopped tomatoes, clam juice, chicken broth, wine, tomato paste, sugar and ½ teaspoon of the black pepper. Bring the mixture to a boil, then reduce the heat to low, cover and simmer while you prepare the remaining ingredients.

Step 6

5 In a small bowl, blend the remaining 2 tablespoons butter with the parsley and remaining ¼ teaspoon black pepper. Halve the bread lengthwise. Spread the bread with the parsley butter. Preheat the broiler or a toaster oven. Broil the bread until toasted, then cut into 4-inch lengths.

6 Cut the fish into 1-inch cubes. Uncover the tomato mixture and bring it to a boil over medium-high heat. Add the fish and cook until it just flakes when tested with a fork, about 6 minutes.

7 Just before serving, stir the crabmeat into the stew and cook until heated through. Serve with the parsley toasts on the side.

Values are approximate per serving: Calories: 413 Protein: 23 gm Fat: 11 gm
Carbohydrates: 52 gm Cholesterol: 75 mg Sodium: 996 mg

Step 7

Snapper with Red Pepper-Cream Sauce

▼

Here is a great way to make a rich-tasting sauce without heavy cream or butter, and it's all done in a food processor. Cream cheese is puréed with a bit of yogurt, tomato paste and cooked vegetables to create a velvety, blush-pink topping for red snapper fillets. The finished dish has a simple elegance that belies its minimal preparation time. Serve it with steamed vegetables, such as carrots and broccoli.

Working time: 10 minutes
Total time: 25 minutes

Snapper with Red Pepper-Cream Sauce

4 Servings

½ small red bell pepper
½ small onion
1 clove garlic, peeled
¼ cup water
2 tablespoons distilled white vinegar
3 tablespoons cream cheese (half a 3-ounce package)
1 tablespoon tomato paste

1 tablespoon plain yogurt
1 teaspoon chili powder
¼ teaspoon salt
Pinch of black pepper
4 red snapper fillets (about 1¼ pounds total) or other firm-fleshed white fish
2 tablespoons chopped chives (optional)

1 Preheat the broiler. Line a broiler pan with foil.

2 In a small saucepan, combine the bell pepper, onion and garlic with the water and vinegar. Bring the mixture to a boil over medium-high heat. Reduce the heat to medium-low, cover and simmer until the vegetables are tender, about 10 minutes.

3 Meanwhile, in a food processor, blend the cream cheese, tomato paste and yogurt.

4 Drain the vegetables. Add them to the food processor and process until smooth. Blend in the chili powder, salt and black pepper.

5 Place the fish on the prepared broiler pan. Dividing evenly, coat each fillet with the red pepper-cream sauce.

6 Broil the fish 4 inches from the heat until it is firm and just flakes when tested with a fork, about 9 minutes.

7 Serve with a sprinkling of chives if desired.

TIME-SAVERS

■ *Do-ahead: The red pepper-cream sauce (Steps 2 through 4) can be made ahead.*

Step 3

Step 4

Step 5

Values are approximate per serving: Calories: 192 Protein: 30 gm Fat: 6 gm
Carbohydrates: 3 gm Cholesterol: 64 mg Sodium: 299 mg

Shrimp with Green-Chili Creole Sauce

▼

A typical Creole sauce is tomato-based and seasoned with onions, green bell pepper, garlic and hot pepper. Instead of green pepper, this sauce uses a yellow bell pepper and canned green chilies, which add just a touch more spiciness. In New Orleans a Creole-style dish such as this would most likely be served over rice, but it also goes well with pasta; try it over orzo, a rice-shaped pasta.

Working time: 25 minutes
Total time: 30 minutes

Shrimp with Green-Chili Creole Sauce

4 Servings

1 medium onion
1 tablespoon butter
1 tablespoon olive or other vegetable oil
3 cloves garlic, minced or crushed through a press
1 can (14 ounces) whole tomatoes, with their juice
2 cans (4 ounces each) chopped mild green chilies, drained

½ teaspoon dry mustard
¼ teaspoon black pepper
¼ teaspoon hot pepper flakes
Pinch of sugar
1 pound medium shrimp
1 large yellow or green bell pepper
1 tablespoon cornstarch
¼ cup chicken broth
¼ cup chopped parsley (optional)

Step 3

1 Coarsely chop the onion.

2 In a large skillet, warm the butter in the oil over medium-high heat until the butter is melted. Add the onion and garlic and cook until the mixture begins to brown, about 5 minutes.

3 Add the tomatoes and their juice, the green chilies, mustard, black pepper, hot pepper flakes and sugar, and bring to a boil, breaking up the tomatoes with a spoon. Reduce the heat to low, cover and simmer while you prepare the remaining ingredients (but for at least 10 minutes).

Step 4

4 Shell and devein the shrimp (if desired, the tails can be left on the shrimp to make them more attractive). Cut the bell pepper into bite-size pieces. In a small bowl, combine the cornstarch and chicken broth.

5 Uncover the tomato sauce and bring it to a boil over medium-high heat. Add the shrimp, bell pepper, broth mixture and parsley (if using). Cook, stirring occasionally, until the shrimp are cooked through, the bell pepper is tender and the sauce has thickened slightly, 3 to 4 minutes.

TIME-SAVERS

■ *Do-ahead: The ingredients can all be prepared ahead. The sauce can be made through Step 3. The sauce can also be made through Step 5, but without adding the shrimp; bring the mixture back to a boil, add the shrimp and simmer until they are cooked through.*

Values are approximate per serving: Calories: 216 Protein: 21 gm Fat: 8 gm
Carbohydrates: 14 gm Cholesterol: 148 mg Sodium: 738 mg

Step 5

Skillet-Baked Flounder Provençale

Dishes from Provence, in the south of France, are highly flavored and frequently
include tomatoes, garlic and olives. If you can find them, try Niçoise olives in this
dish (but use only about ½ cup of them). They will have to be pitted, but will
add the characteristically smoky, olive-y taste typical of Provençale cooking. In case you
have no wine on hand, use either chicken broth or additional tomato sauce.

Working time: 15 minutes
Total time: 40 minutes

Skillet-Baked Flounder Provençale

4 Servings

1 medium onion	¼ teaspoon pepper
2 tablespoons olive or other vegetable oil	¾ cup pitted black olives
	¼ cup chopped parsley (optional)
3 cloves garlic, minced or crushed through a press	4 small flounder or other firm-fleshed white fish fillets (about 1½ pounds total)
1½ cups tomato sauce	
¼ cup red wine or chicken broth	2 tablespoons fine unseasoned breadcrumbs
¾ teaspoon tarragon	

1 Coarsely chop the onion.

2 In a large ovenproof skillet (preferably not cast iron), warm 1 tablespoon of the oil over medium-high heat until hot but not smoking. Add the onion and garlic and cook, stirring occasionally, until the mixture begins to brown, about 5 minutes.

Step 3

3 Add the tomato sauce, red wine, tarragon and pepper, and bring the mixture to a boil. Reduce the heat to low, cover and simmer for 15 minutes.

4 Meanwhile, preheat the oven to 375°.

5 Add the olives and 2 tablespoons of the parsley (if using) to the skillet. Add the flounder and spoon some of the sauce over the fillets.

6 Sprinkle the fish with the breadcrumbs and drizzle with the remaining 1 tablespoon oil. Place the skillet in the oven and bake, uncovered, for 10 minutes, or until the fish just flakes when tested.

7 Serve hot, garnished with the remaining parsley, if desired.

Step 5

TIME-SAVERS

■ *Microwave tip: In a shallow microwave-safe baking dish, combine the onion (finely, not coarsely, chopped), garlic, tomato sauce, wine, tarragon and pepper. Cover loosely with waxed paper and cook at 100% for 4 minutes, or until the liquid boils. Stir, then cook at 50% for 10 minutes. Stir in the olives and parsley (if using) and then arrange the fish fillets on top. (Omit the oil and breadcrumbs, or toast the crumbs separately in a toaster oven and sprinkle over the fish before serving.) Re-cover the fish and cook at 100% for 6 minutes, or until it just flakes when tested with a fork.*

■ *Do-ahead: The sauce can be made ahead through Step 5. Bring the sauce back to a simmer before adding the fish and baking.*

Step 6

Values are approximate per serving: Calories: 296 Protein: 34 gm Fat: 12 gm
Carbohydrates: 13 gm Cholesterol: 82 mg Sodium: 937 mg

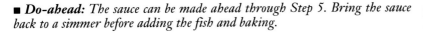

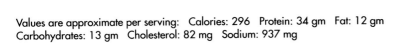

Linguine with Herbed Meat Sauce (page 179)

CHAPTER 4
PASTA

Macaroni and Cheddar Bake

There are countless variations on macaroni and cheese, the classic American comfort food. In this recipe, green peas add color and texture, while cottage cheese and sour cream replace the usual white sauce. To cut calories, use low-fat cottage cheese and reduced-calorie sour cream. There really is no substitute, however, for tantalizingly sharp Cheddar cheese.

Working time: 10 minutes
Total time: 50 minutes

Macaroni and Cheddar Bake

6 Servings

1 cup cottage cheese
1 tablespoon Dijon mustard
⅔ cup sour cream
½ teaspoon pepper
1½ cups small elbow macaroni
   (about ½ pound)

2 cups grated sharp Cheddar
   cheese (about ½ pound)
1 package (10 ounces) frozen peas
3 tablespoons minced chives or
   scallion (optional)

1 Bring a large pot of water to a boil.

2 Meanwhile, in a food processor, blend the cottage cheese and mustard until smooth. Transfer the cottage cheese mixture to a large bowl and stir in the sour cream and pepper.

Step 2

3 Add the macaroni to the boiling water and cook until al dente, 9 to 12 minutes or according to package directions.

4 Meanwhile, preheat the oven to 400°. Butter a 1½-quart baking dish.

5 Drain the macaroni well and add it to the cottage cheese mixture. Add 1½ cups of the Cheddar, the peas and chives (if using), and stir to blend well.

6 Turn the mixture into the prepared baking dish and top it with the remaining ½ cup Cheddar. Bake for about 25 minutes, or until lightly browned on top.

Step 5

TIME-SAVERS

■ *Microwave tip: Prepare Steps 1, 2, 3 and 5 above. Spoon the mixture in a 1½-quart microwave-safe baking dish. Loosely cover with waxed paper and cook at 50% for 15 minutes (stirring once), or until heated through. Top with the remaining ½ cup Cheddar, re-cover and let stand for 2 minutes.*

■ *Do-ahead: The sauce (Step 2) can be made ahead. The whole dish can be assembled ahead of time and then baked later. Or the whole dish can be baked ahead of time and reheated in the oven. (The dish can also be reheated in the microwave, but this may toughen the cheese.)*

Step 6

Values are approximate per serving: Calories: 424 Protein: 22 gm Fat: 20 gm
Carbohydrates: 38 gm Cholesterol: 56 mg Sodium: 521 mg

Vermicelli with Tomato-Bacon Sauce

This robust pasta dish was inspired by carbonara sauce, which is made with bacon, garlic and eggs. This lighter version is made with a quick tomato sauce flavored with bacon, garlic, basil and red wine. (If you prefer not to cook with wine—or don't have any on hand—use chicken broth instead.) A sprinkling of chopped cilantro adds an unusual note, but you can either leave it out or use fresh parsley instead.

Working time: 10 minutes
Total time: 25 minutes

Vermicelli with Tomato-Bacon Sauce

4 Servings

¼ **pound bacon (4 to 6 slices)**
1 **medium onion**
3 **cloves garlic, minced or crushed through a press**
¼ **cup dry red wine**
12 **ounces vermicelli or spaghettini**
1 **can (14 ounces) whole tomatoes with their juice**
1 **can (8 ounces) tomato sauce**
1 **bay leaf**
2 **tablespoons minced fresh basil or 1 teaspoon dried**
¼ **teaspoon pepper**
¼ **cup chopped cilantro or parsley (optional)**

1 Bring a large pot of water to a boil.

2 In a large skillet, cook the bacon over medium heat until crisp, about 10 minutes. Drain the bacon on paper towels.

3 Meanwhile, coarsely chop the onion.

Step 4

4 Pour off all but 2 tablespoons of bacon fat from the skillet. Over medium heat, sauté the garlic and onion in the bacon fat until the onion is translucent, about 5 minutes.

5 Add the wine and cook for 1 minute.

6 Add the pasta to the boiling water and cook until al dente, 10 to 12 minutes, or according to package directions.

7 Meanwhile, add the tomatoes and their juice, the tomato sauce, bay leaf, basil and pepper to the skillet. Break the tomatoes up slightly with a spoon, then reduce the heat to medium-low, cover and simmer for 10 to 12 minutes. Remove and discard the bay leaf.

Step 5

8 Drain the pasta and serve it topped with sauce. Crumble the bacon and sprinkle it on top along with the cilantro or parsley (if using).

TIME-SAVERS

■ *Microwave tip: Cook the pasta as described above. In a 3-quart microwave-safe casserole, arrange the bacon and cover loosely with waxed paper. Cook at 100% for 5 minutes, or until the bacon is browned and crisp. Pour off all but a thin coating of the bacon fat. Add the garlic and onion, re-cover and cook at 100% for 3 minutes. Stir in the wine, tomatoes and their juice, tomato sauce, bay leaf, basil and pepper. Re-cover and cook at 100% for 5 minutes, or until the mixture comes to a boil. Cook at 50% for 10 minutes to blend the flavors, stirring occasionally. Top the cooked pasta with sauce and cilantro or parsley (if using) and serve sprinkled with crumbled bacon.*

Values are approximate per serving: Calories: 305 Protein: 10 gm Fat: 7 gm Carbohydrates: 50 gm Cholesterol: 8 mg Sodium: 448 mg

Step 7

Fettuccine Carbonara with Spring Vegetables

▼

In this variation on the classic Italian pasta dish, hot noodles are tossed with peas, carrots, Parmesan cheese, beaten egg and slivers of ham. The recipe uses a couple of tricks to cut down on cooking times and the number of pots and pans needed: The peas and carrots are cooked along with the pasta; then the heat from the pasta and vegetables is used to cook the egg and cheese sauce right in the serving bowl.

Working time: 15 minutes
Total time: 30 minutes

Fettuccine Carbonara with Spring Vegetables

4 Servings

¼ **pound sliced lean ham (smoked or boiled)**
2 carrots
3 eggs
½ **cup grated Parmesan cheese (about 2 ounces)**

¼ **teaspoon pepper**
½ **pound fettuccine or other broad noodles**
1 package (10 ounces) frozen peas, thawed

1 Bring a large pot of water to a boil.

2 Meanwhile, keeping the ham slices in a stack, cut the ham into ½-inch-wide strips. Cut the carrots into very thin (⅛-inch) rounds.

3 In a small bowl, beat the eggs, Parmesan and pepper together.

4 Add the fettuccine to the boiling water and cook until almost done, 8 to 10 minutes. Add the carrots and peas and cook the pasta and vegetables for 2 minutes longer, or until the pasta is al dente and the carrots are crisp-tender.

5 Place a colander over a large heatproof serving bowl. Drain the pasta and vegetables into the colander, letting the boiling water heat the bowl. Pour the water out of the bowl and add the drained hot pasta and vegetables. Immediately pour the beaten egg mixture over the hot pasta and toss to cook the eggs and coat the pasta.

6 Add the ham and toss. Serve hot.

TIME-SAVERS

■ *Do-ahead: The ham and carrots can be prepared ahead.*

■ *Microwave tip: The peas can be thawed in the microwave.*

■ *Substitution: If you use fresh fettuccine, you can cut the cooking time by as much as 10 minutes. Add the pasta, peas and carrots at the same time and cook until the pasta is al dente and the carrots are crisp-tender, 2 to 3 minutes. If you use fresh noodles that are thinner than fettuccine, they will cook more quickly, so add the peas and carrots first and let them cook for about 1 minute before adding the pasta.*

Step 2

Step 3

Step 5

Values are approximate per serving: Calories: 439 Protein: 28 gm Fat: 12 gm
Carbohydrates: 55 gm Cholesterol: 238 mg Sodium: 719 mg

Pasta Twists with Shrimp, Peas and Tomato

▼

Happily, variations on the pasta-and-sauce theme seem virtually limitless.
There's always a different pasta shape to try, another form of tomatoes (fresh,
canned, sun-dried), a new combination of herbs and seasonings. Here
springy pasta twists are tossed with a fresh tomato sauce, shrimp and green peas.
Add a sprinkling of Parmesan, if you like.

Working time: 25 minutes
Total time: 40 minutes

Pasta Twists with Shrimp, Peas and Tomato

4 Servings

2 medium tomatoes
1 medium onion
1 tablespoon olive or other vegetable oil
3 cloves garlic, minced or crushed through a press
⅓ cup white wine or chicken broth (if using broth, omit the salt)
¾ teaspoon basil

½ teaspoon salt
¼ teaspoon pepper
½ pound pasta twists, such as fusilli, rotini or rotelle (about 2 cups)
¾ pound medium shrimp
1 cup frozen peas
2 tablespoons butter

Step 4

1 Coarsely chop the tomatoes and set aside. Coarsely chop the onion.

2 In a large skillet, warm the oil over medium-high heat until hot but not smoking. Add the onion and garlic, and stir-fry until the onion begins to brown, about 5 minutes.

3 Bring a large pot of water to a boil.

4 Meanwhile, add the chopped tomatoes, wine (or broth), basil, salt and pepper to the skillet. Bring the mixture to a boil over medium-high heat. Reduce the heat to medium-low, cover and simmer for 10 minutes.

5 Add the pasta to the boiling water and cook until al dente, 10 to 12 minutes, or according to package directions.

6 Meanwhile, shell and devein the shrimp.

Step 7

7 Bring the tomato mixture back to a boil. Add the shrimp and frozen peas and bring back to a boil. Reduce the heat to medium-low, cover and simmer, stirring occasionally, until the shrimp are cooked through, about 5 minutes.

8 Stir the butter into the sauce.

9 Drain the pasta well and toss it with the shrimp and tomato sauce.

TIME-SAVERS

■ *Do-ahead: The shrimp can be shelled and deveined ahead. The sauce can be made ahead through Step 4; bring the sauce back to a boil before proceeding.*

Values are approximate per serving: Calories: 416 Protein: 24 gm Fat: 12 gm
Carbohydrates: 53 gm Cholesterol: 121 mg Sodium: 486 mg

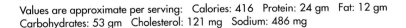
Step 8

Double-Mushroom Pasta

▼

You could buy the dried mushrooms called for in this recipe in a fancy gourmet shop, but you would pay a premium price for them. Instead, check your supermarket's fancy food shelves for a small container of dried mushrooms, often imported from Poland, which are almost identical in flavor to their higher priced Italian and French cousins. Two ½-ounce packages, costing less than a dollar apiece, are all you'll need for this recipe.

Working time: 25 minutes
Total time: 35 minutes

Double-Mushroom Pasta

4 Servings

1 cup chicken broth	¾ pound fresh mushrooms
1 ounce dried mushrooms (about 1 cup)	2 teaspoons oregano
	Pinch of salt
1 medium onion	¼ teaspoon pepper
4 tablespoons butter	¾ pound bow-tie pasta
2 tablespoons olive oil	⅓ cup grated Parmesan cheese
3 cloves garlic, minced or crushed through a press	

Step 2

1 Bring a large pot of water to a boil.

2 Meanwhile, in a small saucepan, bring the chicken broth to a boil. Place the dried mushrooms in a large measuring cup and pour the chicken broth over them. Let the mushrooms soak while you prepare the remaining sauce ingredients.

3 Cut the onion into thin slices.

4 In a large skillet, warm 2 tablespoons of the butter in the oil over medium-high heat until the butter is melted. Add the onion and garlic, and sauté until the onion begins to brown, about 5 minutes.

5 Meanwhile, cut the fresh mushrooms into ¼-inch slices. Add the mushrooms to the skillet and stir-fry until the mushrooms begin to wilt, 1 to 2 minutes.

Step 5

6 To the skillet, add the reconstituted dried mushrooms and ½ cup of their soaking liquid (carefully leaving any grit behind in the measuring cup). Add the oregano, salt and pepper. Bring the mixture to a boil over medium-high heat. Reduce the heat to low and simmer, uncovered, while you cook the pasta.

7 Add the pasta to the boiling water and cook until al dente, 10 to 12 minutes, or according to package directions.

8 Drain the pasta. Stir the remaining 2 tablespoons butter into the mushrooms. Serve the drained pasta topped with the mushrooms, and pass the Parmesan separately.

TIME-SAVERS

■ *Do-ahead: The dried mushrooms can be soaked ahead. The mushroom sauce can be made ahead through Step 6; reheat gently and then stir in the 2 tablespoons of butter.*

Values are approximate per serving: Calories: 568   Protein: 17 gm   Fat: 23 gm
Carbohydrates: 75 gm   Cholesterol: 36 mg   Sodium: 533 mg

Step 6

Linguine with Herbed Meat Sauce

▼

Many cooks feel that there are only two choices when it comes to tomato sauce for pasta: homemade sauce that takes all day to make, or a jar of storebought. Here is a family-pleasing third option: a 20-minute tomato-and-beef sauce seasoned with five herbs—basil, rosemary, thyme, bay and oregano. Of course if you have any extra time, the sauce can only get better if you simmer it a while longer.

Working time: 15 minutes
Total time: 35 minutes

Linguine with Herbed Meat Sauce

4 Servings

1 small onion
1 teaspoon olive or other vegetable oil
3 cloves garlic, minced or crushed through a press
¾ pound lean ground beef
1 can (14 ounces) whole tomatoes, with their juice
1 can (8 ounces) tomato sauce

½ teaspoon basil
½ teaspoon oregano
½ teaspoon rosemary, crumbled
½ teaspoon thyme
¼ teaspoon red pepper flakes
¼ teaspoon black pepper
1 bay leaf
¾ pound linguine or spaghetti
½ cup grated Parmesan cheese

Step 1

1 Coarsely chop the onion.

2 In a medium saucepan, warm the oil over medium-high heat until hot but not smoking. Add the onion and garlic, and cook until the mixture begins to brown, 2 to 3 minutes.

3 Crumble the beef into the saucepan and cook, stirring, until the meat is no longer pink, about 4 minutes.

4 Bring a large pot of water to a boil.

5 Meanwhile, to the saucepan, add the tomatoes and their juice, the tomato sauce, basil, oregano, rosemary, thyme, red pepper flakes, black pepper and bay leaf. Bring to a boil over medium-high heat, breaking up the tomatoes with a spoon. Reduce the heat to low and simmer uncovered for 15 minutes, stirring occasionally.

Step 3

6 About 10 minutes before the sauce is done, add the pasta to the boiling water and cook until al dente, 7 to 9 minutes, or according to package directions.

7 Drain the pasta. Remove the bay leaf from the sauce. Serve the pasta topped with sauce and pass the Parmesan on the side.

TIME-SAVERS

■ *Microwave tip: In a 2-quart microwave-safe casserole, combine the chopped onion, garlic and crumbled ground beef; omit the oil. Cover loosely with waxed paper and cook at 100% for 4 to 5 minutes, or until the beef is cooked, stirring once to break up the meat. Stir in the tomatoes and their juice, the tomato sauce, basil, oregano, rosemary, thyme, red pepper flakes, black pepper and bay leaf. Re-cover and cook at 100% for 6 to 7 minutes, or until the mixture comes to a boil. Cook at 50% for 8 minutes to blend the flavors. Cook the linguine in the conventional manner and serve as above.*

Values are approximate per serving: Calories: 643   Protein: 33 gm   Fat: 24 gm
Carbohydrates: 17 gm   Cholesterol: 72 mg   Sodium: 758 mg

Step 5

Red, Gold and Green
Skillet Casserole

▼

This hearty entrée can be as mellow or spicy-hot as you like. You can leave out the canned green chilies, using a second bell pepper instead. Or, if your family goes for zesty Tex-Mex fare, substitute pepper jack cheese (which contains bits of jalapeño) for the regular Monterey jack, or simply add a seeded, chopped jalapeño pepper. If you can't find ditalini pasta (the name means "little thimbles"), use elbow macaroni .

Working time: 15 minutes
Total time: 30 minutes

Red, Gold and Green Skillet Casserole

6 Servings

- 1 medium onion
- 4 medium plum tomatoes
- 1 medium green bell pepper
- 1 tablespoon butter
- 1 tablespoon olive or other vegetable oil
- 2 cloves garlic, minced or crushed through a press
- 2 cups chicken broth

- 1 can (4 ounces) chopped mild green chilies (optional), drained
- ½ teaspoon oregano
- ¼ teaspoon black pepper
- ½ pound small tube pasta, such as ditalini (about 2¼ cups)
- 1½ cups grated Monterey jack cheese

Step 1

1 Coarsely chop the onion and set aside. Coarsely chop the tomatoes and bell pepper.

2 In a large ovenproof skillet, warm the butter in the oil over medium-high heat until the butter is melted. Add the onion and garlic, and sauté until the onion begins to brown, about 5 minutes.

3 Preheat the broiler.

4 Add the tomatoes, bell pepper, chicken broth, chopped chilies (if using), oregano and black pepper to the skillet. Bring to a boil over high heat and add the pasta. Reduce the heat to low, cover and simmer, stirring frequently, until the pasta is al dente, about 9 minutes.

Step 4

5 Stir in 1 cup of the cheese. Sprinkle the remaining ½ cup cheese evenly over the top. Place the skillet under the broiler and broil 4 inches from the heat until golden brown on top, 3 to 5 minutes.

TIME-SAVERS

■ *Do-ahead: The dish can be made ahead up to the point of adding the pasta (Step 4). Bring the mixture back to a boil (adding a bit of water if it has gotten too thick), add the pasta and proceed with the recipe.*

Step 5

Values are approximate per serving: Calories: 311 Protein: 14 gm Fat: 14 gm
Carbohydrates: 33 gm Cholesterol: 30 mg Sodium: 508 mg

Pasta Primavera Salad

▼

Pasta primavera takes a summery turn here, transformed with a lemon-Dijon dressing into a cool main-dish salad. Frozen peas and asparagus cut the preparation time, especially with the quick trick of using the boiling water from the noodles to thaw the vegetables. Note that the noodles are rinsed under cold water; this not only cools the pasta, but also removes excess surface starch that might result in a gummy salad.

Working time: 20 minutes
Total time: 30 minutes

Pasta Primavera Salad

6 Servings

4 plum tomatoes
3 scallions
½ cup (packed) basil leaves or 2 teaspoons dried
3 tablespoons olive or other vegetable oil
2 tablespoons lemon juice
1 tablespoon Dijon mustard
2 teaspoons grated lemon zest (optional)

¼ teaspoon red pepper flakes
½ teaspoon salt
¼ teaspoon black pepper
3 cloves garlic, peeled
½ pound egg noodles
1 package (10 ounces) frozen peas
1 package (10 ounces) frozen asparagus
2 tablespoons grated Parmesan cheese

Step 2

1 Bring a large pot of water to a boil.

2 Meanwhile, coarsely chop the tomatoes and scallions. Mince the basil.

3 In a large salad bowl, combine the basil, olive oil, lemon juice, mustard, lemon zest (if using), red pepper flakes, salt and black pepper.

4 Add the garlic and noodles to the boiling water and cook until the noodles are al dente, 8 to 10 minutes, or according to package directions.

5 Meanwhile, place the frozen peas and asparagus in a colander. When the noodles are done, drain them into the colander (the hot water will thaw the peas and asparagus). Run the noodles and vegetables under cold water to cool them; drain well. Cut the asparagus into ½- to ¾-inch lengths.

Step 6

6 Press the garlic cloves through a press (or mash with a fork) and add it to the dressing in the salad bowl; whisk to blend well. Add the noodles, vegetables and Parmesan to the bowl and toss to combine with the dressing.

TIME-SAVERS

■ ***Do-ahead:*** *The dressing (Step 3) can be prepared ahead. Or the whole salad can be assembled ahead and served chilled.*

Step 6

Values are approximate per serving: Calories: 274 Protein: 11 gm Fat: 9 gm
Carbohydrates: 38 gm Cholesterol: 37 mg Sodium: 357 mg

Spaghetti with Shrimp and Mushrooms

▼

Tossing hot spaghetti with beaten egg adds richness—for a minimum of calories—to this simple pasta dish. For a less expensive version, cut back on the shrimp and increase the amount of mushrooms; this will not affect the cooking times. If you don't care for anchovies, leave them out. However, you may find that as a result the dish needs a bit more salt or Parmesan.

Working time: 40 minutes
Total time: 40 minutes

Spaghetti with Shrimp and Mushrooms

4 Servings

¾ **pound medium shrimp**
¼ **pound mushrooms**
1 bunch scallions (6 to 8)
½ **pound spaghetti**
1 egg
½ **cup half-and-half or light cream**
½ **cup grated Parmesan cheese
(about 2 ounces)**
¼ **cup chopped parsley (optional)**

**4 teaspoons anchovy paste or 4 flat
anchovies, minced (optional)**
½ **teaspoon dry mustard**
¼ **teaspoon pepper**
**3 tablespoons olive or other
vegetable oil**
**2 cloves garlic, minced or crushed
through a press**

Step 4

1 Bring a large pot of water to a boil.

2 Meanwhile, shell and devein the shrimp. Slice the mushrooms. Coarsely chop the scallions.

3 Add the pasta to the boiling water and cook until al dente, 10 to 12 minutes.

4 Meanwhile, in a serving bowl, beat the egg. Stir in the half-and-half, Parmesan, parsley (if using), anchovy paste (if using), mustard and pepper. Set aside.

5 In a large skillet, warm 2 tablespoons of the oil over medium-high heat until hot but not smoking. Add the mushrooms and garlic and stir-fry until the mushrooms are almost limp, about 5 minutes.

Step 6

6 Add the remaining 1 tablespoon oil and the shrimp and stir-fry for 2 minutes. Add the scallions and stir-fry until the shrimp turn pink and opaque, 1 to 2 minutes longer.

7 Drain the pasta in a colander. Add the hot pasta to the beaten egg mixture and toss to cook the eggs as well as coat the pasta. Add the shrimp-vegetable mixture and toss to distribute evenly. Serve hot.

TIME-SAVERS

■ *Do-ahead: The shrimp can be shelled and deveined ahead. The mushrooms and scallions can be cut up ahead. And the beaten egg mixture can be prepared a short while before cooking.*

Values are approximate per serving: Calories: 494 Protein: 29 gm Fat: 20 gm
Carbohydrates: 48 gm Cholesterol: 193 mg Sodium: 322 mg

Step 7

Pork and Pepper Lo Mein

▼

Lo mein is the Chinese name for thin noodles; linguine, used in this recipe, is similar in size and shape. The pork and vegetables are stir-fried in the time-honored Chinese manner, but a food processor updates the recipe by quickly slicing the garlic, scallions, mushrooms and bell pepper. The dish is made with a moderate amount of soy sauce; if you wish, offer additional soy sauce at the table.

Working time: 30 minutes
Total time: 30 minutes

Pork and Pepper Lo Mein

4 Servings

2 cloves garlic
1 bunch scallions (6 to 8)
¼ pound mushrooms
1 large red bell pepper
¾ pound pork tenderloin
3 tablespoons cornstarch
¼ cup vegetable oil
2 teaspoons Oriental sesame oil

3 quarter-size slices (¼ inch thick)
   fresh ginger, unpeeled
½ pound linguine or spaghetti
1 cup beef broth
2 tablespoons reduced-sodium or
   regular soy sauce
¼ teaspoon black pepper

1 Bring a large pot of water to a boil.

2 Meanwhile, in a food processor with the metal blade, chop the garlic. Add the scallions and coarsely chop them. Remove and set aside.

3 In the same work bowl, but with the slicing blade, slice the mushrooms and the bell pepper. Remove and set aside.

Step 3

4 Cut the pork in half lengthwise and then cut each strip crosswise into ¼-inch-wide slices. Place the cornstarch in a shallow bowl. Dredge the pork in the cornstarch. Set the excess cornstarch aside.

5 In a large skillet, warm 2 tablespoons of the vegetable oil and 1 teaspoon of the sesame oil over medium-high heat until hot but not smoking. Add the garlic, scallions and ginger and stir-fry until the scallions are limp, 2 to 3 minutes.

6 Add the pasta to the boiling water and cook until al dente, 14 minutes, or according to package directions.

Step 4

7 Meanwhile, add the pork to the skillet and stir-fry until the meat begins to brown, about 5 minutes. Remove the pork and scallion mixture to a plate and set aside. Add the remaining 2 tablespoons vegetable oil and 1 teaspoon sesame oil to the skillet. Add the mushrooms and bell pepper and cook, stirring frequently, until the vegetables begin to wilt, about 5 minutes.

8 Meanwhile, add the beef broth, soy sauce and black pepper to the reserved cornstarch and stir to blend. When the vegetables have cooked for 5 minutes, stir in the broth mixture. Return the pork and scallions to the skillet and bring the liquid to a boil. Cook until the sauce thickens slightly, about 3 minutes.

9 Drain the pasta and toss with the pork and vegetables.

Values are approximate per serving: Calories: 402 Protein: 22 gm Fat: 16 gm
Carbohydrates: 43 gm Cholesterol: 44 mg Sodium: 445 mg

Step 8

Bow Ties with Tomatoes and Italian Sausage

▼

The bold flavor and chunky texture of this sauce are rounded out by a topping of mozzarella; if your family loves cheese, pass a bowl of additional shredded mozzarella at the table. Bow tie pasta (sometimes called butterflies or farfalle) is a good match for this sauce, but you could also serve it over rigatoni, ziti or penne—tube-shaped pastas that will hold the sauce well.

Working time: 25 minutes
Total time: 45 minutes

Bow Ties with Tomatoes and Italian Sausage

6 Servings

1 large green bell pepper	**1 teaspoon basil**
1 medium onion	**1 teaspoon oregano**
3 cloves garlic	**½ teaspoon salt**
½ pound sweet Italian sausage	**¼ teaspoon black pepper**
2 cans (16 ounces each) whole tomatoes in purée	**2 cups bow tie or other small pasta shapes (about 8 ounces)**
2 tablespoons tomato paste	**½ cup shredded mozzarella cheese**
1 bay leaf	

Step 2

1 In a food processor, coarsely chop the green pepper, onion and garlic.

2 Remove the sausages from their casings. In a large skillet, cook the sausage, breaking it up with a spoon, over medium heat until the meat has lost its pinkness, about 5 minutes.

3 Add the green pepper-onion mixture and cook until the onion is translucent and beginning to brown, about 8 minutes, stirring frequently.

4 Stir in the tomatoes and purée, tomato paste, bay leaf, basil, oregano, salt and black pepper. Bring to a boil over medium-high heat, reduce the heat to medium-low, cover and simmer for 15 to 20 minutes. Discard the bay leaf.

5 Meanwhile, bring a large pot of water to a boil. Add the pasta to the boiling water and cook until al dente, 11 to 13 minutes, or according to package directions.

6 Drain the pasta and serve it topped with the sauce and sprinkled with the mozzarella.

Step 3

TIME-SAVERS

■ *Microwave tip: In a 3-quart microwave-safe casserole, combine the crumbled sausage with the green pepper-onion mixture. Cover and cook at 100% for 6 minutes, or until the sausage is no longer pink, stirring once to break up the meat. Drain off the sausage fat. Add the tomatoes, tomato paste and seasonings, re-cover and cook at 100% for 8 minutes, or until the mixture comes to a boil. Cook at 50% for 10 minutes, stirring once, to blend the flavors. Prepare and serve the pasta as directed above.*

■ *Do-ahead: The sauce can be made well ahead of time, refrigerated (or frozen) and reheated.*

Values are approximate per serving: Calories: 355 Protein: 14 gm Fat: 15 gm
Carbohydrates: 42 gm Cholesterol: 36 mg Sodium: 781 mg

Step 4

▼

Cooking pasta right in the sauce is a clever way to make an already uncomplicated dish even simpler. This recipe can serve as a basic pattern; use it to create ethnic variations by adding different herbs and spices. For example, add some cinnamon for a Middle Eastern flavor or cumin and chopped cilantro for a Mexican version. If you do not have tomato juice on hand, use half water and half tomato sauce or purée.

Working time: 25 minutes
Total time: 35 minutes

Skillet Macaroni with Zucchini

4 Servings

1 **large or 2 small zucchini (about ½ pound)**
1 **medium onion**
1 **tablespoon olive or other vegetable oil**
2 **cloves garlic, minced or crushed through a press**
½ **pound ground round**
2 **cups elbow macaroni (about ½ pound)**
1 **can (18 ounces) tomato juice**
1 **cup beef broth**
½ **teaspoon oregano**
⅛ **teaspoon pepper**

Step 1

1 Halve the zucchini lengthwise and then cut the halves crosswise into ¼-inch-thick half-rounds; set aside. Coarsely chop the onion.

2 In a large skillet, warm the oil over medium-high heat until hot but not smoking. Add the onion and garlic, and sauté until the onion is translucent, 2 to 3 minutes.

3 Crumble in the ground beef and cook, stirring to break up the meat, until the meat is no longer pink and is slightly browned, about 5 minutes.

4 Add the macaroni, tomato juice, beef broth, oregano and pepper and bring to a boil. Cover, reduce the heat to medium-low and simmer, stirring occasionally, for 10 minutes.

5 Stir the zucchini into the mixture and continue cooking until the macaroni and zucchini are tender, about 3 minutes longer. Serve hot.

Step 3

TIME-SAVERS

■ *Do-ahead: The zucchini and onion can be prepared ahead of time. You can also make the entire dish and reheat it, although you might want to undercook the pasta very slightly so that it does not overcook in the reheating.*

Step 4

Values are approximate per serving: Calories: 462 Protein: 19 gm Fat: 20 gm
Carbohydrates: 52 gm Cholesterol: 48 mg Sodium: 744 mg

Egg Noodles with Pork Balls and Tomato-Pepper Sauce

▼

Instead of the usual spaghetti-and-meatball combination, try these ground-pork balls in a tomato-and-bell-pepper sauce served over egg noodles. The meatballs have a pinch of cayenne in them, but if you like spicy food, increase the amount or add extra hot pepper flakes. Serve with slices of buttery garlic bread and a tossed salad dressed with a light herbal vinaigrette.

Working time: 25 minutes
Total time: 35 minutes

Fettuccine with Chicken and Scallion Sauce

4 Servings

4 skinless, boneless chicken breast halves (about 1¼ pounds total)
1 bunch scallions (6 to 8)
2 cloves garlic
¼ cup olive or other vegetable oil
1 teaspoon oregano
½ pound fettuccine or other broad noodles

1 cup cottage cheese
¼ cup chicken broth
⅓ cup plus 3 tablespoons grated Parmesan cheese
½ teaspoon salt
¼ teaspoon pepper

Step 5

1 Bring a large pot of water to a boil.

2 Meanwhile, cut the chicken into ¼-inch-wide strips. In a food processor, coarsely chop the scallions and garlic.

3 In a medium skillet, warm 2 tablespoons of the oil over medium heat. Add the scallions, garlic and oregano and stir-fry until the scallions are limp, about 5 minutes. Remove the mixture from the skillet and set aside.

4 Add the fettuccine to the boiling water and cook until al dente, 10 to 12 minutes, or according to package directions.

5 Meanwhile, in the same food processor work bowl (there is no need to clean it), purée the cottage cheese. Transfer the cottage cheese to a small bowl. Stir in the chicken broth and ⅓ cup of the Parmesan.

Step 6

6 Add the remaining 2 tablespoons oil to the skillet and warm it over medium-high heat until hot but not smoking. Add the chicken and stir-fry until it is firm and cooked through, about 5 minutes. Stir in the reserved scallions and garlic, the remaining 3 tablespoons Parmesan and the salt and pepper.

7 Drain the pasta well, then add it to the skillet. Add the cottage cheese mixture and the chicken-scallion mixture and toss to combine.

TIME-SAVERS

■ ***Do-ahead:*** *The cottage cheese mixture (Step 5) can be made ahead.*

Step 7

Values are approximate per serving: Calories: 616 Protein: 53 gm Fat: 24 gm
Carbohydrates: 45 gm Cholesterol: 154 mg Sodium: 890 mg

Penne with Crabmeat and Fresh Tomatoes

▼

Fresh tomatoes, black olives and succulent lumps of crabmeat go into this chunky pasta topping. Meaty plum tomatoes work well in this recipe, but you can substitute beefsteak tomatoes when nice local ones are available. Beefsteaks are juicier than plum tomatoes, however; to keep their juices from thinning the sauce, halve the tomatoes and let them drain cut-side down on paper towels for a few minutes.

Working time: 20 minutes
Total time: 35 minutes

Penne with Crabmeat and Fresh Tomatoes

4 Servings

¾ cup pitted black olives
6 plum tomatoes
2 medium onions
¼ cup (packed) fresh dill sprigs or
   1¼ teaspoons dried
¼ cup (packed) cilantro sprigs
   (optional)
1 tablespoon butter
2 tablespoons olive or other
   vegetable oil

3 cloves garlic, minced or crushed
   through a press
2 tablespoons tomato paste
¼ teaspoon sugar
½ teaspoon salt
½ teaspoon pepper
¾ pound penne or other tube-
   shaped pasta
½ pound lump crabmeat

Step 2

1 Bring a large pot of water to a boil.

2 Meanwhile, slice the olives. Coarsely chop the tomatoes. Cut the onions into thin wedges. Mince the dill and the cilantro (if using).

3 In a medium skillet, warm the butter in the oil over medium-high heat until the butter is melted. Add the onions and garlic, and stir-fry until the onions begin to brown, about 5 minutes.

4 Add the tomatoes, olives, dill, cilantro (if using), tomato paste, sugar, salt and pepper. Reduce the heat to low, cover and simmer while you cook the pasta.

Step 4

5 Add the pasta to the boiling water and cook until al dente, 7 to 9 minutes, or according to package directions.

6 Stir the crabmeat into the tomato mixture. Drain the pasta and serve topped with the sauce.

TIME-SAVERS

■ *Do-ahead: The sauce can be made ahead through Step 4.*

Step 6

Values are approximate per serving: Calories: 526   Protein: 24 gm   Fat: 15 gm
Carbohydrates: 74 gm   Cholesterol: 65 mg   Sodium: 759 mg

Southwestern Lasagna

▼

This recipe transforms a favorite family dish by substituting Southwestern flavors for Italian ingredients and seasonings. Monterey Jack cheese replaces the usual mozzarella, while chili powder and cumin take the place of the typically Italian oregano and basil. For a nice contrast to the spiciness of the lasagna, serve a white wine sangria garnished with sliced apples and oranges.

Working time: 30 minutes
Total time: 1 hour 50 minutes

Southwestern Lasagna

8 Servings

2 medium onions
2 tablespoons olive oil
2 cloves garlic, minced or crushed
  through a press
1 can (28 ounces) whole tomatoes,
  with their juice
1 can (8 ounces) tomato sauce
1 can (4 ounces) chopped mild
  green chilies (optional)

3 tablespoons chili powder
1 tablespoon cumin
½ teaspoon salt
½ teaspoon pepper
1 pound lasagna noodles
½ pound Monterey Jack cheese
¾ cup grated Parmesan cheese
1 pound cottage cheese, preferably
  small curd

Step 6

1 Coarsely chop the onions. In a medium saucepan, combine the oil, onions and garlic and cook over medium-high heat for 5 minutes.

2 Add the tomatoes and their juice, the tomato sauce, green chilies (if using), chili powder, cumin, salt and pepper. Bring the mixture to a simmer over medium heat. Reduce the heat to medium-low and simmer, uncovered, for 35 minutes, stirring occasionally.

3 Meanwhile, bring a large pot of water to a boil. Cook the lasagna noodles until al dente, 10 to 12 minutes.

4 While the sauce and noodles are cooking, grate the Monterey Jack. In a medium bowl, toss the Monterey Jack and Parmesan together.

5 Preheat the oven to 350°. Rinse the lasagna noodles under cold water and drain well.

Step 6

6 Spoon some sauce into the bottom of a 13 x 9 x 2-inch baking dish. Make three layers, using the following sequence of ingredients: noodles, cottage cheese, sauce and grated cheeses (using only about three-fourths of the grated cheeses).

7 Top the lasagna with any remaining sauce and the remaining grated cheeses. Bake for 35 minutes. Let stand for 15 minutes.

TIME-SAVERS

■ *Microwave tip: In a medium microwave-safe bowl or casserole, combine the oil, onions and garlic. Cover loosely and cook at 100% 5 to 6 minutes. Add the tomatoes, tomato sauce, chilies, chili powder, cumin, salt and pepper and stir to blend. Re-cover and cook at 100% for 5 minutes. Cook at 50% for 5 minutes. Cook the noodles and assemble the lasagna (in a microwave-safe dish)as described above. Cover and cook at 50% for 15 to 20 minutes, rotating the dish twice, or until heated through. Let stand for 7 minutes.*

Step 7

Values are approximate per serving: Calories: 486 Protein: 26 gm Fat: 18 gm
Carbohydrates: 55 gm Cholesterol: 39 mg Sodium: 1023 mg

Pasta Twists with Pepper-Pepperoni Sauce

▼

*Visit a "salumeria" (deli or sausage shop) in an Italian neighborhood, and you'll find a
mouthwatering array of dried sausages suspended from the ceiling. Most familiar to
American palates is zesty pepperoni, a dried beef or pork sausage spiced with red and
black pepper, often used as a pizza topping. For this pizza-like dish, either buy a chunk
of pepperoni at your supermarket deli counter, or use packaged slices and sliver them.*

Working time: 15 minutes
Total time: 30 minutes

6 Servings

1 can (16 ounces) crushed tomatoes
1 can (8 ounces) tomato sauce
3 cloves garlic, minced or crushed
   through a press
1½ teaspoons oregano
¼ teaspoon black pepper
1 large carrot
1 medium red onion

1 large red bell pepper
¼ cup (packed) fresh basil leaves or
   1½ teaspoons dried
¾ pound pasta twists (about
   4½ cups)
½ pound pepperoni
1 cup shredded mozzarella cheese
   (about ¼ pound)

Step 3

1 Bring a large pot of water to a boil.

2 Meanwhile, in a medium saucepan, combine the crushed tomatoes, tomato sauce, garlic, oregano and black pepper. Bring the mixture to a boil over medium-high heat. Reduce the heat to low, cover and simmer while you prepare the vegetables.

3 In a food processor, one at a time, coarsely chop the carrot, onion, bell pepper and fresh basil.

4 Add the vegetables and basil to the tomato sauce and return to a boil over medium-high heat. Reduce the heat to low, cover and simmer while you cook the pasta and prepare the remaining ingredients.

Step 4

5 Add the pasta to the boiling water and cook until al dente, 10 to 12 minutes, or according to package directions.

6 Meanwhile, remove the thin papery casing from the pepperoni and cut the sausage into scant ½-inch slices, then cut the slices into cubes. Add them to the sauce and continue simmering while the pasta cooks.

7 Drain the pasta and serve topped with pepper-pepperoni sauce. Pass the shredded mozzarella separately.

TIME-SAVERS

■ *Do-ahead: The pepper-pepperoni sauce can be prepared well in advance.*

Step 6

Values are approximate per serving: Calories: 498 Protein: 21 gm Fat: 22 gm
Carbohydrates: 54 gm Cholesterol: 45 mg Sodium: 1205 mg

Pasta and Chicken Gratin

▼

*Three cheeses go into this golden gratin: Grated Swiss and mozzarella are
mixed into the chicken and pasta, and the dish is topped with Parmesan breadcrumbs.
The pasta is simmered in chicken broth with a clove of garlic for extra flavor.
You can vary this recipe by using different kinds of cheese; for instance, substitute
Gruyère for the Swiss, provolone for the mozzarella, or romano for the Parmesan.*

Working time: 30 minutes
Total time: 40 minutes

Pasta and Chicken Gratin

6 Servings

2 cups chicken broth
3 cloves garlic, minced or crushed
   through a press
1 cup orzo or other small pasta
   shape
¼ pound Swiss cheese, unsliced
2 medium zucchini
1 large onion
½ pound skinless, boneless chicken
   breast
3 tablespoons olive or other
   vegetable oil

1½ teaspoons oregano
¼ teaspoon salt
½ teaspoon pepper
1 tablespoon fine unseasoned
   breadcrumbs
1 tablespoon grated Parmesan
   cheese
½ cup grated mozzarella cheese
¼ cup chopped parsley (optional)

Step 2

1 In a medium saucepan, bring the chicken broth and 1 clove of the garlic to a boil over high heat. Add the pasta; reduce the heat to low, cover and simmer until al dente, 9 to 11 minutes, or according to package directions. Remove from the heat when done; do not drain.

2 Meanwhile, grate the Swiss cheese. Cut the zucchini into ½-inch dice. Thinly slice the onion. Cut the chicken across the grain into ¼-inch-wide slices.

3 In a large broilerproof skillet, warm 1 tablespoon of the oil over medium-high heat until hot but not smoking. Add the remaining 2 cloves garlic and the onion, and stir-fry until the onion is beginning to brown, about 5 minutes.

Step 4

4 Add the zucchini, oregano, salt and pepper, and cook, stirring, until the zucchini begins to soften, about 3 minutes. Remove the vegetables to a plate and cover loosely to keep warm.

5 Preheat the broiler. In a small bowl, combine the breadcrumbs and the Parmesan.

6 Add 1 tablespoon of the oil to the skillet and heat until hot but not smoking. Add the chicken and stir-fry until the chicken is barely cooked, about 3 minutes. Reduce the heat to medium.

7 Return the vegetables to the skillet. Add the cooked pasta and broth, Swiss cheese, mozzarella and parsley (if using), and stir to combine. Sprinkle the breadcrumb mixture over the pasta mixture and drizzle with the remaining 1 tablespoon oil. Broil 4 inches from the heat until golden, 3 to 5 minutes. Serve directly from the skillet.

Step 7

Values are approximate per serving: Calories: 360 Protein: 23 gm Fat: 16 gm
Carbohydrates: 31 gm Cholesterol: 47 mg Sodium: 556 mg

Vegetable Lo Mein

This meatless main dish is based on the lo mein ("mixed noodle") dishes found in many Chinese restaurants. Here, five different vegetables are mixed with thin noodles in a light broth-based sauce. Feel free to try other vegetables: for instance, Napa cabbage or bok choy instead of regular cabbage, and Swiss chard in place of spinach. And if you have any leftover chicken, shred it and add it at the end, with the pasta.

Working time: 30 minutes
Total time: 30 minutes

Vegetable Lo Mein

4 Servings

- 5 quarter-size slices (¼ inch thick) fresh ginger, unpeeled
- 3 cloves garlic
- 4 scallions
- ¼ cup (packed) cilantro sprigs (optional)
- 1 large red bell pepper
- Half a small head cabbage
- ¼ pound small mushrooms
- ¼ pound fresh spinach
- ¾ pound linguine or spaghetti
- 2 tablespoons vegetable oil
- ¼ pound bean sprouts
- ⅔ cup chicken broth
- ¼ cup reduced-sodium soy sauce
- 1 tablespoon cornstarch
- 1 tablespoon dry sherry (optional)
- 3 drops hot pepper sauce
- ¼ teaspoon red pepper flakes
- ¼ teaspoon black pepper

Step 2

1 Bring a large pot of water to a boil.

2 Meanwhile, in a food processor, mince the ginger and garlic; set aside. Coarsely chop the scallions; set aside. Add the cilantro (if using) and pulse on and off to finely chop; set aside. Coarsely chop the bell pepper; set aside. Shred the cabbage with a knife; set aside.

3 If the mushrooms are small, leave them whole; otherwise, halve or quarter them. Leave the spinach leaves whole unless they are very large, in which case, tear them into smaller pieces.

4 Add the pasta to the boiling water and cook until al dente, 10 to 12 minutes, or according to package directions.

5 Meanwhile, in a large skillet or wok, warm 1 tablespoon of the oil over medium-high heat until hot but not smoking. Add the ginger-garlic mixture and stir-fry until fragrant, about 2 minutes.

Step 6

6 Add the remaining 1 tablespoon oil and then the scallions, bell pepper, cabbage, mushrooms, spinach and bean sprouts. Cook, stirring, until the vegetables begin to soften, about 4 minutes.

7 In a small bowl, combine the chicken broth, soy sauce, cornstarch, sherry (if using), hot pepper sauce, red pepper flakes and black pepper.

8 Drain the pasta and add it to the skillet along with the cornstarch-broth mixture. Bring the mixture to a boil, tossing to combine the pasta, vegetables and sauce. Add the cilantro (if using) and cook until the mixture is heated through, about 2 minutes.

Step 8

Values are approximate per serving: Calories: 445 Protein: 16 gm Fat: 9 gm
Carbohydrates: 77 gm Cholesterol: 0 mg Sodium: 808 mg

Fettuccine with
Scallops Provençale

▼

This recipe calls for either tiny bay scallops or the larger sea scallops. Although the small scallops will be sweeter and more tender, they are not always readily available —their prime season is fall and winter—and they are generally more expensive. Whichever type of scallop you use, it is best not to prepare the dish in advance and reheat it, as shellfish (and scallops especially) will toughen if overcooked.

Working time: 15 minutes
Total time: 25 minutes

Fettuccine with Scallops Provençale

4 Servings

1 medium onion
¼ pound small mushrooms
1 tablespoon olive or other
   vegetable oil
3 cloves garlic, minced or crushed
   through a press
1 pint cherry tomatoes (about
   ¾ pound)
1 cup tomato sauce
1 tablespoon tomato paste

1 teaspoon basil
½ teaspoon thyme
¼ teaspoon salt
¼ teaspoon pepper
¾ pound fettuccine or other broad
   noodles
1 small yellow squash
½ pound bay or sea scallops
⅓ cup sour cream

Step 2

1 Bring a large pot of water to a boil.

2 Meanwhile, coarsely chop the onion. If the mushrooms are small, leave them whole; otherwise, halve or quarter them; set aside.

3 In a large skillet, warm the oil over medium-high heat until hot but not smoking. Add the onion and garlic and cook until the mixture begins to brown, about 5 minutes.

4 Add the mushrooms, cherry tomatoes, tomato sauce, tomato paste, basil, thyme, salt and pepper, and bring the mixture to a boil. Reduce the heat to low, cover and simmer while you prepare the rest of the ingredients.

5 Add the pasta to the boiling water and cook until al dente, 8 to 10 minutes, or according to package directions.

6 Meanwhile, halve the squash lengthwise, then cut crosswise into ¼-inch half-rounds. If using sea scallops, quarter them.

Step 4

7 Return the tomato sauce to a boil over medium-high heat. Add the squash, scallops and sour cream, and return to a low boil. Cook, stirring, until the scallops are cooked through and the sauce has thickened slightly, about 4 minutes.

8 Drain the pasta and serve topped with the scallops and sauce.

TIME-SAVERS

■ *Do-ahead: The sauce can be made ahead through Step 4. The squash can be cut up ahead.*

Values are approximate per serving: Calories: 507   Protein: 25 gm   Fat: 12 gm
Carbohydrates: 77 gm   Cholesterol: 108 mg   Sodium: 665 mg

Step 7

Warm Pasta Salad with Sautéed Vegetables

▼

This unusual entrée is a welcome surprise—lighter than a heavily sauced pasta dish, yet more substantial than most salads. It combines small pasta shapes such as orzo (rice-shaped pasta) with crisp-tender vegetables and cubes of turkey or ham (if you use ham, you may want to slightly reduce the amount of salt). If zucchini is not available, cut-up green beans, broccoli florets or asparagus can be substituted.

Working time: 20 minutes
Total time: 25 minutes

Warm Pasta Salad with Sautéed Vegetables

4 Servings

3 cloves garlic
1 medium red onion
1 large carrot
1 medium zucchini
½ pound cooked turkey or ham, unsliced
½ pound small pasta, such as small shells or orzo

2 tablespoons vegetable oil
⅓ cup grated Parmesan cheese
3 tablespoons lemon juice
2 tablespoons Dijon mustard
1 teaspoon oregano
½ teaspoon salt
½ teaspoon pepper

1 Bring a large pot of water to a boil.

2 Meanwhile, in a food processor, chop the garlic. Add the onion and coarsely chop. Remove the garlic and onion and set aside. In the same work bowl, coarsely chop the carrot and zucchini.

3 Cut the turkey (or ham) into ½-inch dice.

4 Add the pasta to the boiling water and cook until al dente, 10 to 12 minutes, or according to package directions.

5 Meanwhile, in a large skillet, warm 1 tablespoon of the oil over medium-high heat until hot but not smoking. Add the garlic and onion and sauté until the onion begins to brown, about 5 minutes.

6 Add the remaining 1 tablespoon oil to the skillet. Add the carrot and zucchini and sauté until the carrot is just tender, about 5 minutes. Remove from the heat.

7 Drain the pasta and transfer it to a serving bowl. Stir in the sautéed vegetables and diced turkey. Stir in the Parmesan.

8 In a small bowl, whisk together the lemon juice, mustard, oregano, salt and pepper. Add the dressing to the salad and toss to evenly distribute. Serve warm or at room temperature.

TIME-SAVERS

■ **Do-ahead:** *The vegetables and meat can be cut up ahead. The dressing (Step 8) can be made ahead. The whole dish can be made ahead and served at room temperature or chilled.*

Values are approximate per serving: Calories: 443 Protein: 28 gm Fat: 13 gm
Carbohydrates: 51 gm Cholesterol: 50 mg Sodium: 708 mg

Step 2

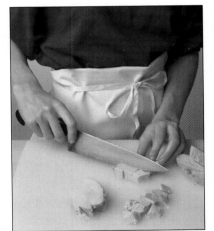
Step 3

Step 7

Wagon Wheels with Homemade Sausage Sauce

▼

You can announce in all honesty that this robust dish contains your own homemade sausage: When you combine the ground pork and turkey, vinegar, fennel, oregano and red pepper, you've made Italian country sausage. You can use the sausage mixture in other recipes that call for bulk sausage, but cook it the day it's made, as fresh sausage is very perishable.

Working time: 25 minutes
Total time: 40 minutes

210

4 Servings

4 cloves garlic
1 medium onion
1 rib celery
1 medium green bell pepper
½ pound mushrooms
2 tablespoons olive oil
½ pound ground turkey
¼ pound lean ground pork
1 tablespoon red wine vinegar or
balsamic vinegar
1 teaspoon fennel seeds

1 teaspoon oregano
¼ teaspoon red pepper flakes
1 can (14 ounces) whole tomatoes,
with their juice
1 can (8 ounces) tomato sauce
2 tablespoons tomato paste
1 teaspoon sugar
½ teaspoon salt
¾ pound wagon wheel pasta
¼ cup grated Parmesan cheese

Step 1

1 In a food processor, mince the garlic. Add the onion and coarsely chop; remove and set aside. Add the celery and bell pepper and chop; remove and set aside. Add the mushrooms and coarsely chop.

2 In a large saucepan, warm the oil over medium-high heat until hot but not smoking. Add the garlic-onion mixture and stir-fry until the onion begins to brown, about 5 minutes.

3 Crumble in the turkey and pork and cook, breaking it up with a spoon, until the meat is no longer pink, about 3 minutes. Add the vinegar, fennel, oregano and red pepper flakes, and cook until fragrant, about 30 seconds.

Step 3

4 Add the celery, bell pepper, mushrooms, tomatoes and their juice, the tomato sauce, tomato paste, sugar and salt to the saucepan and bring the mixture to a boil. Reduce the heat to medium-low and simmer uncovered, stirring frequently, for at least 15 minutes.

5 Meanwhile, bring a large pot of water to a boil. Add the pasta to the boiling water and cook until al dente, 8 to 10 minutes, or according to package directions.

6 Drain the pasta and top with the sauce and Parmesan cheese.

TIME-SAVERS

■ *Microwave tip: To make the sauce, prepare the vegetables as directed in Step 1. In a 2-quart casserole, combine 1 tablespoon of oil, the garlic-onion mixture, celery and bell pepper. Cover and cook at 100% for 5 minutes. Stir in the pork and turkey, and cook, covered, at 100% for 5 minutes, stirring once. Add the remaining sauce ingredients, cover with waxed paper and cook at 100% for 8 minutes and then at 50% for 5 minutes.*

Step 4

Values are approximate per serving: Calories: 641 Protein: 31 gm Fat: 21 gm
Carbohydrates: 82 gm Cholesterol: 66 mg Sodium: 1025 mg

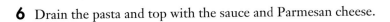

Baked Radiatore with Salmon and White Cheddar Sauce

Radiatore, a relative newcomer to the pasta shelf, are short ruffles of pasta supposedly modeled on the shape of a radiator. Whether you see the resemblance or not, you'll appreciate the knack this pasta has for holding onto a sauce, such as this creamy Cheddar-dill blend. This pasta shape is also marketed under the name ruffles.

Working time: 20 minutes
Total time: 40 minutes

Baked Radiatore with Salmon and White Cheddar Sauce

6 Servings

1 cup grated white Cheddar cheese
  (about ¼ pound)
1 medium red bell pepper
1 medium green bell pepper
¾ pound radiatore pasta (about
  4½ cups)
4 tablespoons butter
2 cloves garlic, minced or crushed
  through a press

⅓ cup flour
1¼ cups milk
1½ teaspoons dill
½ teaspoon salt
¼ teaspoon pepper, preferably
  white
1 can (7½ ounces) salmon, drained
3 tablespoons grated Parmesan
  cheese

Step 1

1 Bring a large pot of water to a boil. Meanwhile, grate the Cheddar. Dice the bell peppers.

2 Preheat the oven to 425°. Lightly grease a 13 x 9-inch baking dish.

3 Add the pasta to the boiling water and cook until al dente, 10 to 12 minutes, or according to package directions.

4 Meanwhile, in a medium saucepan, melt the butter over medium heat. Add the garlic and cook until fragrant, about 1 minute. Add the flour and stir until the flour is no longer visible, about 30 seconds.

5 Slowly add the milk, stirring constantly to keep the sauce smooth. Stir in the Cheddar, dill, salt and pepper, and cook, stirring, until the cheese is melted. Remove from the heat and set aside, covered.

Step 5

6 Drain the pasta and return it to the cooking pot. Add the bell peppers, the cheese sauce and the salmon and stir gently to combine.

7 Turn the mixture into the prepared baking dish. Sprinkle the top with the Parmesan. Bake for 15 minutes, or until heated through and beginning to brown on top.

TIME-SAVERS

■ *Microwave tip: To make the white sauce: In a medium bowl, combine the butter and garlic, cover and cook at 100% for 1 minute. Stir in the flour, then slowly add the milk. Cover and cook at 50% for 5 minutes, stirring once, until the sauce is smooth. To make the whole dish: Prepare the cheese and pasta mixture through Step 6. Turn the mixture into a shallow, ungreased microwave-safe baking dish, but do not sprinkle on the Parmesan. Cover with waxed paper and cook at 100% for 5 minutes. Stir gently, then sprinkle on the Parmesan. Re-cover and cook at 50% for 5 minutes, or until heated through.*

Values are approximate per serving: Calories: 472 Protein: 22 gm Fat: 19 gm
Carbohydrates: 52 gm Cholesterol: 61 mg Sodium: 598 mg

Step 7

Spaghetti Primavera with Chicken

Strictly speaking, an Italian pasta "primavera" would be made with young spring vegetables—primavera means spring—but this adaptation uses mushrooms, scallions and bell pepper, which are available all year long. For a change of pace, substitute oregano or basil (either dried or, if available, fresh minced) for the dill.

Working time: 20 minutes
Total time: 20 minutes

4 Servings

¾ pound skinless, boneless
  chicken breast
½ pound mushrooms
1 medium yellow or green bell
  pepper
1 bunch scallions (6 to 8)
½ pound spaghetti
5 tablespoons light olive or other
  vegetable oil

2 cloves garlic, minced or crushed
  through a press
¼ cup chopped fresh dill or 1
  teaspoon dried
¾ teaspoon salt
¼ teaspoon black pepper

Step 4

1 Bring a large pot of water to a boil.

2 Meanwhile, cut the chicken into 1-inch cubes. Cut the mushrooms into ¼-inch-thick slices. Cut the bell pepper into slivers. Coarsely chop the scallions.

3 Add the spaghetti to the boiling water and cook until al dente, 10 to 12 minutes or according to package directions.

4 Meanwhile, in a large skillet or flameproof casserole, warm 2 tablespoons of the oil over medium-high heat until hot but not smoking. Add the chicken and sauté until the chicken turns white, 2 to 3 minutes.

Step 5

5 Add the mushrooms, bell pepper, scallions, garlic and remaining 3 tablespoons oil and sauté until the vegetables are softened but not browned, 2 to 3 minutes.

6 Drain the spaghetti and add it to the skillet, along with the dill, salt and black pepper. Gently toss the ingredients together and serve hot.

TIME-SAVERS

■ *Do-ahead: The chicken, mushrooms, bell pepper and scallions can be cut up ahead of time.*

Step 6

Values are approximate per serving: Calories: 481 Protein: 29 gm Fat: 19 gm
Carbohydrates: 48 gm Cholesterol: 49 mg Sodium: 473 mg

Pasta Jambalaya

▼

Jambalaya, one of the signature dishes of Cajun-Creole cuisine, usually comes with a built-in carbohydrate component: Rice is cooked right along with the poultry, sausage, ham, oysters and shrimp that are traditionally among its main ingredients. This simplified jambalaya, made with chicken and hot sausage, simmers alone for twenty minutes to a stew-like thickness, and is then served over a plate of pasta.

Working time: 25 minutes
Total time: 35 minutes

4 Servings

- 3 cloves garlic
- 1 large onion
- 1 large green bell pepper
- 1 rib celery
- ¼ pound hot sausage
- 1 teaspoon olive or other vegetable oil
- 1 can (14½ ounces) whole tomatoes, with their juice
- ¼ teaspoon hot pepper sauce
- Pinch of cayenne pepper
- ½ teaspoon salt
- 1 bay leaf
- ¾ pound fusilli or other medium pasta shape
- ½ pound skinless boneless chicken breast

Step 2

1 In a food processor, mince the garlic. Add the onion and coarsely chop; remove and set aside. In the same work bowl, coarsely chop the bell pepper and celery. Remove the sausage from its casings.

2 In a large skillet, warm the oil over medium-high heat until hot but not smoking. Crumble in the sausage and cook until the meat is no longer pink, 2 to 3 minutes.

3 Bring a large pot of water to a boil.

4 Meanwhile, add the garlic-onion mixture to the skillet and stir-fry until the onion begins to brown, about 5 minutes.

5 Add the bell pepper, celery, tomatoes with their juice, hot pepper sauce, cayenne, salt and bay leaf, and bring to a boil. Reduce the heat to low, cover and simmer while you cook the pasta.

Step 5

6 Add the pasta to the boiling water and cook until al dente, 10 to 12 minutes, or according to package directions.

7 Meanwhile, cut the chicken across the grain into ¼-inch-wide strips. Uncover the sauce and bring it to a boil over medium-high heat. Add the chicken and cook, stirring frequently, until the chicken is cooked through, about 5 minutes.

8 Drain the pasta. Remove the bay leaf from the sauce and serve over the pasta.

TIME-SAVERS

■ *Do-ahead: The chicken mixture can be made ahead and served over freshly cooked pasta.*

Values are approximate per serving: Calories: 553 Protein: 29 gm Fat: 15 gm
Carbohydrates: 74 gm Cholesterol: 52 mg Sodium: 692 mg

Step 7

Ham and Cheese Lasagna
with Spinach

In this so-called white lasagna, a rich filling of ricotta, cottage cheese and Parmesan replaces the usual beef and tomato sauce. The cheese mixture is combined with chopped spinach and layered with lasagna noodles and slivered Swiss cheese and ham (try smoked ham for a nice contrast with the rich cheese filling). The lasagna can be assembled ahead and frozen, then baked, unthawed and covered, in a 350° oven.

Working time: 30 minutes
Total time: 1 hour 15 minutes

Ham and Cheese Lasagna with Spinach

8 Servings

½ pound fresh spinach or
   1 package (10 ounces) frozen
   spinach, thawed
½ pound lasagna noodles
1 container (15 ounces) part-skim
   ricotta cheese
1 pound cottage cheese
1 cup grated Parmesan cheese

¼ cup flour
1 teaspoon nutmeg
½ teaspoon salt
½ teaspoon pepper
3 eggs
¼ pound sliced ham (boiled,
   baked or smoked)
¼ pound sliced Swiss cheese

Step 5

1 Bring a large pot of water to a boil.

2 Meanwhile, cook the fresh spinach in ½ cup of boiling water until just wilted, 1 to 2 minutes. (Or thaw the frozen spinach in the microwave.) Drain the spinach and set aside to cool slightly.

3 Add the pasta to the boiling water and cook until al dente, 10 to 12 minutes, or according to package directions. Rinse the pasta under cold running water until it is cool enough to handle.

4 While the pasta is cooking, combine the ricotta, cottage cheese, Parmesan, flour, nutmeg, salt and pepper in a large bowl. Lightly beat the eggs and then stir into the cheese mixture.

5 Squeeze the spinach in paper towels to remove any excess moisture. Finely chop the spinach and stir into the cheese mixture.

6 Preheat the oven to 375°. Lightly grease a 13 x 9-inch baking pan. Cut the ham and Swiss cheese into thin strips.

Step 6

7 Layer the lasagna in the following manner: one-third of the noodles, one-third of the Swiss cheese strips, one-third of the ham strips, one-third of the spinach-cheese mixture. Repeat for two more layers.

8 Bake the lasagna for 45 minutes, or until the top is golden brown.

TIME-SAVERS

■ *Microwave tip: Prepare the recipe through Step 7 using a 13 x 9-inch microwave-safe baking dish. Loosely cover with waxed paper. Place an inverted pie plate in the microwave and place the baking dish on top of it. Cook at 100% for 6 minutes; then cook at 50% for about 20 minutes, rotating the dish occasionally, until the lasagna is hot all the way through. If desired, brown the top under the broiler before serving.*

Values are approximate per serving: Calories: 407 Protein: 31 gm Fat: 17 gm
Carbohydrates: 31 gm Cholesterol: 133 mg Sodium: 875 mg

Step 7

Mexican-Style Pasta with Chicken and Peppers

▼

This chili-spiked pasta dish was inspired by the Mexican "sopa seca" or dry soup. Obviously a contradiction in terms, a sopa seca is made by cooking pasta, rice or tortilla strips in broth until the liquid is absorbed. Here, vermicelli, which resembles Mexican fideos (noodles), is cooked with tomatoes, scallions and bell peppers. The south-of-the-border flavor comes from chili powder, cumin, green chilies and cilantro.

Working time: 20 minutes
Total time: 35 minutes

Mexican-Style Pasta with Chicken and Peppers

6 Servings

4 cups low-sodium chicken broth
1 clove garlic, minced or crushed
   through a press
1 teaspoon cumin
½ teaspoon chili powder
4 plum tomatoes or 6 whole canned
   tomatoes, well drained
3 scallions
1 large green bell pepper
¾ pound vermicelli or other thin
   pasta

½ pound skinless, boneless chicken
   breast
1 tablespoon vegetable oil
1 can (4 ounces) chopped mild
   green chilies, drained
¼ teaspoon salt
¼ cup (packed) cilantro sprigs
   (optional)

Step 4

1 In a medium saucepan, bring the chicken broth, garlic, cumin and chili powder to a boil over medium-high heat.

2 Meanwhile, coarsely chop the tomatoes, scallions and bell pepper. Break the vermicelli into 2-inch pieces.

3 Add the chicken to the boiling broth, reduce the heat to medium-low, cover and simmer until the chicken is cooked through, about 10 minutes. Remove the chicken and set it aside to cool slightly.

4 In a large nonstick skillet, warm the oil over medium-high heat until hot but not smoking. Add the vermicelli and cook, stirring, until the vermicelli is lightly browned, about 2 minutes.

5 Add the broth mixture, tomatoes, scallions, bell pepper, green chilies and salt, and bring to a boil over medium-high heat. Reduce the heat to low, cover and simmer, stirring occasionally, until the pasta is cooked, about 7 minutes.

Step 5

6 Meanwhile, shred the chicken. Mince the cilantro (if using).

7 Stir the shredded chicken and cilantro into the pasta mixture and serve hot.

TIME-SAVERS

■ *Do-ahead: The vegetables can be chopped in advance. The chicken can be cooked and shredded (Steps 1, 3 and 6) ahead; just be sure to bring the broth mixture back to a boil before adding it to the pasta in Step 5.*

Step 6

Values are approximate per serving: Calories: 311 Protein: 18 gm Fat: 5 gm
Carbohydrates: 47 gm Cholesterol: 22 mg Sodium: 275 mg

Pasta with Three-Tomato Sauce

Pasta entrées do not always have to be served hot, nor does cold pasta always have to be a salad. In this main dish, freshly cooked linguine is tossed with herbed olive oil and an uncooked topping of tomato sauce and sun-dried and fresh tomatoes. Serve the dish warm, or let it come to room temperature. If you're unable to find sun-dried tomatoes, use two additional plum tomatoes and a tablespoon of tomato paste.

Working time: 20 minutes
Total time: 25 minutes

4 Servings

4 medium plum tomatoes or 6 whole canned tomatoes, well drained

8 oil-packed sun-dried tomato halves, drained

⅓ cup (packed) fresh basil leaves or 1 tablespoon dried basil

4 scallions

¾ pound linguine or spaghetti

3 tablespoons of the oil from the sun-dried tomatoes or 3 tablespoons olive oil

2 cloves garlic, minced or crushed through a press

1 teaspoon oregano

¼ teaspoon red pepper flakes

¼ teaspoon black pepper

1 can (8 ounces) tomato sauce

Step 2

1 Bring a large pot of water to a boil.

2 Meanwhile, keeping them separate, coarsely chop the fresh (or canned) plum tomatoes, sun-dried tomatoes, fresh basil and scallions.

3 Add the pasta to the boiling water and cook until al dente, 10 to 12 minutes, or according to package directions.

4 Meanwhile, in a small skillet, warm the oil over medium-high heat until hot but not smoking. Add the scallions and garlic and cook, stirring, until the garlic is fragrant, about 2 minutes.

5 Stir in the basil, oregano, red pepper flakes and black pepper, and remove the skillet from the heat.

Step 5

6 Drain the pasta and transfer to a serving bowl. Toss the hot pasta with the canned tomato sauce, plum tomatoes, sun-dried tomatoes and scallion-herb oil.

7 Serve the pasta warm or at room temperature.

TIME-SAVERS

■ *Do-ahead: The canned tomato sauce, fresh (or canned) plum tomatoes, sun-dried tomatoes and scallion-herb oil can all be prepared and combined ahead of time. To serve, cook the pasta and toss it with the sauce. The entire dish can also be made ahead and served at room temperature.*

Values are approximate per serving: Calories: 522   Protein: 14 gm   Fat: 19 gm
Carbohydrates: 77 gm   Cholesterol: 0 mg   Sodium: 363 mg

Step 6

Macaroni with Turkey Chili

*Ground turkey, with less fat and calories than ground beef, can help
to lighten many home-cooked favorites; this chili-macaroni dish is a perfect
example. To keep the carbohydrate content healthfully high, bell pepper,
onion, tomatoes and beans go into the chili; to further lower fat and sodium, the
cheese is kept to a minimum—less than one tablespoon per person.*

Working time: 15 minutes
Total time: 25 minutes

Macaroni with Turkey Chili

6 Servings

1 large green bell pepper
1 medium onion
**1 can (14 ounces) whole tomatoes,
  with their juice**
½ pound ground turkey
2 tablespoons tomato paste
**4 cloves garlic, minced or crushed
  through a press**

3 tablespoons chili powder
¼ teaspoon black pepper
**½ pound elbow macaroni (about
  2 cups)**
¼ cup chicken broth
1 tablespoon cornstarch
1 cup canned kidney beans
⅓ cup grated Cheddar cheese

1 Bring a large pot of water to a boil.

2 Meanwhile, dice the bell pepper. Coarsely chop the onion.

3 In a medium saucepan, combine the tomatoes and their juice, the bell pepper, onion, turkey, tomato paste, garlic, chili powder and black pepper. Bring to a boil over medium-high heat, breaking up the tomatoes and the turkey with a spoon. Reduce the heat to low, cover and simmer, stirring occasionally, while you cook the pasta.

Step 3

4 Add the pasta to the boiling water and cook until al dente, 10 to 12 minutes, or according to package directions.

5 Meanwhile, in a small bowl, combine the chicken broth and cornstarch. Drain the beans, rinse them under running water and drain well. Just before the pasta is done, bring the chili to a boil over medium-high heat. Stir in the broth mixture and the drained beans and cook, stirring, until the mixture thickens and the beans are heated through, 1 to 2 minutes.

Step 5

6 Drain the pasta and toss it with the chili. Serve the chili and pasta topped with the Cheddar.

TIME-SAVERS

■ ***Do-ahead:*** *The turkey chili (Steps 2, 3 and 5) can be made ahead.*

Values are approximate per serving: Calories: 300 Protein: 17 gm Fat: 7 gm
Carbohydrates: 43 gm Cholesterol: 34 mg Sodium: 366 mg

Step 6

Egg Noodles with Basil Vegetables and Pine Nuts

Meatless dishes are pleasantly light in warm weather, and this is a real summer dish, at its best when red-ripe local tomatoes and fresh basil are available. The tomatoes, zucchini and mushrooms are not cooked very long, so they retain their fresh flavor. A little cornstarch added to the sauce thickens it lightly without hours of simmering. Pine nuts can be found in small jars in the gourmet food section of most supermarkets.

Working time: 25 minutes
Total time: 25 minutes

Egg Noodles with Basil Vegetables and Pine Nuts

4 Servings

¼ cup pine nuts

⅓ cup (packed) fresh basil leaves or 2½ teaspoons dried

1 large or 2 small zucchini (about ½ pound)

½ pound mushrooms

1 pound plum tomatoes or 10 whole canned tomatoes, well drained

¾ pound egg noodles

2 tablespoons butter

2 tablespoons olive or other vegetable oil

3 cloves garlic, minced or crushed through a press

1 tablespoon chicken broth or water

1 teaspoon cornstarch

½ teaspoon salt

¼ teaspoon pepper

1 Bring a large pot of water to a boil.

2 Meanwhile, in a small ungreased skillet, cook the pine nuts over medium heat, shaking the pan, until toasted, 5 to 7 minutes.

Step 2

3 Mince the basil. Cut the zucchini and mushrooms into thin slices. Cut the tomatoes into bite-size chunks.

4 Add the noodles to the boiling water and cook until al dente, 8 to 10 minutes, or according to package directions.

5 Meanwhile, in a large skillet, warm the butter in the oil over medium-high heat until the butter is melted. Add the basil and garlic, and cook, stirring, until the flavors are released, about 5 minutes.

6 In a small bowl, combine the chicken broth and cornstarch. Increase the heat under the skillet to medium-high and add the zucchini, mushrooms and tomatoes. Stir in the cornstarch mixture and cook, stirring, until the vegetables are tender, about 6 minutes. Stir in the salt and pepper.

Step 5

7 Drain the noodles and top with the vegetable mixture. Sprinkle with the pine nuts.

Values are approximate per serving: Calories: 534 Protein: 17 gm Fat: 21 gm
Carbohydrates: 73 gm Cholesterol: 96 mg Sodium: 379 mg

Step 6

Four-Cheese Pasta Casserole with Sweet Peppers

Cottage cheese and cream cheese make a velvety coating for the pasta in this baked casserole; a blend of Parmesan and Romano gives it an irresistible aroma and savor. Although similar in appearance, Parmesan and Romano differ somewhat in flavor—Romano is more pungent and saltier. You might also try asiago or an aged Monterey jack cheese, both of which are excellent for grating over pasta.

Working time: 15 minutes
Total time: 50 minutes

Four-Cheese Pasta Casserole with Sweet Peppers

6 Servings

1 clove garlic
2 cups cottage cheese
1 package (3 ounces) cream cheese
½ cup milk
¼ teaspoon nutmeg
¼ teaspoon salt
¼ teaspoon black pepper

½ cup grated Parmesan cheese
½ cup grated Romano cheese
1 medium red bell pepper
1 medium green bell pepper
¾ pound medium pasta shells
   (about 5 cups)

Step 3

1 Preheat the oven to 375°. Butter a 2-quart baking dish.

2 Bring a large pot of water to a boil.

3 Meanwhile, in a food processor, finely chop the garlic. Add the cottage cheese and cream cheese and process until smooth. Add the milk and process to blend. Add the nutmeg, salt and black pepper, and blend.

4 In a small bowl, blend the Parmesan and Romano cheeses and set aside. Cut the bell peppers lengthwise into thin strips.

Step 4

5 Add the pasta to the boiling water and cook until al dente, 9 to 11 minutes, or according to package directions. Three minutes before the pasta is done, add the bell peppers.

6 Drain the pasta and peppers well and place them in a large bowl. Add the cheese sauce and ¾ cup of the Parmesan-Romano mixture, and toss to combine.

7 Turn the mixture into the baking dish. Dust the top of the casserole with the remaining ¼ cup Parmesan-Romano mixture and bake for 25 to 30 minutes, or until golden on top.

TIME-SAVERS

■ ***Microwave tip:*** *Prepare the recipe as directed above, using a 2-quart microwave-safe baking dish. Place the dish on an inverted plate in the oven and cover loosely with waxed paper. Cook at 100% for 5 minutes; cook at 50% for 10 minutes, rotating the dish once or twice, until the dish is heated through.*

■ ***Do-ahead:*** *The cheese sauce (Step 3) can be made and the pasta and peppers cooked in advance. The whole casserole can be assembled ahead and baked later or baked ahead and reheated.*

Step 6

Values are approximate per serving: Calories: 408   Protein: 23 gm   Fat: 14 gm
Carbohydrates: 48 gm   Cholesterol: 41 mg   Sodium: 634 mg

Spaghettini with Mushroom-Herb Sauce

▼

*Three members of the onion family—shallots, garlic and chives—assure
a robust flavor in this pasta dish. The shallots, with their mildly garlicky taste,
add a special note, but yellow onions or the white parts of scallions will
do if shallots are not available. Keep a close eye on the shallots during cooking
because, like garlic, they become bitter if overcooked.*

Working time: 25 minutes
Total time: 35 minutes

230

Spaghettini with Mushroom-Herb Sauce

4 Servings

¾ **pound mushrooms**
¾ **cup chopped shallots (about 4**
ounces) or scallion whites
1 **tablespoon butter**
2 **tablespoons olive or other**
vegetable oil
3 **cloves garlic, minced or crushed**
through a press
2 **tablespoons flour**

¾ **cup chicken broth**
1 **teaspoon basil**
½ **teaspoon tarragon**
¼ **teaspoon pepper**
¾ **pound spaghettini**
3 **tablespoons chopped chives or**
scallion greens
½ **cup heavy cream**
½ **cup grated Parmesan cheese**

Step 2

1 Bring a large pot of water to a boil.

2 Meanwhile, slice the mushrooms. Coarsely chop the shallots (or scallion whites).

3 In a large skillet, warm the butter in 1 tablespoon of the oil over medium-high heat until the butter is melted. Add the shallots and garlic and cook until the mixture begins to brown, about 5 minutes.

4 Add the remaining 1 tablespoon oil and the mushrooms and cook until the mushrooms begin to soften, 3 to 5 minutes.

5 Add the flour and stir until it is no longer visible, about 30 seconds. Add the chicken broth, basil, tarragon and pepper, and bring the mixture a boil, stirring constantly. Reduce the heat to low, cover and simmer for 10 minutes.

6 Meanwhile, add the pasta to the boiling water and cook until al dente, 9 to 11 minutes, or according to package directions.

7 Chop the chives (or scallion greens).

8 Return the mushroom-herb mixture to a boil over medium-high heat. Add the cream, reduce the heat to medium and cook, uncovered, for 2 minutes. Stir in 2 tablespoons of the chives.

9 Drain the pasta and serve topped with the sauce, a sprinkling of the Parmesan and the remaining chives. Pass the remaining Parmesan on the side.

TIME-SAVERS

■ *Do-ahead: The mushroom-herb sauce can be made ahead through Step 5.*

Step 4

Step 8

Values are approximate per serving: Calories: 617 Protein: 19 gm Fat: 26 gm
Carbohydrates: 78 gm Cholesterol: 56 mg Sodium: 426 mg

Scampi-Style Shrimp Over Linguine

▼

In the restaurant favorite called "scampi" (which is simply the Italian word for prawns), shrimp are sautéed in butter with garlic and a splash of wine. In this variation, chopped tomatoes are added for color and flavor and the wine is omitted—although if you have some dry white wine on hand, you may add a tablespoon or two to the skillet when you add the tomatoes.

Working time: 35 minutes
Total time: 35 minutes

Scampi-Style Shrimp Over Linguine

4 Servings

1 pound large or medium shrimp
5 scallions
2 medium tomatoes or 5 whole
    canned tomatoes, well drained
¾ pound linguine or spaghetti
1 tablespoon butter
1 tablespoon olive or other
    vegetable oil

4 cloves garlic, minced or crushed
    through a press
½ cup chicken broth
¼ cup chopped parsley (optional)
½ teaspoon salt
¼ teaspoon pepper
Pinch of sugar
1 tablespoon cornstarch

Step 2

1 Bring a large pot of water to a boil.

2 Meanwhile, shell and devein the shrimp. Coarsely chop the scallions and tomatoes.

3 Add the pasta to the boiling water and cook until al dente, 10 to 12 minutes, or according to package directions.

4 Meanwhile, in a large skillet, warm the butter in the oil over medium-high heat until the butter is melted. Add the scallions and garlic and cook until the scallions are limp, about 1 minute.

5 Add the shrimp to the skillet and cook until they turn pink and are opaque throughout, about 5 minutes.

Step 5

6 Add the chopped tomatoes, all but 1 tablespoon of the chicken broth, the parsley (if using), salt, pepper and sugar. Bring to a boil over medium-high heat, stirring.

7 Blend the reserved 1 tablespoon chicken broth with the cornstarch and stir this mixture into the skillet. Cook, stirring, until the shrimp are cooked through and the sauce is thickened, 1 to 2 minutes.

8 Drain the pasta and serve topped with the shrimp and sauce.

TIME-SAVERS

■ *Do-ahead: The shrimp can be shelled and deveined and the vegetables chopped in advance.*

Values are approximate per serving: Calories: 501   Protein: 31 gm   Fat: 9 gm
Carbohydrates: 71 gm   Cholesterol: 148 mg   Sodium: 574 mg

Step 7

Spaghetti with Ground Turkey-Tomato Sauce

Ground turkey is a flavorful (and low-fat) alternative to beef in this quick spaghetti sauce. Serve the spaghetti with French or Italian bread that has been brushed with a small amount of olive oil, sprinkled with rosemary and grated Parmesan and then browned under the broiler. To complete the meal, serve iced tea and a salad of lettuce, cherry tomatoes and cucumber sticks with a light vinaigrette.

Working time: 15 minutes
Total time: 35 minutes

Spaghetti with Ground Turkey-Tomato Sauce

4 Servings

6 cloves garlic
1 medium onion
½ pound ground turkey
1½ teaspoons oregano
¾ teaspoon salt
½ teaspoon pepper
1 tablespoon olive oil

1 can (35 ounces) low-sodium whole tomatoes, with their juice
2 tablespoons tomato paste
1 bay leaf
½ pound whole wheat or regular spaghetti

Step 3

1 Bring a large pot of water to a boil.

2 Lightly bruise 3 of the garlic cloves and set aside. Mince the remaining 3 garlic cloves or crush them through a press. Coarsely chop the onion.

3 In a small bowl, combine the turkey, crushed garlic, ½ teaspoon of the oregano, ½ teaspoon of the salt and ¼ teaspoon of the pepper.

4 In a medium saucepan, warm the oil over medium-high heat. Add the turkey mixture, the onion and the bruised garlic and cook, stirring frequently to break up the mixture, until the turkey turns white and has just begun to brown, 3 to 5 minutes.

Step 4

5 Add the tomatoes and their juice, the tomato paste, bay leaf and the remaining 1 teaspoon oregano, ¼ teaspoon salt and ¼ teaspoon pepper. Bring the mixture to a boil, breaking up the tomatoes with a spoon. Reduce the heat to medium-low and simmer the sauce, uncovered, for 20 minutes, stirring occasionally. Discard the bay leaf and whole garlic cloves.

6 About 10 minutes before the sauce is done, add the spaghetti to the boiling water and cook until al dente, 10 to 12 minutes or according to package directions.

7 Drain the pasta and divide it among 4 plates. Spoon some sauce over each serving.

TIME-SAVERS

■ **Do-ahead:** *The sauce can be made ahead (through Step 5) and reheated gently on the stovetop or in the microwave.*

Step 5

Values are approximate per serving: Calories: 392   Protein: 22 gm   Fat: 11 gm
Carbohydrates: 58 gm   Cholesterol: 38 mg   Sodium: 567 mg

Szechuan Noodles with Pork and Vegetables

▼

Szechuan dishes are often spicy, and this one is no exception. Fresh ginger and a few drops of hot pepper sauce add a piquancy that complements the richness of the pork and the peanut sauce. Feel free to use less—or more—of the hot sauce, according to your family's tastes. If there's an Asian grocery store near you, you might like to try Chinese egg noodles in this dish; they cook faster than Italian-style linguine.

Working time: 30 minutes
Total time: 40 minutes

Szechuan Noodles with Pork and Vegetables

4 Servings

6 quarter-size slices (¼ inch thick) fresh ginger, unpeeled
4 cloves garlic
4 scallions
¼ cup cilantro sprigs (optional)
⅓ cup creamy peanut butter
3 tablespoons Oriental sesame oil
⅔ cup beef broth
3 tablespoons white wine vinegar or distilled white vinegar

3 tablespoons reduced-sodium or regular soy sauce
5 drops hot pepper sauce
1 tablespoon brown sugar
½ pound fresh green beans or 1 package (10 ounces) frozen, thawed
2 medium carrots
¾ pound lean pork tenderloin
½ pound linguine or spaghetti

Step 4

1 Bring a large pot of water to a boil.

2 Meanwhile, in a food processor, finely chop the ginger and garlic. Add the scallions and pulse until coarsely chopped. Remove the mixture and set aside.

3 In the same processor work bowl, coarsely chop the cilantro (if using). Add the peanut butter, 1 tablespoon of the sesame oil, the beef broth, vinegar, soy sauce, hot pepper sauce and brown sugar, and blend until smooth.

4 Cut the green beans into 2-inch lengths. Cut the carrots into sticks about 2 inches long. Cut the pork crosswise into ¼-inch-thick slices.

5 Add the pasta to the boiling water and cook until al dente, 10 to 12 minutes, or according to package directions.

6 Meanwhile, in a large skillet, warm 1 tablespoon of the sesame oil until hot but not smoking. Add the ginger-scallion mixture and stir-fry until the garlic begins to brown, about 3 minutes.

Step 7

7 Add the remaining 1 tablespoon sesame oil and then add the beans, carrots and pork. Cook, stirring frequently, until the pork is cooked through and the vegetables are crisp-tender, about 5 minutes.

8 Stir the peanut sauce into the skillet and bring the mixture to a boil over medium heat. Remove the skillet from the heat. Drain the pasta and toss it with the pork, vegetables and sauce.

TIME-SAVERS

■ *Do-ahead: The vegetables and pork can be cut up, and the ginger-scallion mixture (Step 2) and peanut sauce (Step 3) can be made ahead.*

Values are approximate per serving: Calories: 591 Protein: 34 gm Fat: 24 gm
Carbohydrates: 61 gm Cholesterol: 55 mg Sodium: 755 mg

Step 8

Herbed Corn on the Cob (page 255)

CHAPTER 5
VEGETABLES & SALADS

Garlic-Sautéed Green Beans

▼

*Inspired by a Chinese preparation called dry-fried beans, this flavorful side
dish uses some of the same techniques but substitutes Italian seasonings. Whole green
beans (or a mixture of green and yellow beans) are stir-fried with garlic, oregano,
shallots and chopped black olives. For a slightly different twist, replace the oregano with
basil and sprinkle on some grated orange zest just before serving.*

Working time: 30 minutes
Total time: 30 minutes

Garlic-Sautéed Green Beans

6 Servings

½ cup black olives
¼ pound shallots or 1 medium
  yellow onion
1½ pounds green beans
1 tablespoon olive or other
  vegetable oil

6 cloves garlic, minced or crushed
  through a press
1 tablespoon butter
1½ teaspoons oregano
¼ teaspoon pepper
½ teaspoon salt

Step 1

1 Chop the olives. Mince the shallots. Trim the beans, but leave them whole.

2 In a large skillet, preferably nonstick, warm the oil over medium-high heat until hot but not smoking. Add the garlic and cook, stirring, until it just begins to brown, about 1 minute.

3 Add the butter and warm until melted. Add the shallots and oregano, and cook until the shallots are softened, about 1 minute.

4 Add the olives, beans and pepper, and cook, stirring constantly, until the beans are crisp-tender, about 9 minutes. Sprinkle on the salt toward the end of the cooking time.

Step 3

TIME-SAVERS

■ **Do-ahead:** *The vegetables can be cut up ahead.*

Values are approximate per serving: Calories: 100 Protein: 3 gm Fat: 6 gm
Carbohydrates: 12 gm Cholesterol: 5 mg Sodium: 309 mg

Step 4

Oven-Fries Italiano

▼

These "fries" are baked in the oven, with a total of just two tablespoons of fat for four servings—quite an improvement over deep-fried french fries. Portions are generous, and the skin is left on the potatoes to cut down on preparation time and provide extra dietary fiber. If you'd like to experiment, replace the Parmesan used here with another grating cheese: Dry jack (aged Monterey jack), Romano and asiago all work well.

Working time: 15 minutes
Total time: 45 minutes

4 Servings

4 large all-purpose potatoes (about 2 pounds), unpeeled	**¾ teaspoon basil**
1 tablespoon butter	**¾ teaspoon oregano**
1 tablespoon olive or other vegetable oil	**½ teaspoon salt**
	¼ teaspoon pepper
2 cloves garlic, minced or crushed through a press	**¼ cup grated Parmesan cheese**

1 Preheat the oven to 425°. Line a baking sheet with foil and lightly grease the foil.

2 Cut the potatoes lengthwise into ½-inch-thick wedges.

Step 2

3 Melt the butter on the stovetop or in the microwave. In a large bowl, combine the melted butter, oil, garlic, basil, oregano, salt and pepper. Add the potatoes and toss to coat well with the herbed butter.

4 Arrange the potatoes on the baking sheet. Sprinkle evenly with the Parmesan.

5 Bake the potatoes for about 30 minutes, or until they are tender and golden. Twice during the cooking time, use a spatula to move the potatoes around to ensure even cooking.

Step 3

TIME-SAVERS

■ ***Do-ahead:*** *The herbed butter can be made ahead.*

Step 4

Values are approximate per serving: Calories: 250 Protein: 7 gm Fat: 8 gm
Carbohydrates: 39 gm Cholesterol: 12 mg Sodium: 412 mg

Asparagus with Creamy Lemon Sauce

▼

Let the flavor of crisp-tender asparagus shine through by dressing it with the lightest of sauces: a lemony yogurt mixture enriched and flavored with olive oil and mustard. The sauce tastes like a tart mayonnaise, but is made without eggs. Prepare some extra sauce and try it in tuna or chicken salad. If you don't have a vegetable steamer, cook the asparagus in a covered skillet in a small amount of water.

Working time: 10 minutes
Total time: 15 minutes

Asparagus with Creamy Lemon Sauce

4 Servings

1 pound asparagus
½ cup plain yogurt
4 teaspoons grated lemon zest
   (optional)
3 tablespoons lemon juice
1 tablespoon olive oil

1 tablespoon Dijon mustard
½ teaspoon dry mustard
1 garlic clove, minced or crushed
   through a press
¼ teaspoon pepper

1 Snap the tough bottoms from the asparagus stems. If the skin seems especially thick, peel the bottom few inches with a vegetable peeler.

2 In a vegetable steamer, steam the asparagus until just tender when pierced with a sharp knife.

3 Meanwhile, in a small bowl, whisk together the yogurt, lemon zest (if using), lemon juice, oil, Dijon and dry mustards, garlic and pepper.

4 Serve the steamed asparagus with the lemon sauce.

TIME-SAVERS

■ *Microwave tip: Place the trimmed asparagus on a microwave-safe plate or in a shallow baking dish. Cover with a wet paper towel (or add 2 tablespoons of water to the dish and cover with plastic wrap). Cook at 100% for 4 to 5 minutes, rearranging the spears once. Prepare the creamy lemon sauce as directed.*

■ *Do-ahead: The asparagus can be trimmed and the lemon sauce made ahead. Or, cook the asparagus ahead and serve it at room temperature or chilled.*

Step 1

Step 1

Step 3

Values are approximate per serving: Calories: 70 Protein: 3 gm Fat: 4 gm
Carbohydrates: 6 gm Cholesterol: 2 mg Sodium: 136 mg

Glazed Carrot Coins

▼

Even children who usually scorn vegetables will take to these bright, shiny carrot rounds, cooked in a sweet, buttery apple glaze. To cut preparation time, use the largest carrots you can find—it takes more time to peel lots of small carrots. Just be sure the carrots will still fit comfortably through your food processor's feed tube.

Working time: 10 minutes
Total time: 20 minutes

Glazed Carrot Coins

4 Servings

6 large carrots (about 1¼ pounds)
⅓ cup apple juice
3 tablespoons butter

2 teaspoons brown sugar
¼ teaspoon salt
1 tablespoon chopped parsley (optional)

Step 1

1 In a food processor with the slicing blade, cut the carrots into thin slices.

2 In a medium saucepan, bring the apple juice, butter and brown sugar to a boil over medium-high heat. Stir in the salt.

3 Add the carrots, reduce the heat to medium, cover and simmer, stirring occasionally, until tender, 5 to 8 minutes. If there is a lot of liquid in the pan, cook the carrots uncovered for the last minute or so to reduce the cooking liquid to a glaze.

4 Toss the carrots with the parsley, if desired, and serve.

TIME-SAVERS

■ ***Microwave tip:*** *Reduce the apple juice to 2 tablespoons and the butter to 1 tablespoon. Combine all the ingredients (except the parsley) in a 1-quart microwave-safe dish. Partially cover with plastic wrap and cook at 100% for 7 minutes, stirring once. Microwaving the carrots will produce more liquid and the carrots will be less "glazed" than with the conventional stovetop method.*

■ ***Do-ahead:*** *The carrots can be cut up ahead. The carrots can also be partially cooked ahead and then finished on the stovetop or in the microwave.*

Step 3

Step 4

Values are approximate per serving: Calories: 155 Protein: 2 gm Fat: 9 gm
Carbohydrates: 19 gm Cholesterol: 23 mg Sodium: 274 mg

Broiled Marinated Vegetables

This versatile recipe makes a generous quantity (about 1 quart) of broiled, marinated vegetables that can be enjoyed in a variety of ways. Serve the freshly cooked vegetables warm and refrigerate the leftovers. Bring the leftovers to room temperature and serve in a salad or as a side dish. Or, for a hearty sandwich, as shown here, layer the vegetables atop some melted mozzarella on French or Italian bread.

Working time: 30 minutes
Total time: 40 minutes

Broiled Marinated Vegetables

6 Servings

1 large zucchini
1 small eggplant (about ¾ pound)
1 large green bell pepper
1 large red bell pepper
1 large yellow bell pepper
½ cup (packed) fresh basil leaves or
  1 tablespoon dried
⅓ cup olive or other vegetable oil

2 tablespoons white wine vinegar
  or cider vinegar
4 cloves garlic, minced or crushed
  through a press
2 teaspoons oregano
¾ teaspoon salt
½ teaspoon black pepper

1 Preheat the broiler. Line a broiler pan with foil. Lightly grease the foil.

2 Cut the zucchini into thin rounds. Halve the eggplant lengthwise, then cut crosswise into ¼-inch-thick half-rounds. Cut the bell peppers into strips about ½ inch wide.

Step 2

3 Coarsely chop the basil. In a large serving bowl, combine the basil, olive oil, vinegar, garlic, oregano, salt and black pepper, and blend well.

4 Arrange the vegetables in a single layer on the broiler pan. Brush the vegetables lightly with the vinaigrette, and broil 4 inches from the heat for 3 to 5 minutes. Turn the vegetables over, brush them with more of the vinaigrette and broil until the vegetables are tender, 3 to 5 minutes. (You may have to do this in batches.)

5 Add the broiled vegetables to the remaining vinaigrette in the serving bowl, and toss gently to coat well.

Step 4

6 Serve the vegetables warm or at room temperature. For later use, store in a covered container in the refrigerator; let the vegetables return to room temperature before serving.

TIME-SAVERS

■ **Do-ahead:** *The vegetables can be broiled and marinated well ahead.*

Values are approximate per serving: Calories: 145 Protein: 2 gm Fat: 12 gm
Carbohydrates: 9 gm Cholesterol: 0 mg Sodium: 280 mg

Step 5

Tarragon Baked Onions

▼

A fine side dish for a weekday roast or a holiday turkey, this sweet-and-sour onion bake is redolent with tarragon. If you can get fresh tarragon, use 3 tablespoons of the chopped leaves in place of the dried herb. Peeled whole small white onions (sometimes called "boiling onions") are an elegant substitute for the onion slices, but will need to be baked for about 45 minutes instead of 15.

Working time: 15 minutes
Total time: 30 minutes

Tarragon Baked Onions

4 Servings

2 pounds large onions
1 tablespoon butter
1 tablespoon olive oil
½ cup chicken broth
1 teaspoon lemon juice
1 tablespoon tarragon

2 teaspoons grated lemon zest
(optional)
¼ teaspoon salt
¼ teaspoon pepper
1 tablespoon sugar

Step 2

1 Preheat the oven to 375°.

2 Cut the onions into ½-inch slices.

3 In a large nonstick skillet, warm the butter in the oil over medium-high heat until the butter is melted. Add the onions and cook, stirring, until the onions begin to brown, about 5 minutes.

4 Transfer the onions to a 1-quart baking dish or gratin dish (or if the skillet is ovenproof, leave the onions in the skillet). Sprinkle the onions with the chicken broth, lemon juice, tarragon, lemon zest (if using), salt and pepper. Sprinkle the sugar on last.

Step 4

5 Cover the dish with foil and bake until the onions are cooked through, about 15 minutes.

TIME-SAVERS

■ *Microwave tip: Arrange the onions in a shallow microwave-safe baking dish. Dot with the butter and oil and sprinkle with all of the remaining ingredients. Cover loosely with waxed paper and cook at 100% for 15 minutes, or until the onions are tender, stirring once.*

■ *Do-ahead: The whole dish can be prepared ahead and served at room temperature or gently reheated.*

Values are approximate per serving: Calories: 144 Protein: 3 gm Fat: 7 gm
Carbohydrates: 19 gm Cholesterol: 8 mg Sodium: 293 mg

Step 5

Cauliflower-Cheddar Gratin

▼

A thick, golden-brown topping of grated Cheddar and herbed breadcrumbs transforms cauliflower into a side dish that can make the meal. The "creamy" texture of cauliflower is a natural for combining with cheese; however, you could prepare steamed broccoli the same way. Since the cheese is so rich and zesty, this recipe is a particularly good accompaniment for simple baked chicken or fish.

Working time: 10 minutes
Total time: 20 minutes

Cauliflower-Cheddar Gratin

6 Servings

1 small head cauliflower
2 tablespoons butter
½ cup fine unseasoned
** breadcrumbs**

½ teaspoon oregano
¼ teaspoon salt
¼ teaspoon pepper
⅓ cup grated Cheddar cheese

Step 1

1 Break the cauliflower into florets. Steam the cauliflower in a steamer until tender, 10 to 12 minutes.

2 Meanwhile, preheat the broiler.

3 Melt the butter on the stovetop or in the microwave.

4 In a medium bowl, combine the breadcrumbs, oregano, salt and pepper. Stir in the melted butter. Stir in the grated cheese.

5 Place the cauliflower in a single layer in a shallow broilerproof baking dish. Sprinkle the cheese-crumb mixture over the top.

6 Broil the cauliflower 4 inches from the heat until golden on top, about 2 minutes.

Step 4

TIME-SAVERS

■ *Microwave tip: Decrease the butter to 1 tablespoon. Melt it in a small microwave-safe bowl and then stir in the breadcrumbs, oregano, salt and pepper. Increase the cheese to ⅔ cup and stir into the breadcrumbs. Arrange the cauliflower florets in an 8-inch round microwave-safe baking dish. Sprinkle with 2 tablespoons hot water. Cover and cook at 100% for 8 minutes, or until just tender, stirring once. Sprinkle the hot cauliflower with the breadcrumb-cheese mixture, cover and let stand until the cheese melts. If the cheese does not completely melt with the residual heat, put the dish back in the microwave and cook at 50% for about 1 minute.*

■ *Do-ahead: The cauliflower can be steamed ahead.*

Step 5

Values are approximate per serving: Calories: 99 Protein: 3 gm Fat: 6 gm
Carbohydrates: 8 gm Cholesterol: 17 mg Sodium: 234 mg

Herbed Corn on the Cob

▼

*If your family is like most, you will want to make two ears of corn per
person, if not more. For each ear of corn you add to this recipe, increase the butter by
1 tablespoon, the basil and oregano by ⅛ teaspoon each and the salt and pepper
by a pinch each. If you are barbecuing, you can cook foil-wrapped corn on the grill:
It should take about 20 minutes over medium-hot coals.*

Working time: 15 minutes
Total time: 45 minutes

Herbed Corn on the Cob

4 Servings

4 ears corn, unhusked
¼ cup butter, softened to room
temperature
½ teaspoon basil

½ teaspoon oregano
¼ teaspoon salt
¼ teaspoon pepper

1 Preheat the oven to 375°. Cut four large squares of foil.

2 Peel back but do not remove the corn husks. Remove the corn silk.

3 In a small bowl, blend together the butter, basil, oregano, salt and pepper.

4 Spread about 1 tablespoon of herbed butter on each ear of corn, then close the husk around the corn.

5 Wrap each ear of corn tightly in foil and bake for 30 minutes, or until tender.

TIME-SAVERS

■ ***Microwave tip:*** *Spread the butter on the corn, as in Step 4, then sprinkle a few drops of water over the kernels. Arrange the corn in a shallow, microwave-safe baking dish, or on paper towels, loosely cover with plastic wrap and cook at 100% for 13 to 15 minutes, rearranging the corn about halfway through the cooking. Let stand 3 minutes.*

■ ***Do-ahead:*** *The herbed butter (Step 3) can be made well ahead. In fact, you can double or triple the quantities and keep it on hand, frozen, for any time you serve corn on the cob.*

Step 2

Step 4

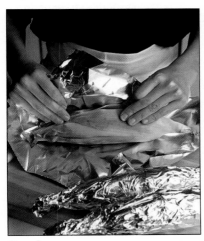
Step 5

Values are approximate per serving: Calories: 180   Protein: 3 gm   Fat: 13 gm
Carbohydrates: 17 gm   Cholesterol: 31 gm   Sodium: 266 mg

Parmesan Potatoes

Parmesan cheese and garlic lift this simple mashed potato dish out of the ordinary. Unpeeled garlic cloves are boiled along with the potatoes, which subdues the garlic's flavor to a savory mildness. Then, when you drain the potatoes after cooking, remove the garlic cloves, slip off their skins and mash them with the potatoes.

Working time: 10 minutes
Total time: 35 minutes

256

Parmesan Potatoes

6 Servings

12 small red potatoes (about 1½ pounds)
4 cloves garlic
½ cup plus 2 tablespoons grated Parmesan cheese
4 tablespoons butter

2 tablespoons milk
½ teaspoon salt
¼ teaspoon pepper, preferably white
2 tablespoons chopped parsley (optional)

1 Bring a 3-quart saucepan of water to a boil.

2 Meanwhile, in a food processor with the slicing blade, slice the unpeeled potatoes.

3 Add the potatoes and unpeeled garlic cloves to the boiling water and cook until the potatoes are tender, about 15 minutes.

4 Preheat the broiler. Butter a shallow 1-quart baking dish.

5 Drain the potatoes and garlic well. Slip the garlic cloves out of their skins.

6 In a shallow bowl, coarsely mash the potatoes and garlic with a potato masher or a fork (do not use a food processor; it will make the potatoes gluey).

7 Add ½ cup of the Parmesan, the butter, milk, salt and pepper to the mashed potatoes and mix thoroughly. Spread the potatoes in the prepared baking dish and sprinkle the remaining 2 tablespoons Parmesan evenly on top.

8 Broil the potatoes 4 inches from the heat until the top is lightly browned, about 6 minutes.

9 Serve the potatoes garnished with the chopped parsley if desired.

TIME-SAVERS

■ ***Do-ahead:*** *The whole dish can be prepared through Step 7 ahead of time, but do not sprinkle the Parmesan over the potatoes until ready to broil them.*

Step 2

Step 6

Step 7

Values are approximate per serving: Calories: 243 Protein: 7 gm Fat: 11 gm Carbohydrates: 28 gm Cholesterol: 29 mg Sodium: 464 mg

Herbed Summer Squash and Onions

This zucchini and yellow squash side dish is a real "flash in the pan"—
both types of squash cook quickly and need not be peeled. Try it with the new golden
zucchini, such as Gold Rush, which has a smooth, golden skin and a rich,
sweet flavor. Flower-shaped, greenish-white pattypan squash (also called scallop or
cymling) is another possibility for this recipe.

Working time: 25 minutes
Total time: 25 minutes

Herbed Summer Squash and Onions

4 Servings

1 large zucchini, unpeeled
1 large yellow squash, unpeeled
1 small onion
1 tablespoon vegetable oil
¼ cup chicken broth

1 tablespoon butter
½ teaspoon basil
½ teaspoon oregano
¼ teaspoon salt
¼ teaspoon pepper

1 Cut the zucchini and yellow squash into small cubes or large dice. Cut the onion into wedges.

2 In a large skillet, warm the oil over medium-high heat until hot but not smoking. Add the onion and sauté until light golden, 5 to 8 minutes.

3 Add the chicken broth, butter, basil, oregano, salt and pepper. Bring the liquid to a boil and add the squash. Reduce the heat to medium, cover and simmer, stirring frequently, until the squash is just tender, 5 to 8 minutes.

TIME-SAVERS

■ *Microwave tip:* Omit the oil. Reduce the broth to 2 tablespoons (or use water). In a 3-quart microwave-safe casserole, combine the squash, onion, broth, butter, basil, oregano, salt and pepper. Cover loosely and cook at 100% for 6 minutes, stirring once or twice, until the squash is crisp-tender.

■ *Do-ahead:* The vegetables can be cut up ahead. The whole dish can be made ahead and gently reheated in the microwave.

Step 1

Step 2

Step 3

Values are approximate per serving: Calories: 81   Protein: 2 gm   Fat: 7 gm
Carbohydrates: 5 gm   Cholesterol: 8 mg   Sodium: 229 mg

Red Pepper and Corn
Stir-Fry

▼

This colorful side dish would be good with anything from stuffed roast chicken to hamburgers. The stir-fried vegetables can also be served atop generous portions of white rice as a main dish. If your family doesn't care for spinach (or if fresh spinach is not available), you can either use another green leafy vegetable or replace it with strips of green bell pepper.

Working time: 15 minutes
Total time: 20 minutes

Red Pepper and Corn
Stir-Fry

4 Servings

2 large red bell peppers
1 medium onion
¼ pound fresh spinach
1¼ cups chicken broth
2 tablespoons cornstarch
¼ teaspoon black pepper

½ teaspoon red pepper flakes
2 tablespoons vegetable oil
2 cloves garlic, minced or crushed
  through a press
1 package (10 ounces) frozen corn,
  thawed and drained

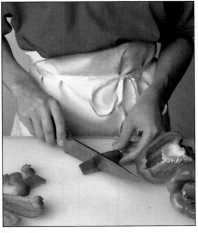

Step 1

1 Cut the bell peppers into bite-size pieces (about ¾ inch). Cut the onion into small wedges. Stem the spinach and tear it into bite-size pieces.

2 In a small bowl or measuring cup, combine the chicken broth with the cornstarch, black pepper and red pepper flakes.

3 In a large skillet or wok, warm the oil over medium-high heat until hot but not smoking. Add the onion and garlic and stir-fry until the onion begins to brown, about 5 minutes.

4 Add the bell peppers, spinach and corn. Stir the cornstarch mixture to reblend the ingredients and add it to the skillet. Bring the mixture to a boil, stirring until slightly thickened. Reduce the heat to medium-low, cover and simmer until the vegetables are crisp-tender, 2 to 3 minutes.

Step 1

TIME-SAVERS

■ *Do-ahead: All of the vegetables can be cut up ahead. The whole dish can also be made ahead and gently reheated on the stovetop or in the microwave.*

Step 4

Values are approximate per serving: Calories: 173 Protein: 4 gm Fat: 8 gm
Carbohydrates: 24 gm Cholesterol: 0 mg Sodium: 329 mg

Grated Skillet Potatoes

▼

*Shredded potatoes are put to delicious use in several European cuisines:
Swiss rösti, French potato galette and German potato kugel are all variations on
the same theme. This recipe, like the kugel, includes eggs to bind it. The
potatoes and scallions can be grated in seconds in a food processor. If you don't have
one, grate the potatoes on the coarse side of a grater and coarsely chop the scallions.*

Working time: 25 minutes
Total time: 25 minutes

Grated Skillet Potatoes

Makes 2 Cakes/6 Servings

¾ **pound red potatoes, unpeeled**
1 bunch scallions (6 to 8)
2 eggs
¼ **teaspoon salt**
⅛ **teaspoon pepper**

1 cup grated Swiss cheese (about
  ¼ **pound)**
4 tablespoons butter
2 tablespoons olive or other
  vegetable oil

1 In a food processor with the shredding blade, shred the potatoes and scallions.

2 In a medium bowl, beat the eggs with the salt and pepper. Add the grated potatoes and scallions and toss to mix. Add the grated cheese and toss to mix.

Step 1

3 In a 10-inch skillet, preferably nonstick, warm 2 tablespoons of the butter in 1 tablespoon of the oil over medium-high heat until hot but not smoking. Add half the potato mixture and press down with a spatula to form a flat cake. Cook over medium-high heat, pressing down with a spatula, until the bottom begins to brown and form a crust, about 4 minutes.

4 Loosen the cake and slide it onto a plate. Invert the pancake onto a second plate and carefully slide it back into the skillet. Cook, pressing down with a spatula, until the second side is crusty and browned, about 4 minutes.

5 Drain cake on paper towels and reserve in a warm oven while you make the second cake, using the remaining oil and butter.

Step 3

Values are approximate per serving: Calories: 254 Protein: 9 gm Fat: 19 gm
Carbohydrates: 12 gm Cholesterol: 109 mg Sodium: 243 mg

Step 4

Cucumber-Pepper Salad
with Dilled Sour Cream Dressing

▼

For a change of pace, try Kirby cucumbers in this salad; they are small and crisp, and have a minimum of seeds. Or try a European cucumber, which is long, thin, seedless and occasionally marketed as a "burpless" cucumber. The tangy, dill-flavored sour cream dressing could also be used on leftover cooked, chilled vegetables such as sliced yellow squash, zucchini or carrots.

Working time: 15 minutes
Total time: 15 minutes

Cucumber-Pepper Salad
with Dilled Sour Cream Dressing

4 Servings

2 medium cucumbers
1 large yellow or green bell pepper
1 bunch scallions (6 to 8)
¼ cup chopped fresh dill or 3
   teaspoons dried
⅓ cup sour cream
⅓ cup plain yogurt

¼ cup lemon juice
1 tablespoon Dijon mustard
1 tablespoon grated lemon zest
   (optional)
¼ teaspoon salt
¼ teaspoon black pepper

Step 1

1 Peel the cucumbers, leaving some strips of cucumber skin on for a decorative effect. Cut the cucumbers into ¼-inch-thick slices.

2 Cut the bell pepper into bite-size pieces. Coarsely chop the scallions. Finely chop the fresh dill (if using).

Step 2

3 In a large serving bowl, combine the dill (fresh or dried), sour cream, yogurt, lemon juice, mustard, lemon zest (if using), salt and black pepper.

4 Add the cucumbers, bell pepper and scallions and toss to combine.

TIME-SAVERS

■ ***Do-ahead:*** *The dressing (Step 3) can be made ahead of time.*

Step 3

Values are approximate per serving: Calories: 102   Protein: 4 gm   Fat: 5 gm
Carbohydrates: 13 gm   Cholesterol: 9 mg   Sodium: 289 mg

Shredded Carrot Salad with Pecans and Red Onion

▼

Always welcome in a lunch box or picnic basket, carrot salad also brightens up weekday suppers. This tangy version, made with red onion and seasoned with mustard and pepper, goes well with simple fare such as fried chicken, salmon patties or pork chops. The food processor shreds carrots quickly, and the dressing is stirred together right in the serving bowl. Walnuts or even unsalted peanuts can stand in for the pecans.

Working time: 10 minutes
Total time: 10 minutes

Shredded Carrot Salad
with Pecans and Red Onion

6 Servings

6 medium carrots (about 1 pound)
1 small red onion
⅓ cup mayonnaise
½ cup plain yogurt
3 tablespoons lemon juice
2 teaspoons grated lemon zest
  (optional)

1 tablespoon Dijon mustard
1 teaspoon dry mustard
¼ teaspoon pepper
¼ teaspoon sugar
1 cup chopped pecans
1 cup raisins

1 In a food processor, shred the carrots.

2 By hand, halve the onion lengthwise and then cut crosswise into thin half-rings.

3 In a large bowl, combine the mayonnaise, yogurt, lemon juice, lemon zest (if using), Dijon and dry mustards, the pepper and sugar.

4 Add the carrots, onion, pecans and raisins, and toss to combine.

TIME-SAVERS

■ *Do-ahead: The individual components can be prepared or the whole salad assembled ahead of time.*

Step 1

Step 2

Step 4

Values are approximate per serving: Calories: 333   Protein: 4 gm   Fat: 23 gm
Carbohydrates: 33 gm   Cholesterol: 8 mg   Sodium: 188 mg

Spinach and Artichoke Salad with Garlic Dressing

▼

The dressing for this substantial salad is a lemony mayonnaise flavored with whole garlic cloves, which are removed before serving. If you prefer, you can crush the garlic through a press, but use just one clove instead of three and stir the crushed garlic into the mayonnaise mixture. Serve the salad either as a light entrée or to accompany a meat, fish or pasta dish.

Working time: 20 minutes
Total time: 20 minutes

Spinach and Artichoke Salad with Garlic Dressing

4 Servings

½ pound fresh spinach
3½ cups shredded red cabbage
   (about ½ pound)
1 large yellow or green bell pepper
1 can (14 ounces) artichoke hearts,
   drained, or 2 jars (6 ounces each)
   artichoke hearts, drained

3 cloves garlic
1 cup mayonnaise
2 tablespoons lemon juice
2 teaspoons Worcestershire sauce

1 Stem the spinach, then wash and drain well. Tear it into bite-size pieces and place in a large serving bowl.

2 Cut the cabbage into thin shreds. Cut the bell pepper into ¼-inch-wide strips.

Step 2

3 If the artichoke hearts are large, halve them.

4 Peel the garlic and bruise the cloves lightly with the side of a knife.

5 Make the dressing: In a small bowl, combine the mayonnaise, lemon juice and Worcestershire sauce. Stir the bruised garlic into the mayonnaise dressing. Cover and refrigerate the dressing until ready to serve (the longer it sits, the stronger the garlic flavor will be). Remove the garlic cloves before serving the dressing.

6 Add the cabbage, bell pepper and artichoke hearts to the spinach and toss to distribute the ingredients evenly. Toss the salad with the dressing or serve it on the side.

Step 3

TIME-SAVERS

■ *Do-ahead: All of the vegetables can be cut up and the dressing made ahead, but do not assemble the salad until shortly before serving.*

Step 4

Values are approximate per serving: Calories: 296 Protein: 3 gm Fat: 29 gm
Carbohydrates: 8 gm Cholesterol: 22 mg Sodium: 273 mg

Melon Salad
with Tangerine-Lime Dressing

▼

Combining honeydew and cantaloupe makes this fruit salad more colorful. For convenience, however, you might prefer to use all one kind of melon. Just keep in mind that you will need approximately five cups of cubed melon in all. The average cantaloupe will yield about four cups of cubes; the average honeydew will yield about six cups.

Working time: 20 minutes
Total time: 20 minutes

Melon Salad
with Tangerine-Lime Dressing

4 Servings

1 teaspoon grated lime zest (optional)
3 tablespoons lime juice
2 tablespoons frozen tangerine or orange juice concentrate
¼ teaspoon ground coriander or vanilla extract

½ cantaloupe
½ honeydew melon
1½ cups seedless red grapes (about 10 ounces)

Step 1

1 Make the dressing: Grate the lime zest (if using). In a medium bowl, stir together the lime zest, lime juice, tangerine juice and the coriander or vanilla.

2 Cut each melon half into 1-inch-wide wedges. Then, using a sharp knife, remove the rind.

3 Cut the melon wedges crosswise into ¾-inch pieces.

4 Add the melon to the dressing, then add the grapes and toss gently to combine. Cover the bowl loosely with plastic wrap and refrigerate, stirring occasionally, until serving. If possible, refrigerate until well chilled, about 2 hours.

Step 2

TIME-SAVERS

■ *Do-ahead: The dressing can be made and the melon cubed ahead of time. The entire salad can also be assembled ahead of time. In fact, it is best served chilled, so making it and then refrigerating it for several hours before serving is all to the benefit of the salad's flavor.*

Step 3

Values are approximate per serving: Calories: 141 Protein: 2 gm Fat: .6 gm Carbohydrates: 37 gm Cholesterol: 0 mg Sodium: 26 mg

Broccoli Salad with Red Onion and Yellow Pepper

The recipe for this tricolor dish offers a good tip for preparing salad and dressing ingredients simultaneously. Whole, unpeeled garlic cloves are steamed along with the broccoli, rendering the garlic sweet and mild and a snap to peel. Another quick trick: Put the mashed garlic and other dressing ingredients in a small, wide-mouthed jar, cover it tightly, and shake it just until the dressing is well blended.

Working time: 15 minutes
Total time: 20 minutes

Broccoli Salad with Red Onion and Yellow Pepper

6 Servings

3 stalks broccoli
2 cloves garlic, unpeeled
1 large yellow bell pepper
1 small red onion
¼ cup olive or other vegetable oil
2 tablespoons red wine vinegar

1½ teaspoons dry mustard
½ teaspoon salt
¼ teaspoon black pepper
**3 tablespoons chopped chives or
    scallion greens (optional)**

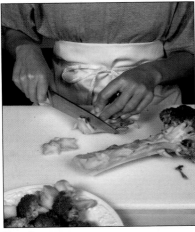
Step 1

1 Cut the tops off the broccoli stalks. Cut the stalks into bite-size pieces and separate the tops into florets.

2 Steam the broccoli and the garlic in a steamer until the broccoli is tender, 5 to 8 minutes.

3 Meanwhile, cut the bell pepper into thin strips. Cut the onion into thin slices.

4 Remove the garlic cloves from the steamer and set aside. Cool the broccoli by refreshing it under cold running water; drain well.

5 In a small bowl, whisk together the oil, vinegar, mustard, salt, black pepper and chives (if using). Peel the cooked garlic and mash it with a fork; add it to the dressing, whisking well to blend.

Step 5

6 Place the broccoli, bell pepper, onion and vinaigrette in a salad bowl and toss to combine.

TIME-SAVERS

■ *Microwave tip: To cook the broccoli, place the florets and stem pieces in a single layer in a 1½-quart microwave-safe baking dish with the garlic and 2 tablespoons of water. Cover and cook at 100% for 7 minutes, stirring once.*

■ *Do-ahead: The broccoli can be steamed and the other vegetables cut up ahead. The dressing can also be made ahead. If you make the dressing ahead without steaming the garlic, reduce the garlic to only 1 clove and crush it through a press (or mince it) before adding it to the dressing*

Step 6

Values are approximate per serving: Calories: 117 Protein: 3 gm Fat: 10 gm
Carbohydrates: 7 gm Cholesterol: 0 mg Sodium: 209 mg

Mixed Vegetable Salad with Toasted Almond Dressing

▼

Your mother or grandmother probably had a curved chopper and a well-worn wooden bowl for making chopped vegetable salads and slaws. Nowadays, the food processor takes over nearly all the work of cutting up the vegetables, and in this case even the dressing is blended by machine. More substantial than a leafy salad, this colorful mixture works well with barbecue or picnic fare, or as a light meal with sandwiches.

Working time: 20 minutes
Total time: 20 minutes

Mixed Vegetable Salad with Toasted Almond Dressing

6 Servings

⅓ cup sliced almonds
2 medium carrots
1 medium zucchini
¼ pound green beans
1 medium yellow or red bell pepper
2 ribs celery
4 scallions
1 can (11 ounces) corn, drained
1 cup frozen peas, thawed

1 clove garlic
½ cup olive or other vegetable oil
⅓ cup white wine vinegar or cider vinegar
2 plum tomatoes
¼ cup (packed) fresh basil leaves
¾ teaspoon salt
Pinch of cayenne pepper

Step 1

1 In a medium ungreased skillet, cook the almonds, shaking frequently, until toasted, 5 to 7 minutes.

2 In a food processor, one at a time, coarsely chop the carrots, zucchini, green beans, bell pepper, celery and scallions. As the vegetables are chopped, transfer them to a salad bowl. Add the corn and peas.

3 In the same processor work bowl, mince the garlic. Add the almonds and finely chop (being careful not to turn the almonds into a paste).

4 To the processor, add the oil, vinegar, tomatoes, basil, salt and cayenne, and process very briefly, just to blend.

Step 2

5 Add the dressing to the vegetables and toss to combine.

TIME-SAVERS

■ *Do-ahead: The vegetables can be chopped several hours ahead; the dressing (Steps 1, 3 and 4) can be made well ahead. The salad can be assembled a short time before serving.*

Step 5

Values are approximate per serving: Calories: 271 Protein: 5 gm Fat: 21 gm
Carbohydrates: 19 gm Cholesterol: 0 mg Sodium: 327 mg

Walnut-Orange Salad with Tangy Citrus Dressing

▼

A sophisticated blend of sharp, sweet and nutty flavors, this salad could be served as a side salad, as a first course for a festive dinner or with some cheese and French bread for a light lunch. Red leaf lettuce makes it especially appealing, but any soft leaf lettuce could be used. Adding a small amount of walnut oil (available in gourmet shops and some supermarkets) to the dressing would emphasize the flavor of the nuts.

Working time: 20 minutes
Total time: 20 minutes

Walnut-Orange Salad with Tangy Citrus Dressing

6 Servings

¾ cup walnut halves or pieces
1 small red onion
2 oranges
1 head red leaf lettuce
2 tablespoons olive or other
   vegetable oil

1 tablespoon orange juice
1 tablespoon lemon juice
1½ teaspoons Dijon mustard
¼ teaspoon basil
Pinch of salt
Pinch of pepper

1 Toast the walnuts at 375° on a baking sheet in a preheated oven or in a toaster oven for 5 to 8 minutes, stirring occasionally.

2 Meanwhile, cut the onion into very thin rings.

3 Peel the oranges, removing as much of the bitter white pith as possible. Separate the oranges in half lengthwise and then cut the oranges crosswise into thin half-moons.

Step 3

4 Tear the lettuce into bite-size pieces.

5 In a small bowl, combine the olive oil, orange juice, lemon juice, mustard, basil, salt and pepper.

6 In a medium bowl, toss the walnuts, onion and oranges together. Serve on beds of lettuce with some of the dressing spooned on top. Pass any additional dressing on the side.

Step 3

TIME-SAVERS

■ **Microwave tip:** *Toss the walnuts with 2 teaspoons olive or other vegetable oil to coat well. Place them in a shallow microwave-safe bowl or plate lined with paper towels and cook at 100% for 30 seconds. Let the nuts cool slightly before combining them with the salad greens.*

■ **Do-ahead:** *The walnuts can be toasted, the onion and oranges cut up, and the dressing (Step 5) made well ahead.*

Step 6

Values are approximate per serving: Calories: 156 Protein: 3 gm Fat: 13 gm
Carbohydrates: 11 gm Cholesterol: 0 mg Sodium: 65 mg

Potato-Pepper Salad with Yogurt Dressing

▼

*Using reduced-calorie mayonnaise—and combining it with an equal
portion of yogurt—cuts the fat content of this potato salad by 75 percent. Mustard,
vinegar, dill and celery seed are added to keep the flavor lively. The salad
is best warm (the potatoes are "dressed" right after they're cooked), but it can also
be served at room temperature or chilled.*

Working time: 20 minutes
Total time: 30 minutes

Potato-Pepper Salad with Yogurt Dressing

6 Servings

15 small red potatoes (about 1½ pounds), unpeeled
4 scallions
3 stalks celery
1 large red bell pepper
½ cup plain yogurt
½ cup light mayonnaise or regular mayonnaise

1 tablespoon Dijon mustard
1 tablespoon white wine vinegar or distilled vinegar
1 teaspoon dill weed
½ teaspoon celery seed
½ teaspoon salt
¼ teaspoon black pepper

Step 2

1 Bring a large saucepan of water to a boil.

2 Meanwhile, cut the potatoes into quarters. Add the potatoes to the boiling water. Reduce the heat to medium-low, cover and simmer until tender, 15 to 18 minutes.

3 Meanwhile, coarsely chop the scallions and celery. Cut the red pepper into bite-size pieces.

4 In a small bowl, combine the yogurt, mayonnaise, mustard, vinegar, dill, celery seed, salt and black pepper.

5 Drain the potatoes well, transfer them to a large serving bowl and toss them with the scallions, celery, bell pepper and yogurt dressing.

6 Serve warm or refrigerate until serving time.

Step 3

TIME-SAVERS

■ *Do-ahead: The yogurt dressing (Step 4) can be made ahead. The entire salad can also be assembled well ahead and refrigerated.*

Values are approximate per serving: Calories: 172   Protein: 4 gm   Fat: 6 gm
Carbohydrates: 26 gm   Cholesterol: 8 mg   Sodium: 406 mg

Step 5

Glazed Strawberry-Banana Cream Pie (page 311)

CHAPTER 6
DESSERTS

Strawberry Cheesecake Pie

You can make "homemade" cheesecake from a mix, but it cannot compare with smooth, gently sweet cheesecake made from scratch. This recipe calls for baking a cheesecake filling in either a ready-made or homemade graham cracker crust: To make your own, combine 1¼ cups of graham cracker (or vanilla or chocolate wafer) crumbs with ⅓ cup melted butter and 3 tablespoons of sugar. Pat the mixture into an 8-inch pie plate.

Working time: 15 minutes
Total time: 1 hour 35 minutes

Strawberry Cheesecake Pie

8 Servings

2 packages (8 ounces each) cream cheese, at room temperature
½ cup sugar
1 egg
1 cup sour cream
1½ teaspoons grated lemon zest (optional)

1 tablespoon lemon juice
1 teaspoon vanilla extract
8-inch graham cracker crust, storebought or homemade
1 cup halved strawberries
2 tablespoons red currant or strawberry jelly

1 Preheat the oven to 350°.

2 In a food processor, beat the cream cheese until smooth. Beat in the sugar and egg. Beat in the sour cream, lemon zest (if using), lemon juice and vanilla.

3 Pour the mixture into the graham cracker crust and bake for 35 minutes, or until set.

4 Place the pie on a rack to cool to room temperature and then chill for at least 1 hour, or until serving time.

5 Before serving, halve the strawberries and arrange them around the top edge of the cheesecake pie.

6 Melt the jelly in a small skillet or saucepan, or in the microwave, and spoon or brush the melted jelly over the strawberries to glaze them.

TIME-SAVERS

■ *Microwave tip: Prepare the filling and pour into the pie crust as directed above, being sure it is in a glass or other microwave-safe pie plate. Place an inverted saucer or several custard cups in the microwave and place the pie plate on top. Cook at 50% until the pie is set, about 15 minutes, rotating the pie plate once or twice. Note that the center will be a little bit softer than that of a cheesecake pie baked in a conventional oven.*

Step 3

Step 5

Step 6

Values are approximate per serving: Calories: 444 Protein: 7 gm Fat: 32 gm
Carbohydrates: 34 gm Cholesterol: 107 mg Sodium: 344 mg

Giant Chocolate-Chocolate-Chip Cookies

▼

Bake a whole batch of cookies and keep them on hand in the freezer for a quick and simple dessert. You can serve one of these giant cookies topped with a scoop of ice cream. Or, with a little advance planning, you can make ice cream sandwiches: press slightly softened ice cream between two cookies; then, if you're not serving them right away, return them to the freezer.

Working time: 20 minutes
Total time: 35 minutes

Giant Chocolate-Chocolate-Chip Cookies

Makes about 1 dozen

1 package (6 ounces) semisweet
   chocolate chips
2 tablespoons milk
1 cup plus 2 tablespoons flour
2 tablespoons unsweetened cocoa
   powder

½ teaspoon baking soda
½ teaspoon salt
1 stick (4 ounces) butter, softened to
   room temperature
⅔ cup packed brown sugar
1 egg

1 Preheat the oven to 375°.

2 In a small saucepan, combine ⅓ cup of the chocolate chips and the milk and let sit over very low heat until the chocolate is melted, 5 to 10 minutes. Stir the chocolate mixture until smooth and blended. Remove the pan from the heat and set aside.

3 Meanwhile, in a medium bowl, stir together the flour, cocoa, baking soda and salt.

4 In another medium bowl, cream the butter with the sugar until well blended. Beat in the egg until well blended, then blend in the chocolate mixture.

5 Beat in the dry ingredients just until combined, then stir in the remaining chocolate chips.

6 Drop ¼-cup portions of dough on an ungreased baking sheet, leaving about 3 inches between them.

7 Gently flatten the dough to form 2½-inch rounds.

8 Bake the cookies for 10 to 12 minutes, or until the bottoms are lightly browned. Undercook them somewhat if you prefer chewy cookies. Let the cookies cool slightly on a rack before serving.

Step 2

Step 6

Step 7

TIME-SAVERS

■ *Microwave tip: The chocolate can be melted in the microwave. Place the chocolate chips and milk in a small microwave-safe bowl and microwave at 50% for 3 minutes. The chips will maintain their shape even when melted, so stir them a bit to see if they are melted before cooking them longer.*

■ *Do-ahead: The cookie dough can be made ahead of time and frozen. To freeze, shape the dough into a log about 8 inches long and 2 inches in diameter. Wrap it in plastic wrap and then in aluminum foil. To make the cookies, cut the log into 12 even pieces and bake at 375° for about 12 minutes.*

Values are approximate per cookie: Calories: 239 Protein: 3 gm Fat: 14 gm
Carbohydrates: 30 gm Cholesterol: 44 mg Sodium: 214 mg

Baked Raspberry-Vanilla Pudding

▼

*This delectable dessert is like a French clafouti—a quick combination
of fruit and rich batter that bakes into a sort of pancake/pie. Although a clafouti is
traditionally made with fresh fruits in season, this one is based on sweetened
frozen raspberries. If you are lucky enough to have fresh raspberries, sprinkle them
with a little sugar after placing them in the pie plate.*

Working time: 5 minutes
Total time: 30 minutes

Baked Raspberry-Vanilla Pudding

6 Servings

1 package (10 ounces) frozen
   raspberries in syrup, thawed
4 eggs
½ cup milk

½ cup heavy cream
¼ cup flour
¼ cup plus 1 tablespoon sugar
½ teaspoon vanilla extract

1 Preheat the oven to 375°. Lightly butter a 9-inch pie plate or a 1-quart shallow baking dish.

2 Spread the raspberries and their syrup evenly over the bottom of the pie plate.

3 Make the batter: In a blender or food processor, combine the eggs, milk, cream, flour, ¼ cup of the sugar and the vanilla, and blend well.

4 Pour the batter over the fruit. Sprinkle with the remaining 1 tablespoon sugar.

5 Bake for 20 to 25 minutes, or until the pudding is set and golden around the edges.

Step 2

Step 3

Step 4

Values are approximate per serving: Calories: 239 Protein: 6 gm Fat: 11 gm
Carbohydrates: 29 gm Cholesterol: 172 mg Sodium: 60 mg

Quick Lemon-Lime Mousse

▼

Velvety smooth and gently tart, this mousse is basically a lemon-lime custard lightened with whipped cream. To cut down on preparation time, instead of putting the bowl of custard in the freezer to chill, place it in a larger bowl of ice and water and stir the mixture until well chilled. The mousse can be served as soon as you fold in the whipped cream, or it can be refrigerated and served later.

Working time: 25 minutes
Total time: 55 minutes

Quick Lemon-Lime Mousse

4 Servings

1½ teaspoons grated lemon zest (optional)	3 egg yolks
½ teaspoon grated lime zest (optional)	½ cup sugar
	2 tablespoons cornstarch
	Pinch of salt
¼ cup lemon juice	⅔ cup milk
1 tablespoon lime juice	1 cup heavy cream

1 Put a stainless steel mixing bowl in the freezer to chill.

2 If using a fresh lemon and fresh lime, grate the zests from the fruits and then juice them.

Step 2

3 In a medium saucepan, combine the citrus zests (if using), citrus juices, egg yolks, sugar, cornstarch and salt. Whisk in the milk.

4 Place the saucepan over medium heat and cook, stirring constantly, until the custard has thickened and comes to a boil, about 10 minutes.

5 Remove the saucepan from the heat and transfer the lemon-lime custard to the chilled stainless steel bowl. Place a sheet of plastic wrap directly on the surface of the custard to prevent a skin from forming. Place the bowl in the freezer to quick-cool the custard, stirring occasionally to evenly distribute the cold. Be careful not to leave the custard in too long (no more than 30 minutes and even less if your freezer is very efficient); it should remain soft. If you are making the dessert ahead of time, chill the custard in the refrigerator instead.

Step 5

6 When the lemon-lime custard is cooled, in another bowl, whip the heavy cream until stiff peaks form. Fold the whipped cream into the custard. Spoon the mousse into individual dessert bowls or parfait glasses and refrigerate until serving time.

TIME-SAVERS

■ ***Microwave tip:*** *To make the lemon-lime custard: In a 1-quart glass measuring cup, combine the citrus zests (if using), citrus juices, egg yolks, sugar, cornstarch, salt and milk. Cook at 50% for 7 minutes, stirring twice, or until thickened.*

■ ***Do-ahead:*** *The lemon-lime custard can be made well ahead. The mousse can be made several hours ahead.*

Values are approximate per serving: Calories: 390 Protein: 5 gm Fat: 27 gm
Carbohydrates: 34 gm Cholesterol: 247 mg Sodium: 85 mg

Step 6

Mocha-Pecan Bars
with Mocha Icing

▼

*These snazzy bar cookies take the brownie to new heights. They have a sophisticated
coffee-chocolate flavor and are studded with pecans instead of the usual walnuts.
The glossy mocha glaze on top can be drizzled on from the tip of a spoon, or you can use
a homemade decorating bag: Spoon the icing into a small heavy-duty plastic bag,
then snip a tiny piece off one bottom corner and squeeze the icing through the opening.*

Working time: 25 minutes
Total time: 45 minutes

16 Servings

4 ounces chocolate chips
1 stick (4 ounces) butter
1 cup pecan halves
1⅔ cups (packed) dark brown
    sugar
3 teaspoons instant espresso
    powder or instant coffee granules
1 cup flour

½ teaspoon baking powder
3 eggs
1 teaspoon vanilla extract
¾ cup confectioners' sugar
2 tablespoons unsweetened cocoa
    powder
2 tablespoons hot water

1 Preheat the oven to 375°. Butter and flour a 13 x 9-inch baking pan.

2 In a large heatproof bowl set over a saucepan of simmering water, melt the chocolate chips and butter.

Step 2

3 Meanwhile, finely chop the pecans.

4 Remove the bowl of chocolate from the saucepan and stir in the brown sugar and 2 teaspoons of the espresso powder. Stir to dissolve the sugar. Set the chocolate mixture aside to cool slightly.

5 In a small bowl, blend the flour and baking powder. In another small bowl, beat the eggs until frothy.

6 Stir the eggs and vanilla into the chocolate mixture. Stir in the dry ingredients and the pecans. Scrape the batter into the prepared baking pan and bake for 20 to 25 minutes, or until a toothpick inserted in the center comes out clean. Let the cake cool in the pan on a rack.

Step 6

7 In a small bowl, combine the confectioners' sugar and cocoa. Dissolve the remaining 1 teaspoon espresso powder in the hot water and add to the sugar and cocoa, stirring to blend. Drizzle the glaze over the cooled cake. Let the glaze set before cutting the cake into 16 bars.

TIME-SAVERS

■ *Microwave tip: To melt the chocolate, combine the chocolate and butter in a microwave-safe mixing bowl. Cook at 100% for 1 to 2 minutes, stirring once.*

■ *Do-ahead: You can make the glaze (Step 7) ahead; if it hardens before you drizzle it on the cake, warm it over a pan of water or in the microwave (uncovered, at 100% for 5 to 8 seconds).*

Values are approximate per serving: Calories: 380 Protein: 4 gm Fat: 18 gm
Carbohydrates: 54 gm Cholesterol: 75 mg Sodium: 125 mg

Step 7

Blueberry Walnut Crumble

▼

Crumbles make the best of summer fruits. One of their finest features is speedy preparation: Plump blueberries can emerge from the oven as a glorious dessert in less than an hour. The buttery walnut-oatmeal topping is also delicious with other fruits, such as blackberries, peaches, plums or nectarines. Top the crumble with ice cream for an extra-special treat.

Working time: 10 minutes
Total time: 45 minutes

Blueberry Walnut Crumble

8 Servings

4 cups blueberries, fresh or frozen   ⅓ cup old-fashioned rolled oats
1 tablespoon lemon juice   ⅓ cup brown sugar
3 tablespoons granulated sugar   ¼ teaspoon salt
½ cup plus 3 tablespoons flour   ⅓ cup butter
1 teaspoon allspice   ⅔ cup chopped walnuts

1 Preheat the oven to 375°. Butter and flour a shallow 1½-quart baking dish.

2 In a large bowl, toss the blueberries with the lemon juice, granulated sugar, 3 tablespoons of the flour and ½ teaspoon of the allspice. Transfer the mixture to the prepared baking dish.

Step 2

3 In a small bowl, combine the remaining ½ cup flour with the oats, brown sugar, salt and the remaining ½ teaspoon allspice.

4 With a pastry blender or two knives, cut in the butter until the mixture is coarse and crumbly. Stir in the chopped walnuts.

5 Sprinkle the walnut topping over the blueberries and bake for 30 minutes, or until the topping begins to brown.

Step 4

TIME-SAVERS

■ *Microwave tip: Prepare the fruit and topping as directed. Do not butter and flour the pan. Arrange the fruit in a microwave-safe 9-inch deep-dish pie plate. Sprinkle the topping over the berries. Cook at 100% for 3 minutes. Rotate the dish and cook for another 2 minutes at 100%. Watch the blueberries carefully to be sure they do not bubble up or they will be overcooked.*

Values are approximate per serving: Calories: 277 Protein: 4 gm Fat: 14 gm
Carbohydrates: 36 gm Cholesterol: 20 mg Sodium: 154 mg

Step 5

Chocolate-Butterscotch Pudding Cake

▼

This old-fashioned pudding cake is full of surprises: Before baking the cake you pour a cup of hot water over the batter. And when you cut into the cake, you'll find that it has formed a top layer that's like the richest of fudge brownies—chock-full of melted butterscotch chips—and a bottom layer of spoonable hot fudge sauce. Try other flavored chips, such as semisweet, milk chocolate or mint, for a variation.

Working time: 15 minutes
Total time: 50 minutes

Chocolate-Butterscotch Pudding Cake

6 Servings

1 cup flour
1 cup (packed) brown sugar
½ cup unsweetened cocoa powder
1 tablespoon instant coffee
1½ teaspoons baking powder
½ teaspoon salt
½ cup butterscotch chips

½ cup milk
2 tablespoons vegetable oil
1 teaspoon vanilla extract
1 cup hot water
Whipped cream (optional)

1 Preheat the oven to 350°. Butter an 8-inch round cake pan.

2 In a medium bowl, thoroughly blend the flour, ½ cup of the brown sugar, ¼ cup of the cocoa, the coffee, baking powder and salt. Stir in the butterscotch chips.

3 In a small bowl, blend the milk, oil and vanilla. Add the wet ingredients to the dry ingredients and stir until blended.

4 Pour the batter into the prepared cake pan and spread it evenly.

5 Blend together the remaining ½ cup brown sugar and ¼ cup cocoa. Sprinkle this mixture on top of the cake batter. Pour the hot water evenly over the surface of the batter.

6 Bake for 35 to 40 minutes, until the top looks cakelike and dry.

7 Serve the pudding cake with whipped cream if desired.

Values are approximate per serving: Calories: 363 Protein: 5 gm Fat: 11 gm
Carbohydrates: 66 gm Cholesterol: 3 mg Sodium: 323 mg

Step 2

Step 5

Step 5

Cookie Crust Fruit Tart

▼

In a European-style fruit tart, the fruit usually tops a layer of cooked, flour-thickened custard called "crème pâtissière," or pastry cream. In this simplified version, the pastry cream is replaced with a velvety mixture of cream cheese and sour cream flavored with almond extract. The tart's crust, which tastes like a buttery almond cookie, is easy to mix in a food processor.

Working time: 20 minutes
Total time: 40 minutes

Cookie Crust Fruit Tart

8 Servings

⅓ cup sliced almonds
1½ cups flour
¼ cup sugar
½ teaspoon salt
10 tablespoons chilled butter, cut into pieces
2 packages (3 ounces each) cream cheese, at room temperature

1⅓ cups sour cream
1 teaspoon almond extract
3 cups mixed sliced fruit, fresh or frozen
2 tablespoons strawberry jelly

1 Preheat the oven to 450°.

2 In a food processor, finely chop the almonds (do not overprocess or the almonds will turn into a paste).

Step 4

3 Add the flour, 3 tablespoons of the sugar and the salt, and process to blend. Add the butter and pulse until the dough just holds together.

4 Press the dough evenly into the bottom and up the sides of a 9-inch tart pan with a removable bottom. Bake the tart shell for 5 minutes (the dough will puff slightly). Remove the tart shell from the oven but leave the oven on.

5 Meanwhile, in the same processor work bowl (no need to clean it), blend the cream cheese, sour cream, almond extract and the remaining 1 tablespoon sugar.

6 Spread the cream cheese mixture evenly in the tart shell and return to the oven. Bake for 7 to 9 more minutes, or until set. Set the tart aside on a rack to cool.

Step 6

7 If using fresh fruit, slice it and toss with some lemon juice to keep it from discoloring. If using frozen fruit, drain the thawed fruit well on paper towels. Arrange the fruit on top of the cooled pie.

8 In a small saucepan over low heat, or in the microwave, melt the strawberry jelly. Spoon or brush the jelly over the fruit.

TIME-SAVERS

■ *Do-ahead: The tart shell and cream cheese filling can be baked and the fruit sliced ahead of time; it's best not to put the fruit topping on until shortly before serving.*

Values are approximate per serving: Calories: 462 Protein: 7 gm Fat: 32 gm
Carbohydrates: 38 gm Cholesterol: 79 mg Sodium: 368 mg

Step 8

Peanut Butter-Chocolate Chip Brownies

▼

The combination of peanut butter and chocolate is irresistible, especially in the form of these chewy bar cookies. The ingredients can be mixed in a food processor, and the brownies bake in just 35 minutes. You don't need to let these cool for long—in fact, they're at their best slightly warm, while the chocolate chips are still melted. Cater to your family's tastes by using semisweet or milk chocolate chips, as they prefer.

Working time: 10 minutes
Total time: 50 minutes

Peanut Butter-Chocolate Chip Brownies

Makes 16 Brownies

1 stick (4 ounces) butter
½ cup chunky peanut butter
1 cup sugar
2 eggs
1 teaspoon vanilla extract

1½ cups flour
¾ teaspoon baking powder
¼ teaspoon salt
1 cup chocolate chips

1 Preheat the oven to 375°. Butter and flour an 8-inch square baking pan.

2 In a food processor, cream the butter and peanut butter. Beat in the sugar. Beat in the eggs, one at a time. Beat in the vanilla.

Step 2

3 In medium bowl, thoroughly combine the flour, baking powder and salt. Add to the food processor and pulse on and off for 5 seconds, or until the dry ingredients are no longer visible.

4 Stir the chocolate chips into the batter.

5 Spread the batter in the prepared baking pan and bake for 35 minutes, or until golden brown on top and a toothpick inserted in the center comes out clean.

6 Let cool in the pan on a rack before cutting into 16 squares.

Step 3

TIME-SAVERS

■ *Microwave tip: Lightly grease (but do not flour) an 8- or 9-inch round baking dish. Prepare the batter as instructed above and spread it in the baking dish. Place an inverted saucer or two custard cups in the middle of the microwave and place the baking dish on top. Cook at 100% for 7 minutes, rotating the dish once. Let stand directly on the counter to cool (do not use a cooling rack).*

Values are approximate per brownie: Calories: 256 Protein: 5 gm Fat: 14 gm
Carbohydrates: 30 gm Cholesterol: 44 mg Sodium: 167 mg

Step 4

Lemon-Poppyseed Cake with Lemon Mousse Filling

▼

A grand finale to a festive weekend dinner, this dessert pairs rich lemon-poppyseed cake with a mousse-like lemon filling, which is made by simply folding whipped cream into a lemon-flavored custard. Most of the "total time" given for the recipe is cooling time for the cake, during which you can attend to other dinner-party details.

Working time: 40 minutes
Total time: 2 hours

8 Servings

1 tablespoon plus 2 teaspoons
  lemon juice
¾ cup milk
1½ cups flour
¼ cup poppyseeds
¼ teaspoon baking soda
¼ teaspoon salt
1 stick (4 ounces) butter, softened

1⅓ cups granulated sugar
2 whole eggs plus 1 egg yolk
2 teaspoons grated lemon zest
  (optional)
½ teaspoon lemon extract
1½ teaspoons cornstarch
½ cup heavy cream
2 teaspoons confectioners' sugar

1 Preheat the oven to 350°. Butter and flour an 8 x 2-inch round cake pan.

2 In a small bowl, stir 1 tablespoon of the lemon juice into ½ cup of the milk and set aside. In a bowl, stir together the flour, poppyseeds, baking soda and salt.

3 In a bowl, cream the butter and 1 cup of the granulated sugar. Beat in the whole eggs one at a time. Beat in 1 teaspoon of the lemon zest (if using) and the lemon extract. Alternately beat in the dry ingredients and the lemon juice-milk mixture.

4 Pour the batter into the pan and bake for 35 to 40 minutes, or until a toothpick inserted in the center comes out clean. Cool the cake in the pan on a rack for 10 minutes; remove from the pan to cool completely.

5 Meanwhile, in a small saucepan, combine the remaining ⅓ cup granulated sugar with the cornstarch and remaining ¼ cup milk. Cook over medium heat, stirring, until thickened, 3 to 4 minutes.

6 In a small bowl, beat the egg yolk. Beat in about 2 tablespoons of the hot cornstarch-milk mixture. Stir the warmed yolk mixture into the saucepan and cook over medium heat for 1 to 2 minutes.

7 Remove the pan from the heat and stir in the remaining 2 teaspoons lemon juice and 1 teaspoon lemon zest (if using). Loosely cover the custard with waxed paper and let cool to room temperature.

8 In a mixing bowl, beat the heavy cream until soft peaks form. Fold the whipped cream into the cooled lemon custard in the saucepan.

9 With a long serrated knife, split the cake in half horizontally. Spread all of the lemon filling over the cut side of the bottom layer. Top with the remaining layer, cut-side down, and dust the cake with the confectioners' sugar.

Values are approximate per serving: Calories: 433 Protein: 6 gm Fat: 21 gm
Carbohydrates: 55 gm Cholesterol: 133 mg Sodium: 254 mg

Step 8

Step 9

Step 9

Honey-Broiled Fruit Kebabs

▼

Hot, honey-glazed fruit is a splendid dessert on its own, or served over pound cake or ice cream. You can broil the skewered fruits in the oven or grill them on the barbecue (as a grown-up alternative to the kids' toasted marshmallows). Simpler still, just combine the cut-up pineapple, peaches and strawberries in a shallow ovenproof dish, drizzle the honey butter over the fruit, and bake at 425° for about 15 minutes.

Working time: 20 minutes
Total time: 25 minutes

Honey-Broiled Fruit Kebabs

4 Servings

Half a small pineapple or 2 cups
    canned pineapple chunks
2 medium peaches (about 6 ounces
    total), unpeeled
16 medium strawberries (about 1
    pint)

2 tablespoons butter
1 tablespoon honey

Step 2

1 Preheat the broiler. Line a broiler pan with foil.

2 Cut the top off the pineapple, then cut off the skin. To remove the eyes, cut out a wedge-shaped groove following the natural line that the eyes form around the pineapple. Halve the pineapple lengthwise and reserve one half for another use. Cut the remaining half lengthwise into quarters. Core the quarters and cut the pineapple crosswise into wedges. Halve the wedges if they are large.

3 Cut the peaches into wedges and cut the wedges in half.

4 Thread the pineapple and peach wedges and the strawberries onto skewers.

5 In a small saucepan, melt the butter over medium heat. Stir in the honey and remove from the heat. Stir the mixture until well combined.

6 Place the fruit kebabs on the broiler pan and brush the honey butter over the fruit. Broil 4 inches from the heat until the fruit is beginning to brown but hasn't lost its shape, 5 to 7 minutes.

Step 2

TIME-SAVERS

■ *Microwave tip: To make the honey butter, place the butter and honey in a small bowl. Cook at 100% for 30 seconds.*

■ *Do-ahead: All of the fruit and the honey butter can be prepared ahead. If using wooden (not metal) skewers, the kebabs can be assembled ahead and kept tightly covered until time to cook.*

Step 6

Values are approximate per serving: Calories: 170 Protein: 1 gm Fat: 7 gm
Carbohydrates: 30 gm Cholesterol: 16 mg Sodium: 61 mg

Devil's Food
Waffle Sundaes

▼

Don't reserve your waffle iron just for breakfast. Use it to "bake" these delicate brownie-like dessert waffles. Serve them warm, topped with ice cream and a simple homemade chocolate sauce, or make waffle ice cream sandwiches: Spread softened ice cream between two waffles, wrap in plastic wrap and freeze until firm. Serve the sandwiches with or without the chocolate sauce.

Working time: 35 minutes
Total time: 35 minutes

Devil's Food Waffle Sundaes

6 Servings

1⅓ cups flour
⅓ cup unsweetened cocoa powder
1½ teaspoons baking powder
1 teaspoon cinnamon
½ teaspoon salt
1 stick (4 ounces) plus 1 tablespoon
  butter
1⅓ cups (packed) light brown
  sugar

2 eggs
1½ teaspoons vanilla extract
⅓ cup milk
3 ounces semisweet chocolate
⅓ cup heavy cream
1 pint vanilla ice cream

Step 4

1 Preheat a waffle iron.

2 In a medium bowl, combine the flour, cocoa powder, baking powder, cinnamon and salt.

3 In another medium bowl, cream 1 stick of the butter with ⅔ cup of the brown sugar. Beat in the eggs one at a time. Beat in 1 teaspoon of the vanilla.

4 Alternating between the two, add the dry ingredients and the milk to the butter-sugar mixture.

5 Pour enough batter into the waffle iron to cover about two-thirds of the surface. Close the waffle iron and cook for approximately the same amount of time it would take to cook an ordinary waffle, about 3 minutes. Repeat with the remaining batter.

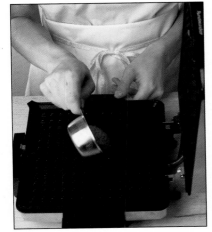

Step 5

6 Meanwhile, in a small saucepan, combine the chocolate, cream, remaining ⅔ cup brown sugar, 1 tablespoon butter and ½ teaspoon vanilla. Cook over medium heat, stirring, until the chocolate is melted and the sauce is smooth, about 10 minutes.

7 Serve the waffle topped with a scoop of ice cream and the chocolate sauce.

TIME-SAVERS

■ *Microwave tip: To make the chocolate sauce: Combine the sauce ingredients in a medium bowl or 4-cup glass measure. Cook at 50% for 4 minutes, stirring twice.*

■ *Do-ahead: The chocolate sauce can be made ahead and reheated. The waffles can be made ahead and toasted lightly for a crisper texture.*

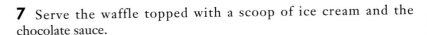

Values are approximate per serving: Calories: 693   Protein: 9 gm   Fat: 35 gm
Carbohydrates: 91 gm   Cholesterol: 157 mg   Sodium: 551 mg

Step 6

Apple-Walnut Upside-Down Cake

▼

Fresh apple adds a tasty autumnal twist to this cake, which is, of course, usually made with canned pineapple. Walnuts and raisins, brown sugar and cinnamon are complementary fall flavors. If you don't have an ovenproof skillet, heat the brown sugar and butter in a skillet on top of the stove, then pour the mixture into a 9 x 2-inch cake pan and continue with the recipe.

Working time: 15 minutes
Total time: 50 minutes

306

Apple-Walnut
Upside-Down Cake

8 Servings

1 large Granny Smith or other tart
  green apple, unpeeled
1 stick (4 ounces) butter, softened
1 cup (packed) brown sugar
2 cups chopped walnuts
1⅓ cups flour
1 teaspoon baking powder

1 teaspoon cinnamon
¼ teaspoon salt
2 eggs
1 teaspoon vanilla extract
⅓ cup milk
½ cup golden raisins

1 Preheat the oven to 350°.

2 Cut the apple into ¼-inch-thick wedges.

3 In a 9-inch ovenproof skillet, melt 4 tablespoons of the butter over medium heat. Add ⅔ cup of the brown sugar and cook, stirring, until the sugar melts, 1 to 2 minutes.

4 Remove the skillet from the heat. Arrange the apple slices in a spoke pattern, starting at the center of the skillet. Scatter 1 cup of the walnuts around the outside of the apples to fill in the gap between the apples and the edge of the pan.

5 In a medium bowl, thoroughly mix the flour, baking powder, cinnamon and salt.

6 In a mixing bowl, cream the remaining 4 tablespoons butter and ⅓ cup brown sugar until light and fluffy. Beat in the eggs, one at a time. Beat in the vanilla.

7 Alternately add the dry ingredients and the milk to the mixing bowl. Add the remaining 1 cup walnuts and the raisins; do not overmix.

8 Spread the batter over the nuts and apples in the skillet. Rap the pan once or twice on the counter to remove any air pockets. Bake for 30 minutes, or until the cake shrinks from the sides of the pan and a toothpick inserted in the cake portion comes out clean.

9 Immediately run a knife around the edges of the cake and carefully invert it onto a serving plate.

TIME-SAVERS

■ *Microwave tip: To soften the butter for easy creaming, stand the stick of butter on end and microwave at 30% for 30 seconds. Turn the butter over and microwave at 30% for another 30 seconds.*

Values are approximate per serving: Calories: 540 Protein: 9 gm Fat: 32 gm
Carbohydrates: 51 gm Cholesterol: 86 mg Sodium: 272 mg

Step 4

Step 8

Step 9

Chocolate Chip-Almond Pound Cake

▼

Here is a big, beautiful cake to serve on special occasions. If you don't have a tube pan, you can use two 9 x 5-inch loaf pans. Start them on two different shelves in the oven and halfway through, switch the pans. The baking time will be about the same. For extra almond flavor, brush almond liqueur (amaretto or crème de noyaux) lightly over the top of the cake while it is still warm.

Working time: 20 minutes
Total time: 2 hours

Chocolate Chip-Almond Pound Cake

16 Servings

1½ cups sliced almonds
3 cups flour
1 teaspoon baking powder
¼ teaspoon salt
3 sticks (12 ounces) butter, at room temperature

2 cups sugar
8 eggs
1½ teaspoons almond extract
1 package (6 ounces) semisweet chocolate chips

1 Preheat the oven to 350°. Butter and flour a 10-inch Bundt or other fluted tube pan.

2 In a large ungreased skillet, toast the almonds over medium heat, stirring frequently so that they toast evenly, about 10 minutes. Remove them from the pan so they will cool while you mix the batter.

Step 2

3 In a medium bowl, combine the flour, baking powder and salt, and thoroughly blend.

4 In a mixing bowl, cream the butter and sugar. Beat the eggs in one at a time, beating well after each addition. Beat in the almond extract.

5 Beat in the dry ingredients. By hand, stir in the chocolate chips and the cooled toasted almonds.

6 Turn the batter into the prepared pan and spread it evenly. Rap the pan on the counter once or twice to remove any air pockets.

7 Bake for 1 hour and 5 minutes, or until a toothpick inserted halfway between the tube and the edge of the pan comes out clean.

Step 4

8 Cool the cake in the pan on a rack for about 30 minutes. Unmold the cake onto the rack and let cool completely.

TIME-SAVERS

■ *Microwave tip: To toast the almonds, place them in a glass pie plate and drizzle with 1 teaspoon of oil. Cook at 100% for 4 minutes, stirring once.*

Values are approximate per serving: Calories: 479 Protein: 8 gm Fat: 28 gm
Carbohydrates: 51 gm Cholesterol: 153 mg Sodium: 269 mg

Step 5

Glazed Strawberry-Banana Cream Pie

▼

Here is a simple trick for making a pie that looks and tastes as though you spent hours in the kitchen: Layer fresh fruit and custard in a prebaked pie crust. The crust can be baked and the custard cooked well ahead of time, and the pie assembled at the last minute. For an even faster pie, you could use a storebought vanilla pudding mix in place of the custard.

Working time: 30 minutes
Total time: 45 minutes

Glazed Strawberry-Banana Cream Pie

8 Servings

Unbaked 9-inch pie shell,	**1 teaspoon vanilla**
homemade or storebought	**1 tablespoon butter**
⅓ cup sugar	**4 bananas**
¼ cup flour	**3 tablespoons lemon juice**
3 egg yolks	**2 cups whole strawberries**
1½ cups milk	**⅓ cup strawberry or currant jelly**

Step 1

1 Preheat the oven to 375°. Line the pie shell with aluminum foil and fill with pie weights or dried beans.

2 Bake the pie shell for 10 minutes. Remove the weights and bake for 10 minutes longer, or until the shell is golden. Set the pie shell aside to cool.

3 Meanwhile, in a medium saucepan, combine the sugar and flour. Beat in the egg yolks one at a time. Gradually whisk in the milk. Add the vanilla.

4 Bring the mixture almost to a boil over medium heat, whisking. Reduce the heat to low and simmer, whisking, until the custard is thick enough to coat the back of a spoon, 2 to 3 minutes.

Step 4

5 Remove the custard from the heat, stir in the butter and set aside to cool slightly. Place plastic wrap directly on the surface of the custard and refrigerate until cooled to at least lukewarm.

6 Meanwhile, cut the bananas into ¼-inch slices and toss them with the lemon juice. Halve the strawberries and toss them with the bananas.

7 In a small saucepan, warm the jelly over low heat until melted. Let cool slightly, then gently combine the jelly with the fruit.

8 Spread the custard in the cooled pie shell. Top with the fruit.

TIME-SAVERS

■ *Microwave tip: To melt the jelly, place it in a microwave-safe container and cook at 100% for 45 seconds to 1 minute, stirring once or twice.*

■ *Do-ahead: The pie shell can be prebaked. The custard (Steps 3 through 5) can be made ahead. (To prevent a skin from forming on the custard, be sure to press plastic wrap right onto its surface.)*

Values are approximate per serving: Calories: 323   Protein: 5 gm   Fat: 13 gm
Carbohydrates: 48 gm   Cholesterol: 112 mg   Sodium: 182 mg

Step 8

Golden Nugget Cookie Bars

▼

Make these roasted peanut and chocolate chip blondies once, and you'll never make just a single batch again. Happily, this recipe doubles beautifully (use a 13 x 9-inch pan) and freezes well. To freeze, simple turn out the whole pan of cooled uncut brownies onto a large sheet of plastic wrap and seal it tightly. To recapture their just-baked freshness, briefly warm the thawed bars before serving.

Working time: 10 minutes
Total time: 40 minutes

Golden Nugget
Cookie Bars

16 Servings

¾ cup sugar
⅓ cup butter
½ teaspoon vanilla extract
⅔ cup flour
1 teaspoon baking powder

¼ teaspoon salt
1 cup dry-roasted unsalted peanuts
1 egg
1 cup semisweet chocolate chips

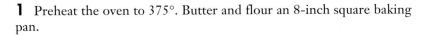

1 Preheat the oven to 375°. Butter and flour an 8-inch square baking pan.

2 In a medium saucepan, combine the sugar and butter, and warm over medium heat until the butter melts. Remove from the heat and stir in the vanilla. Set aside to cool slightly.

Step 2

3 Meanwhile, in a medium bowl, thoroughly blend the flour, baking powder and salt. Coarsely chop the peanuts.

4 When the butter mixture has cooled to at least lukewarm, break the egg into the saucepan and stir immediately to blend.

5 Blend the dry ingredients into the saucepan. Stir in the chocolate chips and peanuts.

Step 4

6 Spread the batter evenly in the baking pan and bake for 25 minutes, or until a toothpick inserted in the center comes out clean.

7 Cool the cake in the pan on a rack before cutting into 16 squares.

TIME-SAVERS

■ *Microwave tip: In a microwave-safe bowl, melt the butter and sugar at 100% for 1 minute 30 seconds; stir and set aside to cool to lukewarm.*

Step 5

Values are approximate per serving: Calories: 201 Protein: 4 gm Fat: 12 gm
Carbohydrates: 22 gm Cholesterol: 24 mg Sodium: 103 mg

Cranberry-Apple
Pandowdy

The enticing aromas of a pandowdy in the oven are much more promising
than this delicious dessert's unassuming name. Here, cranberries, apple
and raisins—sweetened with brown sugar and almond extract—are baked
under a tender and golden sweet-biscuit topping. Vanilla ice cream is
a perfect partner for the pandowdy.

Working time: 15 minutes
Total time: 50 minutes

Cranberry-Apple Pandowdy

6 Servings

3 tablespoons butter
1 Granny Smith apple, unpeeled
1 pound cranberries, fresh or
   frozen, unthawed
½ cup golden raisins
½ cup (packed) plus 2 tablespoons
   dark brown sugar

1½ teaspoons almond extract
1 egg
¼ cup plain yogurt
⅔ cup flour
½ teaspoon baking powder
Pinch of salt

Step 3

1 Preheat the oven to 375°. Butter a shallow 1½-quart baking dish.

2 Melt the butter on the stovetop or in the microwave. Set aside to cool slightly.

3 Cut the apple into ½-inch cubes.

4 In a medium bowl, stir together the apple, cranberries, raisins, ½ cup of the brown sugar and the almond extract. Pour the fruit mixture into the prepared baking dish.

5 In another medium bowl, beat the egg with the yogurt and melted butter. Stir in the flour, the remaining 2 tablespoons brown sugar, the baking powder and salt.

Step 4

6 Spread the batter evenly over the fruit mixture and bake for 30 to 35 minutes, or until the topping is light golden brown.

7 Serve the pandowdy warm or at room temperature.

TIME-SAVERS

■ *Microwave tip: The microwave version of this dish cuts the baking time by 25 minutes, but the topping will not brown, and the end result will not be as attractive. Prepare the recipe as directed, using a microwave-safe baking dish. Loosely cover with waxed paper and place the dish on an inverted plate. Cook at 100% for 3 minutes. Cook at 50% for 5 minutes; uncover and cook an additional 4 minutes, or until the apples are tender and the topping is set.*

■ *Do-ahead: The fruit mixture (Steps 3 and 4) can be prepared ahead.*

Step 6

Values are approximate per serving: Calories: 296 Protein: 4 gm Fat: 7 gm
Carbohydrates: 56 gm Cholesterol: 52 mg Sodium: 140 mg

One-Pan Chocolate Walnut Cake

▼

This homemade one-pan cake has the same convenience as the storebought mixes (you only have to wash a fork, a spatula, and the pan), but is far tastier. The cake is moist and light but with a fudgy walnut-brownie richness. Serve it with vanilla-flavored whipped cream and fresh strawberries for a company-dinner finale; top it with ice cream for a family dessert; or pack it plain for school lunches or picnics.

Working time: 15 minutes
Total time: 50 minutes

One-Pan Chocolate Walnut Cake

10 Servings

1 cup flour	½ cup sour cream
1 cup sugar	¼ cup light vegetable oil
⅔ cup unsweetened cocoa powder	3 eggs
1 teaspoon baking powder	1 teaspoon vanilla extract
½ teaspoon baking soda	1 cup chopped walnuts

1 Preheat the oven to 350°. Butter and flour an 8-inch square or round cake pan, preferably nonstick.

2 In the prepared baking pan, combine the flour, sugar, cocoa, baking powder and baking soda and stir to blend thoroughly. Make a well in the center of the dry ingredients.

3 Place the sour cream, oil, eggs and vanilla in the well. With a fork or small whisk, lightly beat the wet ingredients together.

4 Gradually incorporate all of the dry ingredients into the wet ingredients by pulling the dry ingredients in from the edges as you stir. Stir in the walnuts.

5 Spread the mixture evenly in the pan and rap it once or twice on the counter to remove any air bubbles in the batter.

6 Bake for 25 to 30 minutes, or until a toothpick inserted in the center comes out clean. Cool the cake in the pan on a rack.

Values are approximate per serving: Calories: 312 Protein: 6 gm Fat: 18 gm
Carbohydrates: 35 gm Cholesterol: 69 mg Sodium: 111 mg

Step 2

Step 3

Step 4

INDEX